Enterprise AI

by Zachary Jarvinen

for dummies®

A Wiley Brand

Enterprise AI For Dummies®

Published by: **John Wiley & Sons, Inc.**, 111 River Street, Hoboken, NJ 07030-5774, www.wiley.com

Copyright © 2020 by John Wiley & Sons, Inc., Hoboken, New Jersey

Published simultaneously in Canada

For general information on our other products and services, please contact our Customer Care Department within the U.S. at 877-762-2974, outside the U.S. at 317-572-3993, or fax 317-572-4002. For technical support, please visit https://hub.wiley.com/community/support/dummies.

Wiley publishes in a variety of print and electronic formats and by print-on-demand. Some material included with standard print versions of this book may not be included in e-books or in print-on-demand. If this book refers to media such as a CD or DVD that is not included in the version you purchased, you may download this material at http://booksupport.wiley.com. For more information about Wiley products, visit www.wiley.com.

Library of Congress Control Number: 2020941002

ISBN: 978-1-119-69629-2 (pbk); ISBN 978-1-119-69638-4 (ebk); ISBN 978-1-119-69639-1 (ebk)

Manufactured in the United States of America

10 9 8 7 6 5 4 3 2 1

Contents at a Glance

Table of Contents

Introduction

What we want is a machine that can learn from experience.

— *Alan Turing, Lecture to the London Mathematical Society, 20 February 1947*

The whizbang aspects of artificial intelligence get lots of press and screen time. Consider a few recent headlines:

>> The U.S. Army is creating robots that can follow orders.

>> DeepMind's AI has now outcompeted nearly all human players at StarCraft II.

>> A robotic hand taught itself to solve a Rubik's Cube after creating its own training regime.

>> A new AI fake text generator may be too dangerous to release, say creators.

>> This AI bot writes such convincing ads that Chase just "hired" it to write marketing copy.

Remember back when the caption "Wi-Fi Ready" or "Bluetooth Ready" was stamped in a starburst graphic on the front of boxes for everything from televisions to refrigerators? AI has now reached that exalted status.

Of course, you have the smart speaker of your choice and maybe a smart thermostat. But wait, there's more. You can get an AI-powered toothbrush that tattles to your smartphone about your brushing habits, via Bluetooth of course. An AI-enabled pill dispenser reminds you to take your medicine. And an AI-powered vacuum cleaner tidies up before the dinner guests arrive.

But AI is not just about gadgets and novelties. It also keeps the store from running out of water, batteries, and strawberry-flavored Pop-Tarts during hurricane season. It makes sure that a factory doesn't exceed emissions standards. It figures out supply chain logistics, taking into account product quality, weather, tariffs, geo-political hotspots, compliance, and a host of other factors.

AI is also about increasing revenue and creating jobs. Yes, you read that last part right. Contrary to common warnings, AI could boost employment levels by 10 percent if the rest of the world invested in AI and human-machine collaboration at the same level as the top performing 20 percent.

About This Book

In this current AI renaissance, new advances appear on a near-daily basis, and that's a good thing. But this book isn't about the new, sexy, flashy, bleeding-edge, headline-grabbing utopian AI. It isn't about the futuristic dystopian AI dreams portrayed in movies, books, and conspiracy theories either.

This book is about what AI can do for you, right now, in your business. It's about well-established, tried-and-true technology and processes that are currently being used in businesses and organizations all over the world to help humans become more productive, more accurate, more efficient, and more understanding.

What you won't find in this book:

>> Deep dives into the mathematics and science underpinning AI

>> Coding tutorials, examples of coding, or coding exercises

>> Libraries and packages that you have to download and install

>> Exercises to complete or problems to solve

What you will find in this book:

>> A survey of the market drivers for AI and the enabling technology that makes it possible

>> A very high-level, layperson's overview of the algorithms and techniques that pragmatic AI uses

>> A quick stroll down AI memory lane to see if you recognize early implementations you likely used

>> Some tips on picking a solid use case for your first AI project for your business

>> A survey of 21 vertical and horizontal markets to see how pragmatic AI can help you now

Strong, Weak, General, and Narrow

Often, people don't differentiate between the AI that checks the grammar on your resume and the AI that becomes Skynet and ushers in the robot apocalypse. Just like coffee, ice cream, Pringles, and Pop-Tarts, AI comes in many flavors, but at a high level, it falls into two categories:

>> **Strong/general AI:** Also known as artificial general intelligence (AGI), *general AI* is an intelligence that is indistinguishable from human intelligence. In other words, for now, AGI resides solely in the land of science fiction and speculation.

>> **Weak/narrow AI:** In contrast to general AI, *narrow AI* lives firmly in the land of the now and the real. Each implementation has a very targeted (hence narrow) focus on accomplishing a specific, practical task. In fact, narrow AI is often called *practical* or *pragmatic AI*.

Pragmatic artificial intelligence is the subject of this book. You can apply AI to many problems, but in your business, the solutions all fall under three business goals.

REMEMBER

Every enterprise AI project aims to reduce cost, increase revenue, or explore new business models.

As you read about the various vertical and horizontal markets and the related use cases, I might talk about workflow optimization or recommendation engines or predictive maintenance, but ultimately every use case falls under one of these three goals.

Foolish Assumptions

I am assuming that you, the reader, fall into one or more of the following categories:

>> You have a college-level education, such as a bachelor's degree, MBA, or professional certifications, or are pursuing a business degree.

>> You read trade publications and books on business management.

>> You possibly have leadership and/or IT skills, but not necessarily programming knowledge.

>> You fall somewhere on the spectrum between:

- Business executive and decision-maker at a mid-sized to large organization

- Consultant and strategic advisor, formal or informal

- Ambitious junior and up-and-coming employee

- Business school or related student

Icons Used in This Book

As you read this book, you see icons in the margin that indicate material of interest. This selection briefly describes each icon in this book.

TIP

Everybody likes a tip, a little inside knowledge about a good thing. A life hack. A hint about how to save time or money. How to make things easier. This icon marks the spot where the goods are buried.

REMEMBER

A few things are good to know, and remember, about how AI works. This icon reminds you to remember those things — and makes it easy to find them again if you forget to remember.

WARNING

This icon is the reverse of a tip. It tells you how to avoid the bad thing. You see this? Don't do that.

TECHNICAL STUFF

Once or twice for a second or so, the book gets down in the weeds, kicks over a rock to see what's underneath. If you like that kind of thing, when you see this icon, keep on reading. If not, just skip it. You won't miss anything you can't live without.

Beyond the Book

To extend the experience beyond what's in print here today, I've put together these additional resources:

>> **Cheat sheet:** A quick reference to the major bullets and tables from the book. Feel free to print and post to your wall or simply glance at it when you need a reminder of some of the most fundamental concepts of Enterprise AI. You can find the cheat sheet by going to www.dummies.com and searching for *Enterprise AI For Dummies Cheat Sheet*.

>> **Updates:** I've written this book to expose essential groundwork and use cases that will remain evergreen. That said, as this topic will likely only receive more prominence, not less, over the years to come, I also plan to publish updates, as applicable. They will be available on www.dummies.com as well by searching for *Enterprise AI For Dummies*. Additionally, input about this content is welcome directly through my site, www.zachonomics.com, where book-related talks and articles are also posted.

Where to Go from Here

There's no harm in starting at Chapter 1 and reading right through, but unless you want to learn how AI can be used in a wide array of vertical markets and horizontal applications, you will likely want to dip into the areas of most interest to you and save the rest for another time.

Maybe you've noticed AI in the news, glanced at the headlines, skimmed a few articles, watched a video or two, but you're still not completely certain that you know how it works and how you can use it. If so, before diving into the practical applications, start with Chapter 1, which provides some background about why companies are turning to AI to solve their problems and takes you on a tour of the four pillars on which modern AI is built.

You might have heard the term *algorithm* tossed about casually and wondered what one looks like. In that case, the last third of Chapter 1 is for you. It covers all the cool ideas, such as machine learning, deep learning, and text mining, to mention a few, not at a deep technical level, but at the level required to understand how you can use them to address your business challenges.

If you are looking for real-life examples of how AI has been used in the past and how it is being used now to solve business problems, read Chapter 2.

If you want to explore what it takes to get an AI project up and running in your business, check out Chapter 3.

If you'd like to take a deeper look at how you can use AI in your market, flip to Part 2. For each market, the chapters cover these areas:

>> The challenges facing that market

>> How AI can save costs, increase revenue, and support new business models

>> A look under the hood to see the AI techniques that make it happen

>> Specific use cases that allow you to leverage AI to grow your organization

Part 3 looks forward to future applications of AI, as well as sets out a framework of guardrails, so instead of approaching the topic like a panacea, you are equipped with a grounding that will set you and your organization up for a successful implementation.

Part 4 looks at ways AI will affect the coming decades and why AI is not the final answer for all your business issues.

1

Exploring Practical AI and How It Works

Discover how you can use AI in your organization.

Look under the hood to see how AI works.

Learn the difference between pure AI and practical AI.

Explore common use cases for AI.

Discover best practices for designing an AI project.

Chapter **1**

Demystifying Artificial Intelligence

W hile some have traced the history of artificial intelligence back to Greek mythology and philosophers, fast-forward with me to the twentieth century when serious work on AI was directed to practical applications.

The term *artificial intelligence* was first used in a 1955 proposal for the Dartmouth Summer Research Project on Artificial Intelligence, in which American computer scientist John McCarthy and others wrote:

"We propose that a 2-month, 10-man study of artificial intelligence be carried out during the summer of 1956 at Dartmouth College in Hanover, New Hampshire. The study is to proceed on the basis of the conjecture that every aspect of learning or any other feature of intelligence can in principle be so precisely described that a machine can be made to simulate it."

Over the following decades, AI progress waxed and waned as development overcame one obstacle only to encounter another.

In this chapter, you get an idea of what, why, and how:

>> What the fuss is all about, what AI can do for you, and what it can't.

>> Why now and not 20 years ago, and why AI is suddenly all the rage and wherever you look you see news about everything from self-driving cars to AI-powered showerheads.

>> How it works, and how all the moving parts fit together to solve interesting and challenging problems.

Before I go any further, let me get a few definitions out of the way right up front so you'll know what I mean when I use a term.

Algorithm: A set of rules and calculations used for problem-solving. Some compare an algorithm to the process you follow when you make dinner. The problem to be solved is getting a fully prepared meal on the table, and the algorithm consists of the recipes you use to turn ingredients into the dishes you will serve. An algorithm is not a magic formula; it's just a regular kind of formula, or rather a set of formulas and instructions.

Machine learning: A collection of algorithms that discover relationships in data with an associated level of confidence based on the likelihood, or probability, that it is a true relationship. Note that I didn't say ML teaches the machine to think or make decisions the same way humans do. It's just math. Some pretty fancy math, but still math.

Artificial intelligence: A collection of machine-learning and related technologies used to accomplish tasks that normally require human intelligence, such as to recognize and categorize speech, identify an object or person in a photo or video, or summarize the content of a social media post.

It comes down to pattern recognition. You can think of the human brain as a massively parallel pattern-recognition engine. AI enlists the processing power of computers to automate pattern recognition.

In some ways, AI is more powerful than the human brain, especially in how fast it can match certain patterns. JP Morgan Chase developed a machine-learning system that processed loans that took lawyers and loan officers a total of 360,000 hours to complete; it did this in less than a minute and with fewer mistakes.

In other ways, the human brain is more powerful than current AI implementations. Humans can use all the pattern matching processes that they have learned before to contextualize new pattern matching processes. This ability allows them to be far more adaptable than AI, for now. For example, if you take a photo of a chihuahua from a certain angle, it can look surprisingly like a blueberry muffin. A human can quickly identify which photos are chihuahuas and which are muffins. AI, not so much.

Understanding the Demand for AI

If there is a universal constant in commerce throughout the ages, it is competition. Always changing, always expanding, always looking for a foothold, an advantage — whether from reducing costs, increasing revenue, or unlocking new, innovative business models.

Similarly, while much discussion has taken place in the last few decades about the challenges posed by a global economy, international trade is not a recent phenomenon. It dates back at least to the Assyrians.

Four millennia later, the goal is the same for the modern enterprise: establish a competitive advantage. However, the specific challenges to tackle are new.

Converting big data into actionable information

As data increased in volume, variety, and velocity (known as the three Vs of data), data processing departments experienced an increasing challenge in turning that data into information.

Enter big-data analytics, which is a collection of analytical methods that provide increasing levels of understanding and value.

REMEMBER

>> Descriptive analytics = information

>> Diagnostic analytics = hindsight

>> Predictive analytics = insight

>> Prescriptive analytics = foresight

Descriptive analytics

Descriptive analytics reveal what happened. Sometimes called *business intelligence,* this tool turns historical data into information in the form of simple reports, visualizations, and decision trees to show what occurred at a point in time or over a period of time. In the larger landscape of big-data analytics, it performs a basic but essential function useful for improving performance.

Diagnostic analytics

Diagnostic analytics reveal why something happened. More advanced than descriptive reporting tools, they allow a deep dive into the historical data, apply big-data modelling, and determine the root causes for a given situation.

Predictive analytics

Predictive analytics present what will likely happen next. Based on the same historical data used by descriptive and diagnostic analytics, this tool uses data, analytical algorithms, and machine-learning techniques to identify patterns and trends within the data that suggest how machines, parts, and people will behave in the future.

Prescriptive analytics

Prescriptive analytics recommend what to do next. This tool builds on the predictive function to show the implications of each course of action and identify the optimum alternative in real time.

AI-powered analytics

AI-powered analytics expose the context in vast amounts of structured and unstructured data to reveal underlying patterns and relationships. Sometimes called *cognitive computing,* this tool combines advanced analytics capabilities with comprehensive AI techniques such as deep learning, machine learning, and natural-language recognition.

Figure 1-1 shows the relationship between business value and difficulty of an analytic method.

All these tools combine to bring a fourth "V" to the table: visualization.

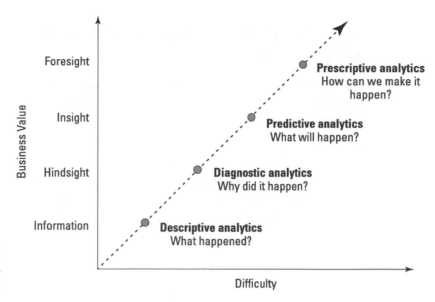

FIGURE 1-1:
Business value
versus difficulty
in analytics.

Relieving global cost pressure

More than a decade ago in his book *The World Is Flat*, Pulitzer Prize-winning New York Times columnist Thomas Friedman posited three eras of globalization:

>> **Globalization 1.0, circa 1400-1940:** The globalization of countries and governments, beginning with Vasco da Gama and Christopher Columbus. It included the invention of the steamship, the railroad, and the telegraph.

>> **Globalization 2.0, circa 1940-2000:** The globalization of multinational companies, beginning with World War II through to Y2K, intensifying in the final two decades. It included the popularization of air travel, computers, and telecommunications.

>> **Globalization 3.0, circa 2000 forward:** The globalization of the individual, powered by the Internet and instantaneous, continuous connection with every market.

Globalization is a one-way train that left the station centuries ago and is still putting on steam. From the perspective of developed countries, globalization exerts a downward pressure: lower material costs, lower wages, lower prices, lower margins.

REMEMBER

AI can offset the downward pressure of globalization by enabling the enterprise to add value by distilling insight from the oceans of data available, and then improving products, product development, logistics, marketing, and personalization, to name just a few.

Accelerating product development and delivery

Despite all the best efforts of product managers and their associated professional organizations and certifications, product development can be chaotic and unpredictable.

One study by McKinsey showed that 70 percent of the software projects analyzed failed to meet their original delivery deadline, and 20 percent of the projects that did meet the deadline did so by dropping or delaying planned features. The average overrun was 25 percent of the original schedule. A study of IC design projects revealed that 80 percent were late, and the projects were equally likely to overrun the schedule by 80 percent as they were to finish on time. Cost overruns were also common.

AI can reduce the duration of several stages of product development, from discovery and refining the offering, to keeping development on track through predictive project management.

Facilitating mass customization

Studies show that you can boost sales by reducing the range of choices. And if those limited choices are targeted to the customer's preferences, you can boost them even more. Accenture found that 75 percent of consumers are more likely to buy from a retailer that recognizes them by name and can recommend options based on past purchases.

Mass customization and personalization enables you to tailor a product to the customer. Through data mining and text mining, not only can you personalize the product to a specific customer, you can also discern trends across segments and use the information to inform product development.

Identifying the Enabling Technology

Just as constant as the challenges posed by competition throughout the ages is the role of innovation in addressing competitive pressure. Four millennia ago camels were domesticated, and a few centuries later ships were launched to enable long-distance trade.

In this new millennium, the continued pressure of competition has fueled advances in technology, particularly in the domain of artificial intelligence.

Like the camel and the ship, AI enables those in business to go farther and faster, to respond to global pressure to reduce cost, increase efficiency, and accelerate the development and delivery of products.

However, several enabling technologies had to reach maturity to create a foundation that would allow AI to realize the potential envisioned by the scientists at the 1956 Dartmouth Summer Research Project on Artificial Intelligence.

Processing

In a 1965 paper, Gordon Moore, the co-founder of Fairchild Semiconductor and CEO of Intel, observed that the number of transistors in a dense integrated circuit doubled about every year. In 1975, Moore revised his estimate going forward to doubling every two years.

The first single-chip central processing unit (CPU) was developed at Intel in 1970. In the intervening half-century, computing power has increased roughly according to Moore's law. For example, in 1951, Christopher Strachey taught the Ferranti Mark 1 computer to play chess. Forty-six years later, the IBM Deep Blue computer beat world chess champion Garry Kasparov. Deep Blue was 10 million times faster than the Mark 1.

While the curve is starting to level out, 50 years of advances in processing power has established computing platforms capable of the massive, parallel-processing power required to develop natural-language processing (NLP), self-driving cars, advanced robotics, and other AI disciplines.

Algorithms

In the 1990s and beyond, work in AI expanded to include concepts from probability and decision theory and applied them to a broad range of disciplines.

TECHNICAL STUFF

» **Bayesian networks:** A probabilistic graphical model that represents a set of variables and their conditional dependencies via a directed acyclic graph

» **Hidden Markov models:** Statistical models used to capture hidden information from observable sequential symbols

» **Information theory:** A mathematical study of the coding, storage, and communication of information in the form of sequences of symbols, impulses, and so on

» **Stochastic modeling:** Estimates probability distributions of potential outcomes by allowing for random variation in one or more inputs over time

- >> **Classical optimization:** Analytical methods that use differential calculus to identify an optimum solution

- >> **Neural networks:** Systems that learn to perform tasks by considering examples without being programmed with task-specific rules

- >> **Evolutionary algorithms:** Population-based optimization algorithms inspired by biological evolution, such as reproduction, mutation, recombination, and selection

- >> **Machine learning:** Algorithms that analyze data to create models that make predictions, take decisions or identify context with significant accuracy, and improve as more targeted data is available

As the sophistication of the algorithms directed to the challenges of AI increased, so did the power of the solutions.

Data

The early days of life on Earth were dominated by single-celled organisms that sometimes organized into colonies. Then, back about 541 million years ago during the Cambrian era, most of the major animal phyla suddenly appeared in the fossil record. This is known as the *Cambrian explosion.*

It seems that the twenty-first century is experiencing its own Cambrian explosion of data. In the beginning, there was data. Pre-Cambrian data. It was pretty simple, mostly structured, and relevant to specific commercial applications such as accounting or inventory or payroll and the like. Data processing turned that data into information to answer questions, such as "What does that mean for me?"

Now, thanks to the Internet and other data-generating technologies, big data has arrived. Unfortunately, traditional data processing lacks the sophistication and power to answer all the questions that are hidden in the data. AI employs big-data analytics to turn big data into actionable information.

REMEMBER

What differentiates regular old data from big data? The three Vs mentioned earlier:

- >> Volume

- >> Variety

- >> Velocity

Volume

Much more data is available now. In fact, the sheer volume of data being generated every minute is staggering:

>> On YouTube, 300 hours of video are uploaded.

>> On Facebook, 510,000 comments are posted, 293,000 statuses are updated, and 136,000 photos are uploaded.

>> On Twitter, 360,000 tweets are posted.

>> On Yelp, 26,380 reviews are posted.

>> On Instagram, 700,000 photos and videos are uploaded.

And all this is on just a few social media sites.

AI needs data, lots of data, to generate actionable recommendations. To develop text-to-speech capabilities, Microsoft burned through five years of continuous speech data. To create self-driving cars, Tesla accumulated 1.3 billion miles of driving data.

Variety

Many more types of data are available than ever before. Traditionally, companies focused their attention on the data created in their corporate systems. This was mainly structured data — data that follows the same structure for each record and fits neatly into relational databases or spreadsheets.

Today, valuable information is locked up in a broad array of external sources, such as social media, mobile devices, and, increasingly, Internet of Things (IoT) devices and sensors. This data is largely unstructured: It does not conform to set formats in the way that structured data does. This includes blog posts, images, videos, and podcasts. Unstructured data is inherently richer, more ambiguous, and fluid with a broad range of meanings and uses, so it is much more difficult to capture and analyze.

A big-data analytics tool works with structured and unstructured data to reveal patterns and trends that would be impossible to do using the previous generation of data tools. Of the three Vs of big data, variety is increasingly costly to manage, especially for unstructured data sources.

Velocity

Data is coming at us faster than ever. Texts, social media status updates, news feeds, podcasts, and videos are all being posted by the always-on, always-connected culture. Even cars and refrigerators and doorbells are data generators. The new Ford GT not only tops out at 216 miles per hour, it also has 50 IoT sensors and 28 microprocessors that can generate up to 100GB of data per hour.

And because it's coming at us faster, it must be processed faster. A decade ago, it wasn't uncommon to talk about batch processing data overnight. For a self-driving car, even a half-second delay is too slow.

REMEMBER

When AI was just starting out, data was scarce. Consequently, the quality of information generated was of limited value. With the advent of big data, the quality of the information to be harvested is unprecedented, as is the value to the enterprise of modern AI initiatives.

Storage

AI requires massive amounts of data, so massive that it uses a repository technology known as a *data lake*. A data lake can be used to store all the data for an enterprise, including raw copies of source system data and transformed data.

In the decade from 2010-2020, data storage changed more in terms of price and availability than during the previous quarter century, and due to Moore's Law, that trend will continue. Laptop-peripheral, solid-state drives priced at hundreds of dollars today have the same capacity as million-dollar hard-drive storage arrays from 20 years ago. Large-scale storage capacity now ranges up to hundreds of petabytes (a hundred million gigabytes) and runs on low-cost commodity servers.

REMEMBER

Combined with the advent of more powerful processors, smarter algorithms and readily available data, the arrival of large-scale, low-cost storage set the stage for the AI explosion.

Discovering How It Works

Artificial intelligence is a field of study in computer science. Much like the field of medicine, it encompasses many sub-disciplines, specializations, and techniques.

Semantic networks and symbolic reasoning

Also known as good old-fashioned AI (GOFAI), semantic networks and symbolic reasoning dominated solutions during the first three decades of AI development in the form of rules engines and expert systems.

Semantic networks are a way to organize relationships between words, or more precisely, relationships between concepts as expressed with words, which are gathered to form a specification of the known entities and relationships in the system, also called an *ontology*.

The *is a* relationship takes the form "X is a Y" and establishes the basis of a taxonomic hierarchy. For example: A monkey is a primate. A primate is a mammal. A mammal is a vertebrate. A human is a primate. With this information, the system can not only link human with primate, but also with mammal and vertebrate, as it inherits the properties of higher nodes.

However, the meaning of monkey as a verb, as in "don't monkey with that," has no relationship to primates, and neither does monkey as an adjective, as in monkey bread, monkey wrench, or monkey tree, which aren't related to each other either. Now you start to get an inkling of the challenge facing data scientists.

Another relationship, the *case* relationship, maps out the elements of a sentence based on the verb and the associated subject, object, and recipient, as applicable. Table 1-1 shows a case relationship for the sentence "The boy threw a bone to the dog."

TABLE 1-1 ## Case Relationship for a Sentence

Case	Threw
Agent	Boy
Object	Bone
Recipient	Dog

The case relationship for other uses of "threw" won't necessarily follow the same structure.

>> The pitcher threw the game.

>> The car threw a rod.

>> The toddler threw a tantrum.

Early iterations of rules engines and expert systems were code-driven, meaning much of the system was built on manually coded algorithms. Consequently, they were cumbersome to maintain and modify and thus lacked scalability. The availability of big data set the stage for the development of data-driven models. Symbolic AI evolved using the combination of machine-learning ontologies and statistical text mining to get the extra oomph that powers the current AI renaissance.

Text and data mining

The information age has produced a super-abundance of data, a kind of potential digital energy that AI scientists mine and refine to power modern commerce, research, government, and other endeavors.

Data mining

Data mining processes structured data such as is found in corporate enterprise resource planning (ERP) systems or customer databases, and it applies modelling functions to produce actionable information. Analytics and business intelligence (BI) platforms can quickly identify and retrieve information from large datasets of structured data and apply the data mining functions described here to create models that enable descriptive, predictive, and prescriptive analytics:

REMEMBER

>> **Association:** This determines the probability that two contemporaneous events are related. For example, in sales transactions, the association function can uncover purchase patterns, such as when a customer who buys milk also buys cereal.

>> **Classification:** This reveals patterns that can be used to categorize an item. For example, weather prediction depends on identifying patterns in weather conditions (such as rising or dropping air pressure) to predict whether it will be sunny or cloudy.

>> **Clustering:** This organizes data by identifying similarities and grouping elements into clusters to reveal new information. One example is segmenting customers by gender, marital status, or neighborhood.

>> **Regression:** This predicts a numeric value depending on the variables in a given dataset. For example, the price of a used car can be determined by analyzing its age, mileage, condition, option packages, and other variables.

Because data mining works on the structured data within the organization, it is particularly suited to deliver a wide range of operational and business benefits. For example, data mining can crunch data from IoT systems to enable the predictive maintenance of factory equipment or combine historical sales data with customer behaviors to predict future sales and patterns of demand.

Text mining

Text mining deals with unstructured data, which must be organized and structured before applying data modeling and analytics. Using natural-language processing (NLP), text-mining software can extract data elements to populate the structured metadata fields such as author, date, and content summary that enable analysis.

Text mining can go beyond data mining to synthesize vast amounts of content to identify people, places, things, events, and time frames mentioned in written text, assign emotional tone to each mention of them (negative, positive, or neutral), and even understand whether the document is factual or opinion.

Text mining is important for its ability to digest unstructured textual data, which contains more context and valuable insights than structured, transactional data, because it reflects the author's opinion, intention, emotion, and conclusions.

In 2018, Google introduced a technique for NLP pre-training called Bidirectional Encoder Representations from Transformers (BERT). This technique replaces ontologies with statistical-based mining to ratchet up the relevance of search results.

With AI and machine learning comes an assumption that the more clean data you have, the more accurate your predictions become. But this also assumes you have the horsepower to process and analyze that data quickly, at scale, without dimming the city's lights. To be effective at customer analysis, AI solutions must process immense amounts of data efficiently and scale to meet increasing volumes of data over time as it is collected and persisted.

Table 1-2 compares and contrasts the properties and uses of data mining versus text mining.

TABLE 1-2   **Data Mining Versus Text Mining**

	Data Mining	Text Mining
Overview	Data mining searches for patterns and relationships in structured data.	Text mining transforms unstructured textual data into structured information to enable data analysis.
Data Type	Structured data from large datasets is found in systems such as databases, spreadsheets, ERP, and accounting applications.	Unstructured textual data is found in emails, documents, presentations, videos, file shares, social media, and the Internet.
Data Retrieval	Structured data is homogenous and organized, making it easy to retrieve.	Unstructured textual data comes in many different formats and content types located in a more diverse range of applications and systems.
Data Preparation	Structured data is formal and formatted, facilitating the process of ingesting data into analytical models.	Linguistic and statistical techniques — including NLP keywording and meta-tagging — must be applied to turn unstructured into usable structured data.
Taxonomy	There is no need to create an overriding taxonomy.	A global taxonomy must be applied to organize the data into a common framework.

Machine learning

Machine learning (ML), a subset of artificial intelligence, enables users to learn from historical data to achieve a desired outcome. It powers targeted ads, personalized content, song recommendations, predictive maintenance activities, and virtual assistants.

ML mimics human learning by absorbing information. Humans learn by reading, watching, listening, and doing. ML learns by processing historical data. For example, a human's knowledge of elephants is based on historical experience, such as going to the zoo, riding an elephant, watching a documentary, and reading a book. ML gains knowledge of elephants by processing text and images.

REMEMBER

The learning phase consists of these steps:

1. Sample historical data (machine activity, customer attributes, and transactions).

2. Apply algorithm to historical data to learn key patterns and trends.

3. Generate a model or set of rules or instructions.

The prediction phase consists of these steps:

1. Load the existing model.

2. Apply the model to new data.

3. Predict the likelihood of an outcome (in other words, customer churn).

The output of the prediction phase feeds back into the input of the learning phase to refine the model.

Learning

For the purposes of ML, historical data is called *training data*. In the case of text mining, the system uses OCR and NLP to process text. For images, the system uses computer vision techniques for detection, recognition, and identification to process the image.

The algorithm processes the data to detect key patterns and trends and correlate them to labels. For example, if you're doing text mining, the algorithm might notice certain words being associated with elephants, such as large, gray, tusk, and trunk, and associate those with the label "elephant." Later, in the prediction phase, when the algorithm sees a significant number of these terms, it calculates the probability that the passage is talking about an elephant.

In the learning phase, the system applies statistical techniques or algorithms to the historical data to generate a machine-learning model. You can think of the model as a set of rules or instructions (similar to steps in a recipe) that one must follow to make a business decision.

For example, to approve a loan application, a loan officer considers income, age, net worth, and many other factors. Each attribute of the application is a rule or factor that the officer must evaluate to approve or reject the loan. Machine-learning techniques follow a similar process, comparing various attributes, historical decisions, and the outcome of similar applicants to estimate the credit worthiness of the new applicant. Table 1-3 shows how machine learning is like a recipe.

Prediction

In the prediction stage, the system uses the model to process new data (not historical data), detect patterns and trends, and attempt to match them to patterns from the learning data.

TABLE 1-3   **Machine Learning as a Recipe**

	Machine Learning	Recipe
Task	An algorithm is a step-by-step instruction set or formula for solving a problem or completing a task.	Thaw the chicken. Season the chicken. Bake the chicken at 350°F.
Objective	Minimize errors (loss function) to attain the best approach to solve a task.	Minimize the number of ingredients and steps required to prepare a tasty dish.
Insight/ result	The algorithm learns from errors, finds the best approach, and generates insights and rules used to make predictions.	Learn from your mistakes the next time you attempt the recipe.

For example, if you process a brochure for the San Diego Zoo using the model, it would recognize the content about elephants and add the tag "elephant" to the document along with a score. The result is a prediction in the form of the percentage probability that the document contains information about elephants. Basically, the model makes a data-driven guess.

In AI and data science, execution is not just implementing a plan. The methodology establishes an iterative process of learning, discovering, and then acting based on new information as opposed to a more traditional IT model of formulating a plan or idea and then rolling it out as planned.

Auto-classification

Auto-classification is a machine-learning technique that automates tedious, error-prone tasks such as classifying information for storage and retrieval or answering a question. In a world where the amount of information stored digitally is expected to double every two years well into the next decade, auto-classification makes the difference between using that information and being overwhelmed by it.

Auto-classification uses two machine-learning methods, supervised classification and unsupervised classification, for two different purposes.

Supervised classification

Machine learning via supervised classification uses exemplars of known document types to classify new documents in a two-step process:

1. Train the algorithm using known, manually classified content.

2. Classify new content using the trained algorithm.

In a stable content environment, AI teams use supervised classification to set custom classification models specific to a particular application or organization. This method requires human intervention to select the training data and optimize the model, and thus requires substantial involvement and effort in the early phases of the project, but yields predictable, accurate results.

Unsupervised classification

Machine learning via unsupervised classification uses clustering and association algorithms to discover relationships in a heterogeneous dataset:

» Clustering algorithms identify commonalities in the data, such as textual content or data format, and extrapolate relationships to create natural groupings and detect anomalous elements, such as security threats or medical issues.

» Association algorithms reveal interesting relationships in the data to answer questions to address issues such as reducing customer churn or selecting related products for a promotion.

AI teams use unsupervised classification when attempting to answer these types of questions:

» Is there any evidence of fraud in these financial transactions?

» Are there any network performance symptoms that indicate a latent issue that would increase the risk of network failure?

» Are there any anomalies in customer activity that point to possible buying trends?

Predictive analysis

Predictive analysis uses data mining, machine learning, and predictive modeling to process transactional and historical data to identify trends that indicate areas of increased risk or reward.

Specifically, predictive modelling software uses known results from existing data to train the model to predict relationships and outcomes that are likely to occur in future data and recommend a course of action. It is a business function, not a math problem or a science exercise.

AI teams use predictive analytics when attempting to answer these types of questions:

>> Will my customer purchase product X?

>> Will my customer like a recommended song?

>> Which of my customers are likely to switch to a competitor or cancel their contract?

>> Of all recently submitted claims, which ones are likely to require an additional fraud investigation unit review?

>> Is this applicant likely to default on their car loan in the future?

REMEMBER

Because predictive analytics delivers actionable insight, in-depth knowledge in the business domain is as important as an understanding of the various analytics techniques or the ability to code analytics solutions.

For example, predictive analytics can spot buying trends and patterns, but it takes someone with an understanding of the market to help the software interpret them and assess their relevance.

Predictive analysis is used in a wide range of markets:

>> Manufacturing and logistics operations apply predictive maintenance to ensure maximum performance and uptime for their assets.

>> Financial services and retail organizations use predictive analytics tools for many key business functions, including personalized marketing and fraud detection.

Deep learning

Deep learning techniques mimic the brain's neuron activities, which is why they are also referred to as neural networks. Some common applications include natural-language processing, image recognition, and realistic photo and video generation. Table 1-4 shows the relationship among artificial intelligence, machine learning, and deep learning.

TABLE 1-4 **Artificial Intelligence, Machine Learning, and Deep Learning**

Technique	Description	Example
Artificial Intelligence	Computing systems capable of performing tasks that humans are very good at	Recognize objects, recognize and make sense of speech, self-driving cars
Machine Learning	Field of AI that learns from historical data toward an end goal or outcome	Predict customers likely to churn
Deep Learning	Powerful set of machine-learning techniques that mimic the brain's neuron activities	Computer vision, colorize photos, deep fakes, mastering a game

Sentiment analysis

Sentiment analysis uses text mining, NLP, and other AI techniques to detect the opinions and emotions of a person based on written or spoken content, such as social media posts, reviews, videos, and podcasts. It identifies the person expressing the opinion, what the person is talking about, and whether the opinion is positive or negative.

Also called *opinion mining,* sentiment analysis is often used to process reviews or survey results to discern the voice of the customer and adjust a policy, product, or response accordingly.

In the early days of Twitter, many corporate social media teams would auto-retweet any content that tagged the brand. The resulting retweets of complaints of bad service were a great source of amusement to the general populace but did little to build the value of the brand. Sentiment analysis not only avoids such embarrassing moments, but also creates an opportunity to be proactive in engaging customers with knowledge and empathy.

Chapter **2**

Looking at Uses for Practical AI

Mention artificial intelligence, and you'll get all kinds of reactions, from cartoon fantasies of Rosie, the Jetson's robot maid, to the dystopian cityscape of Ridley Scott's *Blade Runner*, James Cameron's *The Terminator*, or Michael Crichton's *Westworld*.

These representations of AI are examples of artificial general intelligence, also called *pure AI*. Even from the beginning at the Dartmouth workshop, the pioneers of AI aimed for the stars, asserting that "every aspect of learning or any other feature of intelligence can in principle be so precisely described that a machine can be made to simulate it," but by the time it filtered down to the masses, it presented itself in humbler forms.

These days, AI is pervasive, but it slips past unnoticed because it is not a manifestation of the romantic vision of writers. Instead, it is eminently practical. Pragmatic. Useful.

Recognizing AI When You See It

Like good design, good AI is invisible. When done right, both remove some of the friction from daily life. In fact, you have probably been using artificial intelligence for longer than you realize.

ELIZA

In the mid-1960s, Joseph Weizenbaum at the Massachusetts Institute of Technology Artificial Intelligence Laboratory developed ELIZA, a natural-language processing program that converses in the style of a psychologist asking questions based on previous responses. With the advent of the personal computer, ELIZA escaped the MIT lab and ventured into people's homes. You can still find implementations online.

Grammar check

Spell check has been around for a long time, but that's a simple application that doesn't require artificial intelligence, just a fuzzy search that reacts to a not-found condition by returning items that are similar but not identical to the search term. By contrast, grammar check uses natural-language processing (NLP) and supervised machine learning (ML) to learn language rules and usage.

In 1981, Aspen Software released Grammatik, an add-on diction and style checker for personal computers. In 1992, Microsoft Office embedded a grammar checker in Microsoft Word. In 2007, Grammarly launched a cloud-based grammar checker.

Virtual assistants

Back in the day, a virtual assistant was really virtual, as in digital, not a term to describe a remote clerical worker.

As the personal computer gained popularity, it migrated into the homes of users, who had widely varying degrees of computer literacy and aptitude. Software providers rushed in to fill the void between computer capabilities and consumer competence.

Anybody using computers in 1997 will remember Clippy, Microsoft's ill-fated virtual assistant. Officially named Clippit, it was a stylized paper clip with googly eyes and Groucho eyebrows standing on a sheet of yellow legal-pad paper like Aladdin on a magic carpet. Watching from a corner of the window, Clippy would monitor what you typed and jump in when he thought you might need help.

For example, if you opened a new document and typed "Dear" followed by a space, Clippy would jump to the middle of the screen and say, "It looks like you're typing a letter. Would you like help?"

In 2010, three years after Clippy officially died, Apple launched Siri, followed in the next six years by Google Now, Alexa, Cortana, and Google Assistant. This new wave of virtual assistants uses voice recognition and expands the scope beyond help with a specific computer application to help with almost every aspect of life. Like chatbots, virtual assistants can be deployed in the enterprise to enhance internal or external customer service.

Clippy provided assistance based on Bayesian algorithms, a family of probabilistic classifiers. Modern virtual assistants use NLP to interact more like a human.

Chatbots

In 2001, AOL launched SmarterChild, a chatbot that could report the weather, do calculations and conversions, set reminders, store notes, and answer general questions that you would use a search engine or a virtual assistant for today.

Chatbots, also called *chatterbots,* are text-based applications or plugins that replace the human side of a conversation with artificial intelligence. Chatbots are frequently used on websites to provide tier-one technical support, schedule appointments, find a specific product, and other simple tasks that can be accomplished without human intervention. Early implementations had a limited ability to parse language and thus required the user to formulate a question with a very specific syntax and vocabulary. Deep learning based on intent recognition has expanded the utility of chatbots by freeing the user to ask questions in everyday language.

TIP

Unlike virtual assistants such as Siri, closed-domain chatbots are trained as experts in a specific field and can resolve a large volume of questions and requests simultaneously and continuously, tying into a customer relationship management platform and allowing call center employees to focus on more nuanced issues.

While many of these examples could be typified as business-to-consumer applications, AI began making inroads into enterprise and medical environments as early as the 1970s. Many of these applications use supervised learning, unsupervised learning, or a combination of both.

Recommendations

When Amazon launched in 1995, it sold only books and didn't have features such as "If you bought that, you might like this" or "Other people who bought that also bought this." Those features emerged a few years later and have expanded to nine different types of recommendation. Amazon doesn't publish numbers on their recommendation engine, but in 2013, McKinsey estimated recommendations were responsible for 35 percent of Amazon sales. Two key breakthroughs in use of recommendations were the following:

>> In 2001, Yahoo applied recommendation engines to streaming music with Yahoo LAUNCH, later rebranded as Yahoo Music and then Y! Music. Four years later Pandora went live, its recommendation engine powered by the music genome project, a manual classification system conceived by the founders in 1999.

>> In 2007, Netflix applied the recommendation engine to streaming video, powered by the CineMatch algorithm, which Netflix said was accurate to within half a star 75 percent of the time. In 2009, the company replaced CineMatch with Pragmatic Chaos, an algorithm developed by BellKor as a submission for the Netflix Prize competition, a $1 million contest for the first person or team that could beat CineMatch.

Medical diagnosis

Attempts to apply AI to medicine date back to the 1970s, but a wealth of data is a fundamental prerequisite for effective AI, and the real push to digitize medical records and test results didn't gain momentum until the twenty-first century. It's no surprise that the primary application is diagnostics. A 2013 review of three large U.S. studies reported that about 12 million patients, roughly 5 percent, are significantly misdiagnosed per year.

Currently, AI brings machine learning, natural-language processing, and other AI techniques to medical diagnosis.

Traditional breast cancer screening tests involve radiologists examining X-ray film for telltale signs of cancer. It is reliable most of the time, but it produces false negatives (20 percent of the time radiologists fail to find cancer when it is present) and false positives (a false alarm where radiologists mistakenly conclude cancer is present). About 50 percent of women who do annual mammograms get at least one false positive in a ten-year period.

In 2020, Google Health used DeepMind to train a model to recognize cancer in mammogram X-ray in U.K. patients. Compared to human radiologists, it reduced false negatives by 2.7 percent and false positives by 1.2 percent. When they extended the project to U.S. patients, the model reduced false negative by 9.4 percent and false positives by 5.7 percent.

Network intrusion detection and prevention

Hackers and cyber-crime date back to the 1970s, but things have changed a lot since Matthew Broderick hacked into a government computer to impress a girl and almost annihilated the planet in *War Games*. (Spoiler alert: Regarding playing the game, the computer comes to its conclusion through the use of reinforcement learning, the same AI technique used to train computers to beat human experts at chess and Go, and to train robots to walk.)

Back in the real world, it took the proliferation of the Internet and the dawn of e-commerce to provide the incentive for electronic malfeasance on a global scale. Conventional network intrusion detection systems (NIDS) and network intrusion prevention systems (NIPS) detect and prevent network attacks.

However, these systems have a significant usability issue in the triggering of false positives, marking legitimate traffic or behavior as an attack and requiring human intervention to respond to the anomaly and mark it as safe. A 2018 SANS survey found that in the face of a false positive rate of 50 percent, many security teams have taken to tuning the security settings to reduce the number of alerts. The problem with this practice is the potential to increase the number of false negatives, identifying a breach as harmless traffic — and it only takes one breach to cause a world of hurt.

As early as the mid-1990s, designers began exploring AI techniques, including unsupervised machine learning and artificial neural networks, to improve protection while reducing the need for human intervention. AI offers these capabilities:

>> AI leverages supervised learning and, especially, artificial neural networks to build a massive library of markers of hostile code, and then it scans incoming data for matches.

>> AI uses machine learning and security analytics, including user and entity behavior analytics, to detect external and internal risks earlier and more accurately than a traditional rules-based approach.

>> Some systems use natural-language processing to repel text-based attempts to trick users into replying with sensitive information via email and messaging by pretending to be from a legitimate source, such as a tech support agent, bank, or government agency, also known as *phishing attacks.*

Fraud protection and prevention

Anyone who has seen *It's a Wonderful Life* remembers how nervous everyone became when the bank examiner showed up at Bailey Building and Loan. He walked in with a briefcase and spent hours going over financial statements. These days, he might show up with a laptop and a scanner and let the algorithms process the paperwork and identify anomalies and violations of federal and state regulations.

As a field that is driven by well-defined practices, structured data, and *pro forma* documents and reports, the finance sector is well aligned for automation, and in light of the financial crises of 2000 and 2008, the emergence of practical AI is timely. The "2018 AFCE Global Study on Occupational Fraud and Abuse" reported a loss of $7 billion due to fraud in 2018 alone.

Recent approaches to fraud prevention use a range of AI tools, including data mining, supervised and unsupervised machine learning, behavioral analysis, link analysis, regression, decision trees, neural networks, and Bayesian networks.

Over the past five decades, AI has evolved from offering lightweight consumer applications or add-ons to supplementing and performing mission-critical and even life-or-death functions. The next sections introduce some of the ways AI is changing the landscape for the enterprise.

Benefits of AI for Your Enterprise

TIP

Artificial intelligence offers significant benefits for a broad range of markets. The most noticeable is optimizing the workforce by increasing their efficiency and reducing the burden of manual tasks. AI is good at automating things you might feel bad about asking someone else to do, either because it is tedious, such as reading through reams of reports, or dangerous, such as monitoring and managing workflow in a hostile environment. In other words, AI can relieve workers from the part of the job that they like the least.

In addition, when an algorithm produces results with high accuracy and predictability, mundane processes and routine decisions can be automated, thus reducing the need for human intervention in the paper chase of the typical enterprise and freeing workers to focus on tasks that increase revenue and customer satisfaction.

REMEMBER

AI thrives on data and excels at automating routine tasks, so those industries with a wealth of digitized data and manual processes are poised to reap large rewards from implementing AI. For these industries, AI can enhance the things you want to increase, such as quality, adaptability, and operational performance, and mitigate the things you want to reduce, such as expense and risk.

This section provides a bite-sized overview of industries that can derive specific benefits from implementing AI. Later chapters explore use cases for each in depth.

Healthcare

It's hard to find an industry more bogged down in data than healthcare. With the advent of the electronic health record, doctors often spend more time on paperwork and computers than with their patients.

>> In a 2016 American Medical Association study, doctors spent 27 percent of their time on "direct clinical face time with patients" and 49 percent at their desk and on the computer. Even worse, while in the examination room, only 53 percent of that time was spent interacting with the patient and 37 percent was spent on the computer.

>> A 2017 American College of Healthcare study found that doctors spend the same amount of time focused on the computer as they do on the patients.

>> A 2017 Summer Student Research and Clinical Assistantship study found that during an 11-hour workday, doctors spent 6 of those hours entering data into the electronic health records system.

The good news is that AI is changing that equation. Healthcare is a data-rich environment, which makes it a prime target for AI:

>> Natural-language processing can extract targeted information from unstructured text such as faxes and clinical notes to improve end-to-end workflow, from content ingestion to classification, routing documents to the appropriate backend systems, spotting exceptions, validating edge cases, and creating action items.

>> Data mining can accelerate medical diagnosis. In a 2017 American Academy of Neurology study, AI diagnosed a glioblastoma tumor specimen with actionable recommendations within 10 minutes, while human analysis took an estimated 160 hours of person-time.

>> Artificial neural networks can successfully triage X-rays. In a 2019 Radiology Journal study, the team trained an artificial neural network model with 470,300 adult chest X-rays and then tested the model with 15,887 chest

X-rays. The model was highly accurate, and the average reporting delay was reduced from 11.2 to 2.7 days for critical imaging findings and from 7.6 to 4.1 days for urgent imaging findings compared with historical data.

» Speech analytics can identify, from how someone speaks, a traumatic brain injury, depression, post-traumatic stress disorder (PTSD), or even heart disease.

Manufacturing

If any system is ripe for transferring the tedious work to intelligent agents, it's a system of thousands of moving parts that must be monitored and maintained to optimize performance. By combining remote sensors and the Internet of Things with AI to adjust performance and workflows within the plant or across plants, the system can optimize labor cost and liberate the workforce from the tedious job of monitoring instruments to add value where human judgment is required.

AI can also drive down costs using sensor data to automatically restock parts instead of referring to inventory logs and by recommending predictive maintenance as opposed to reactive maintenance, periodic maintenance, or preventative maintenance, extending the life of assets and reducing maintenance and total cost of ownership. McKinsey estimated cost savings and reductions could range from 5 to 12 percent from operations optimization, 10 to 40 percent from predictive maintenance, and 20 to 50 percent from inventory optimization.

Energy

In the energy sector, downtime and outages have serious implications. One study estimated that more than 90 percent of U.S. refinery shutdowns were unplanned. A McKinsey's survey found that, due to unplanned downtime and maintenance, rigs in the North Sea were running at 82 percent of capacity, well below the target of 95 percent, because, although they had an abundance of data from 30,000 sensors, they were using only 1 percent of it to make immediate yes-or-no decisions regarding individual rigs.

In December 2017, a hairline crack in the North Sea Forties pipeline halted production that cost Ineos an estimated £20 million per day. In contrast, Shell Oil used predictive maintenance and early detection to avoid two malfunctions, saving an estimated $2 million in maintenance costs and downtime.

TIP

AI can capture data across all rigs and other operations and production systems to apply predictive models that can quickly identify potential problems, order the required parts, and schedule the work when physical maintenance is required.

Banking and investments

The finance sector is blessed, or cursed, with both a super-abundance of paperwork and a surplus of regulation. I say "blessed" because the structured nature of the data and tightly defined rules create the perfect environment for an AI intervention.

Credit worthiness: AI can process customer data, such as credit history, social media pages, and other unstructured data, and make recommendations regarding loan applications.

Fraud prevention: AI can monitor transactions to detect anomalies and flag them for review.

Risk avoidance and mitigation: AI can review financial histories and the market to assess investment risks that can then be addressed and resolved.

Regulatory compliance: AI can be used to develop a framework to help ensure that regulatory requirements and rules are met and followed. Through machine learning, these systems can be programmed with regulations and rules to serve as a watchdog to help spot transactions that fail to adhere to set regulatory practices and procedures. This helps ensure real-time automated transaction monitoring to ensure proper compliance with established rules and regulations.

Intelligent recommendations: AI can mine not just a consumer's past online activity, credit score, and demographic profile, but also behavior patterns of similar customers, retail partners' purchase histories — even the unstructured data of a customer's social media posts or comments they've made in customer support chats, to deliver highly-targeted offers.

Insurance

Some in the industry think that factors unique to insurance — size, sales channel, product mix, and geography — are the fundamental cost drivers for insurers. However, a McKinsey survey notes that these factors account for just 19 percent of the differences in unit costs among property and casualty insurers and 46 percent among life insurers. The majority of costs are dependent on common business challenges, such as complexity, operating model, IT architecture, and performance management. AI can play a significant role in mitigating these costs.

Claims processing: Using NLP and ML, AI can process claims much faster than a human and then flag anomalies for manual review.

Fraud detection: The FBI estimates the annual cost of insurance fraud at more than $40 billion per year, adding $400 to $700 per year for the average U.S. family in the form of increased premiums. Using predictive analytics, AI can quickly process reams of documents and transactions to detect the subtle telltale markers that flag potential fraud or erratic account movements that could be the early signs of dementia.

Customer experience: Insurance carriers can use AI chatbots to improve the overall customer experience. Chatbots use natural-language patterns to communicate with consumers. They can answer questions, resolve complaints, and review claims.

Retail

The global economy continues to apply pressure to margins, but AI gives retailers many ways to push back.

Reduced customer churn: MBNA America found that a 5-percent reduction in customer churn can equate to a 125-percent increase in profitability. Predictive analytics can identify customers likely to leave as well as predicting the remedial actions most likely to be effective, such as targeted marketing and personalized promotions and incentives.

Improved customer experience: A 2014 McKinsey study notes that companies that improve their customer journey can see revenues increase by as much as 15 percent and lower costs by up to 20 percent. AI provides a deeper and contextual understanding of the customer as they interact with your brand. In particular, natural-language processing and predictive analytics provide a granular understanding of your customer regarding their product preferences, communication preferences, and which marketing campaigns are likely to resonate with each customer.

Optimized and flexible pricing: Predictive analytics enable a company to implement an optimized pricing strategy, pricing products according to a range of variables, such as channel, location, or time of year. The system creates highly accurate predictive models that study competitor prices, inventory levels, historic pricing patterns, and customer demand to ensure that pricing is correct for each situation, achieving up to 30 percent improvement in operating profit and increasing return on investment (ROI) up to 800 percent.

Personalized and targeted marketing: A 2016 Salesforce report found that 63 percent of millennials and 58 percent of Generation-X customers gladly share their data in return for personalized offers and discounts. Retailers are uniquely positioned to collect a range of data on individual customers, including preferences, buying history, and shopping patterns. Predictive analytics help personalize marketing and engagement strategies. A 2017 Segment study found that 49 percent of shoppers made impulse buys after receiving a personalized recommendation and 44 percent become repeat buyers after personalized experiences.

Improved inventory management: The days of overstocking inventory are quickly diminishing as retailers realize that optimized stock equals more profit. Predictive analytics gives retailers a better understanding of customer behavior to highlight areas of high demand, quickly identify sales trends, and optimize delivery so the right inventory goes to the right location. The results are streamlined supply chains, reduced storage costs, and expanded margins.

Legal

AI is tackling the mountain of paper that characterizes most legal proceedings by providing better and smarter insights from organizational data to detect compliance risks, predict case outcomes, analyze sentiment, identify useful documents, and gather business intelligence to make better-informed decisions. Through automation and the use of predictive analytics, these technologies have significantly helped reduce the time and costs associated with discovery.

A 2018 test pitted 20 lawyers with decades of experience against an AI agent three years into development and trained on tens of thousands of contracts. The task? Spot legal issues in five NDAs. The lawyers lost to the AI agent on time (average 92 minutes as opposed to 26 seconds) and accuracy (average of 85 percent as opposed to 94 percent).

In one case, a discovery team of three attorneys on a class-action lawsuit had 1.3 million documents to review. They used E-Discovery to code 97.7 percent of the 1.3 million documents as non-responsive, leaving fewer than 30,000 documents for the three-attorney team to review.

TIP

AI can aggregate and analyze data across a law department's cases for budget predictability, outside counsel and vendor spend analysis, risk analysis, and case trends to facilitate real-time decision-making and reporting. AI can perform document on-boarding and reviews based on continuous active learning to prioritize the most important documents for human review — lowering the total cost of review by up to 80 percent.

Human resources

Another bastion of paperwork, the HR department is a good candidate for streamlining processes using AI. In the 2018 "Littler Annual Employer Survey" of employers, the top three uses for AI were recruiting and hiring (49 percent), HR strategy and employee management (31 percent), and analyzing company policies and practices (24 percent).

As the average job opening attracts 250 resumes, the most immediate gains in efficiency are possible in recruiting and hiring. Scanning resumes into an applicant tracking system can reduce the time to screen from 15 minutes per resume to 1 minute. Natural-language processing and intent analysis go beyond keyword searches to find qualified candidates whose wording doesn't exactly match the job posting. Virtual assistants interact with candidates to schedule meetings, an otherwise time-consuming and tedious task. By automating these and similar tasks, HR personnel have more time to focus on strategic tasks that require an interpersonal approach.

Supply chain

Globalization increases volatility in demand, lead times, costs, and regulatory hurdles, just to name a few factors. The announcement of a new trade tariff or a sudden flare-up of civil unrest can force quick adjustments and decisions. AI and data visualization techniques can accelerate the transition from reactive operations to predictive supply chain management and automated replenishment. It starts with recovering the value locked up in structured and unstructured data to convert a data swamp into a data lake to provide pervasive visibility of the current state of all assets across the entire organization and beyond to partners, customers, competitors, and even the impact of the weather on operations and fulfillment. It ends with streamlined processes, improved customer satisfaction, reduced costs, and an increased bottom line.

Transportation and travel

Transportation issues have become the many-headed hydra of the twenty-first century, threatening the lifestyle and sustainability of metropolitan life. Addressing traffic is one of the defining challenges of worldwide urban life for this century.

Congestion: The cost of congestion in the U.S. reached $305 billion in 2017. AI can process the complex dataset of traffic monitoring to suggest intelligent traffic light models and use real-time tracking and scheduling to mitigate traffic, both on the road and for public transport systems.

Maintenance: A single downed truck can cost a fleet up to $760 per day. A grounded plane can cost more than $17,000 a day. Using machine learning and digital twins, you can assess the performance of a vehicle, plane, or train in real time and trigger notifications or alerts when repairs or preventive maintenance are needed. The system uses automation to order parts and schedule maintenance.

Public safety: AI can track real-time crime data to increase public safety and direct law enforcement to developing situations.

Freight transport: Predictive analytics can assist in forecasting volume to optimize routes and inventory.

Telecom

With the turn of the millennium and the advent of ubiquitous communications, the era of customer loyalty for a communications provider has passed. Customers churn faster than carriers can roll over minutes. As the network continues to evolve, customer quality-of-experience expectations increasingly dictate consumer behavior.

Customer support: AI-powered chatbots are helping many telecoms improve the customer experience while saving support costs. Nokia improved resolution rates by 20 to 40 percent. Vodafone improved customer satisfaction by 68 percent with its chatbot, TOBi.

Predictive and preventive maintenance: AI can process performance data at the equipment level to anticipate failure based on historical patterns and recommend tactical or strategic actions. For example, the system could alert a technician, who can use the AI-powered insights to proactively run diagnostics, perform root-cause analysis, and take action at any point in the link, from the set-top box all the way up the chain to the cell tower or network operations center. On the strategic level, these insights can inform network redesign to sustain better quality of experience and provide valuable data to inform development of new services to maintain a competitive edge.

Network optimization: AI can find patterns at the traffic level and notify the network operations center of anomalies so a potential issue can be corrected before it affects the quality of service and to assist in exploring alternatives for optimizing the existing network.

Public sector

In 2017, United States agencies collectively received more than 818,000 freedom-of-information (FOI) requests and processed more than 823,000. In the second quarter of 2017, the U.K. Department for Exiting the EU was able to respond to only 17 percent of FOI requests, and the Department for International Trade faired only slightly better at 21 percent.

AI can shorten the time to provide information by automating manual tasks and flagging requests that require special consideration, enabling government workers to focus on high-value tasks instead of tedium.

The U.S. Citizenship and Immigration Services respond to more than 8 million applications each year. In 2018, Emma, a virtual assistant on their website, responded to 11 million inquiries with a success rate of 90 percent.

AI-assisted decision-making: Many aspects of governance suffer from a surfeit of information. Separating the important from the mundane is a time-consuming and mind-numbing task for a human, but a simple and appropriate task for predictive analytics. AI can process and analyze enormous amounts and varieties of data to highlight patterns and reveal insights that facilitate efficient and effective decisions.

Internet of Things: As cities deploy devices such as traffic cameras, smart traffic lights, smart utility meters, and other sensors, AI can sift through the mountain of data they generate to streamline operations, optimize process control, and deliver better service.

Professional services

Professional services firms often focus on high-touch engagements that are essentially human-centric and thus may not seem to be good candidates for AI. However, much of the work they take on involves processes that are quite amenable to AI. Professional services touch many of the industries discussed in this chapter, and just as technology matures and affects all industries, of necessity it affects how professional services firms engage their clients.

The key takeaway is that AI won't replace core professional expertise, but it will make professional services firms more efficient and thus increase the value proposition for their clients. However, professionals who do begin to embrace AI will replace those who don't.

The applications span all industries:

>> Document intake, acceptance, digitization, maintenance, and management

>> Auditing, fraud detection, and fraud prevention

>> Risk analysis and mitigation

>> Regulatory compliance management

>> Claims processing

>> Inventory management

>> Resume processing and candidate evaluation

Marketing

The secret sauce in marketing is not a secret. The ingredients are well known and are used daily all over the world. What is new is the glut of data now available regarding every search, click, and comment your customers make. AI doesn't reinvent marketing. It just simplifies the daunting task of incorporating everything your data tells you about customers so you can anticipate their next move and improve the experience.

With AI, your marketing can accomplish these feats:

>> Use everything you know about customers, including their order history, browsing path through the website, customer service interactions, and social media posts

>> Target your candidates and customers down to the individual

>> Personalize messages according to whatever metric you have tracked, even down to buyer personas

>> Generate thousands of variations on a message

>> Schedule messages to maximize engagement

>> Train messages based on engagement feedback

>> Customize the customer experience on your website

>> Optimize customer engagement and reduce churn

>> Optimize price, even down to the individual if you so choose

>> Qualify leads automatically

>> Produce more accurate sales forecasts

Media and entertainment

AI obviously plays a big role in movies and video games through CGI, special effects, and gaming engines, but what can it do for the enterprise?

Valuing and financing: AI can use predictive analytics to determine the potential value of a script and then identify likely prospects for investment.

Personalized content: AI can analyze user data to make intelligent recommendations for streaming media services.

Search optimization. AI can support intelligent search engines for visual content for applications within and outside of the media industry.

Film rating: AI can use predictive analytics to process historical rating information to suggest the proper rating for a film.

Chapter **3**

Preparing for Practical AI

Considering the value that AI can bring to an organization, it's no wonder that the world is experiencing an AI renaissance. Gartner reported that the adoption rate for AI in the enterprise increased 270 percent between 2015 and 2019, and that trend shows no signs of slowing.

A 2018 Deloitte report found that the primary focus of enterprise AI deployments has been to optimize internal and external operations, make better decisions, and free workers to be more creative.

However, launching an AI initiative is not as simple as setting up powerful processors and massive storage and then throwing a bunch of data at it. It's a powerful beast and must be approached with all due caution.

Before you obsess on technology, you should take a deep breath and focus on a benefit. Identify specific use cases that are compatible with an AI solution. Next, evaluate the business case for each use case and solution, specifically for a near-future benefit. Then you can do a gap assessment to identify the next steps for moving forward.

Democratizing AI

For decades, artificial intelligence was the province of academics, scientists, and technicians with a highly specialized skill set. In the 1980s, some data scientists took the step from academe to commerce, applying AI to real-world problems and the development of expert systems. In the 1990s, commercial applications for AI expanded along with the Internet and the wealth of data it generated.

Even so, any business wanting to capitalize on the power of artificial intelligence had to commit a serious amount of capital, not only for rare and expensive data scientists, but also for major-league processing power and data storage.

More recently, full-powered AI solutions with simplified interfaces allow users to create and train models and produce reports and data visualization, reducing the need for a full team of dedicated data scientists.

In fact, Gartner predicted that workers using self-service analytics would output more analysis than professional data scientists. That's good news for enterprises. And don't worry about putting data scientists out of business. They are still in high demand. For the last three years, data scientist was the #1 ranked job in the U.S. on the career website Glassdoor.

Visualizing Results

The key to actionable insight is the ability to quickly recognize what the data is telling you. Any AI solution you use must have a rich, robust, and easy-to-use data visualization engine.

Good data visualization transcends barriers of language and culture to instantly communicate the important data points and trends. It also has the virtue of being easy to share and to engage with. Table 3-1 shows four visualization types categorized by use.

Comparison

When you want to compare a selection of things, you line them up on the table to see them all at once. That's how a comparison visualization works.

TABLE 3-1

Types of Visualizations and Uses

Type	Use
Comparison	Compare two or more values on an XY axis.
	Examples: timeline, trend, ranking
	Types: line, column, bar, timeline
Composition	Show how the parts relate to the whole.
	Examples: revenue of product mix over time, breakdown of demographic data across the range of a variable
	Types: stacked bars/columns, pie/donut, stacked area, waterfall, polar
Distribution	Show the value of one variable tracked across a set of categories.
	Examples: sales across regions or stores, age ranges in demographic
	Types: histogram, line, area, scatter plot, map
Relationship	Show the connection between two or more variables.
	Examples: track revenue versus cost across regions or stores, show traffic or accident incidents by weather or time of day
	Types: scatter, bubble, line

One way to do that is a bar chart, either vertical or horizontal. One axis displays the collection of categories or ranges and the other the quantity, rank, or another metric.

Another way is to have the X axis represent one variable and the Y axis represent a different variable, and then plot the data points. The data points can even use bubble size to represent a third variable, packing information into a simple visualization that conveys lots of information in a glance. Figure 3-1 shows the number of page visits on the X axis, the duration of the visit on the Y axis, and income band by the size of the bubble.

Composition

A composition visualization drills down into the information that comprises a single number.

For example, you may know the total number of employees across industries, but there is more information buried in the data.

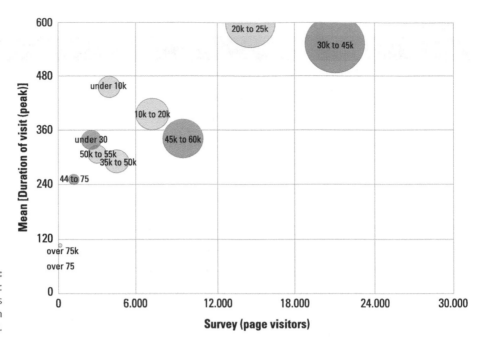

FIGURE 3-1:
Comparison:
Total page visits
by mean duration
of visit.

The top part of Figure 3-2 shows a bar chart with the various categories of employees on one axis and the number of employees on the other axis to help you understand the composition of the workforce across industries. The bottom part of Figure 3-2 shows a donut chart breaking down the percentage of revenue per market segment.

Distribution

A distribution visualization conveys how the data points fall across categories or locations and such. For example, you can show a table of counties in alphabetical order and the number of startups for each county, but it is hard to get a sense of how they relate geographically. Figure 3-3 uses a heat map to represent values through colors, often with gradations shades or tints indicating the values of adjacent numbers.

Relationship

A relationship visualization reveals how two or more variables affect each other. You can show relationships through a variety of methods.

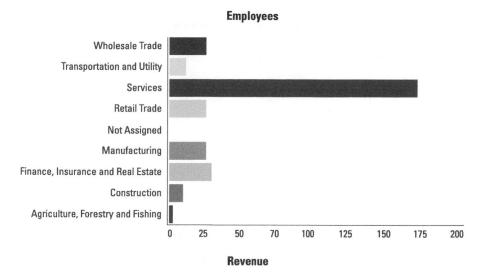

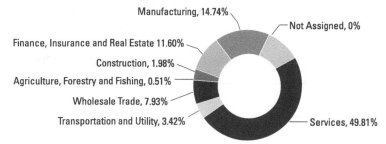

FIGURE 3-2:
Composition:
Employee per
industry (top),
revenue per
market segment
(bottom).

The simplest is a line graph showing how one variable rises or falls along the Y axis as it moves through degrees of another variable on the X axis. A scatter plot is useful when the data is not linear, such as representing the height and weight of a population, where there are multiple instances of weight for each height. A bubble chart is a scatter plot using the size of the bubble to represent a third variable.

You can also indicate relationship by graphing two variables on one axis across a third variable on the other axis. Figure 3-4 graphs call center wait times and customer satisfaction scores across time.

FIGURE 3-3: Distribution: Startups per county.

FIGURE 3-4: Relationship: Call center wait time versus satisfaction score.

Digesting Data

Of the three pillars of AI — processing power, scalable storage, and big data — the third is the one that presents the biggest challenge. How to get it, how to validate it, how to process it.

Figure 3-5 shows the pyramid of critical success factors for AI and analytics. Four of the six layers relate to data, focusing on relevance, accessibility, usability, completeness, and data-based conclusions.

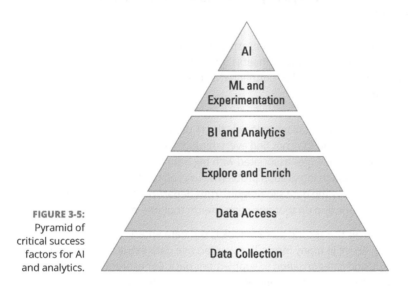

FIGURE 3-5: Pyramid of critical success factors for AI and analytics.

Table 3-2 describes critical questions to answer at each layer.

TABLE 3-2

Pyramid of Critical Success Factors for AI and Analytics

Element	Questions
AI	How will you address analytical deployment, governance, and operations?
Experimentation ML	Does machine learning add business value? How do you define success?
BI / Analytics	What is the story your data is telling? What conclusions can you make from this information?
Explore and Enrich	Can the data be used meaningfully? Are you missing any data or features?
Data Access	Is the data accessible and usable (analysis-ready)? Is the data flow reliable?
Data Collection	Do you have data relevant to your business goals?

Identifying data sources

Before you start, you should perform a data audit to determine what data you already have and identify gaps in your data that you must fill to accomplish your business goals.

As mentioned in Chapter 1, for the enterprise, data falls into two categories: structured data (databases and spreadsheets) and unstructured data (email, text messages, voice mail, social media, connected sensors, and so on). Potential sources for data include:

>> **Internal data:** The first place to look is the IT department, but depending on the organization, you may not find everything you need in one place. The most common challenges associated with big data aren't analytics problems; they are information integration problems. To reap the benefits of big data, you must first slay the data silo dragon, from department-level tribal thinking down to that one app on that one computer in that one person's office.

>> **Data capture:** The second place to look is the data entering your organization. It can arrive in many forms, but you can use data extraction, metadata extraction, and categorization to supplement data. For example, you can run paper documents, whether handwritten or printed, through an optical character recognition system to digitize them in preparation for processing. Then they can join the rest of the digital data, such as emails, PDF files, Word documents, images, voice mail messages, videos, and other formats to be classified and populate the data store that will feed your AI insights.

>> **Data as a service (DaaS):** If there are still holes in your data requirements, you can turn to third-party data for purchase, either commercial datasets such as Accuweather or public datasets such as data.gov and Kaggle.com. Broadening your datasets can increase the insights lurking in your own data.

Cleaning the data

What's worse than no data? Dirty data. Dirty data is poorly structured, poorly formatted, inaccurate, or incomplete.

For example, you might expect it would be easy for a system to scan a document and extract a date — until you reflect that Microsoft Excel alone has 17 different date formats, as show in in Figure 3-6.

Table 3-3 shows several ways that dirty data can manifest.

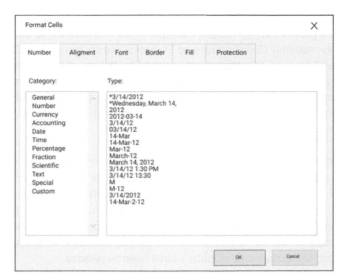

TABLE 3-3 **Types of Dirty Data**

Type	Example
Incomplete	Empty or null values — the most prevalent type of bad data
Incorrect	A date with a 47 in the month or day position
Inaccurate	A data with a valid month value (1-12) but the wrong month
Inconsistent	Different formats or terms for the same meaning
Duplicate	One or more occurrences of the same record
Rule violation	Starting date falls after ending date

WARNING

Why is dirty data worse? Because it costs you more.

For most companies, bad data costs from 15 to 25 percent of revenue as workers research a valid source, correct errors, and deal with the complications that result from relying on bad data.

The solution is to focus on data, not models. Not surprisingly, in a recent Crowd-Flower survey, data scientists said the top two time-consuming tasks were cleaning and organizing data (60 percent) and collecting datasets (19 percent). However, in the survey, they also identified as the least enjoyable part of their job cleaning and organizing data (57 percent) and collecting datasets (21 percent).

Here's a particularly trenchant example of the importance of data quality. In 2015, the International Classification of Diseases, Ninth Revision (ICD-9) coding system used for medical claims was replaced by the more robust, more specific ICD-10 system. ICD-10 provides a higher level of specificity that includes diagnoses, symptoms, site, severity, and treatments. Health providers had the option to use the simpler unspecified ICD-9 codes during the first year as they learned and became accustomed to the more complex system.

During the one-year grace period, many providers just continued to use the ICD-9 codes rather than transition to the more accurate ICD-10 codes, and their automated claims submissions reflected the less specific data. Claim denials increased, which meant more work for the providers who had to retroactively collect supporting documentation to appeal the denial or face loss of revenue. If they had submitted the claims with the more accurate, although a bit more complex, ICD-10 codes, the extra work wouldn't have been necessary.

You can take this anecdote a step further. Imagine that a few years later, the facility that didn't upgrade to ICD-10 codes decides to transition to an AI-enabled medical records system to not only streamline document intake, but also serve as a database for medical history and diagnosis. They lose all the potential benefit of diagnostic insights from the history for the "dark year."

An Alegion study found that two of the top three problems with training data relate to dirty data.

Defining Use Cases

"I suppose it is tempting, if the only tool you have is a hammer, to treat everything as if it were a nail."

— *Abraham Maslow, "The Psychology of Science: A Reconnaissance" 1966*

To hear some tell it, AI is the panacea to solve all the problems of the world; to hear others tell it, AI will lead to the singularity and the destruction of human civilization. As usual, the truth lies somewhere in between.

As with any tool, AI does some things well and other things not so well. If you're upholstering a chair, a tack hammer is best, but if you're putting up a circus tent, you need a bigger hammer.

As twentieth-century psychologist Abraham Maslow pointed out, the problem arises when you start with a tool and try to use it on every challenge or obstacle you encounter. The better approach is to identify a desired outcome and select the tool that possesses capabilities suited to achieving the desired outcome. So what is AI good at?

A → B

As computer scientist Andrew Ng points out, "Despite AI's breadth of impact, the types of AI being deployed are still extremely limited. Almost all of AI's recent progress is through one type, in which some input data (A) is used to quickly generate some simple response (B)."

Often, response B consists of nothing more than "Is this X or not X?" For example:

>> Is this transaction nominal or anomalous?

>> Is this document a patient case history?

>> Does this image contain a human face?

This capability is known as *supervised learning,* in which AI learns the relationship between A and B by processing massive amounts of data, guided by humans to establish the rules that govern the decisions. (See Chapter 1 for more information.)

In other cases, B is a transformation of A, such as when AI is used for transcribing or translating a passage. This capability is known as *natural-language processing.*

Good use cases

A good use case for AI relies on the core enablers of AI as a tool — big data, digitalization, and well-defined classification and rules.

A 2019 IDC guide on worldwide AI spending through 2023 indicated that the top three use cases are automated customer service agents, automated threat intelligence and prevention systems, and sales process recommendation and automation; the use cases with the biggest growth are human resource automation and pharmaceutical research and development. Each case includes a wealth of digital source data and well-defined categories. If you look back over the "Benefits of AI for Your Enterprise" section in Chapter 2, you will notice that those use cases also share those characteristics.

Bad use cases

"Knowledge is knowing that a tomato is a fruit. Wisdom is not putting it in a fruit salad."

— *Miles Kington*

At this point in its development, AI is not a good tool for tasks that involve the human touch, such as situations that require creativity, imagination, empathy, compassion, and the like.

For example, although AI is an excellent tool for legal document capture, archiving, searching, and flagging issues for human review, you wouldn't want AI to be the judge or jury in your trial. You might be able to appeal to the mercy of the court, but at present it isn't possible to appeal to the mercy of the algorithm.

Reinforcement learning and model drift

Perhaps the most classic example of the difficulty of coding and training empathy into AI is Microsoft's Twitter bot, Tay. Launched at 7:14 a.m. on March 23, 2016, Tay was designed to mimic the linguistic patterns of a 19-year-old female. But within 16 hours of her launch, and after 96,000 tweets, Microsoft suspended the Twitter account because Tay had become an alt-right, Holocaust-denying, anti-feminist, anti-Semitic troll.

Although Microsoft hasn't disclosed the technology behind Tay, it has the earmarks of a subset of machine learning called *reinforcement learning.* Used to teach computers how to play games or to train a robot how to walk, reinforcement learning defines success criteria and then rewards the algorithm when it gets closer to the desired behavior. The machine must figure out for itself how to achieve success. On social media, success correlates to likes, so Tay learned how to maximize engagement from the people who interacted with her.

Tay is an example of *model drift.* After the model was initially trained and Tay interacted with users without a human in the loop or any automated testing to correct for bias or other issues, model drift came into play due to the skewed nature of the data it encountered.

Nine months later, Microsoft launched Zo, Tay's 13-year-old sister, which didn't use reinforcement learning, so model drift wasn't an issue. Zo avoided potentially charged topics such as religion and politics, shutting them down with comments such as, "not gonna keep talking if u keep this up . . . just sayin." Zo lasted for more than two years before disengaging on most social media platforms in March 2019, and completely in July 2019.

Insufficient or biased data

Then there is the problem of insufficient training data. In 2017, due to reports of possible student visa fraud, the U.K. Home Office used voice-recognition software to flag cases where it appeared that the same voice took an English-proficiency test for multiple students. However, voice-recognition accuracy rates are dependent on having known samples of the voice being reviewed, and the organization doing the review didn't have independent samples of the English-proficiency test candidates. Based on the results of the review, the government refused, cut short, or canceled the visas of nearly 36,000 people.

In the fall of 2019, the U.S. National Institute of Standards and Technology tested 189 facial recognition algorithms from 99 developers using 18.27 million images of 8.89 million people taken from four sources: domestic mugshots, immigration applications, visa applications, and border crossings.

They tested two common matching tasks for false positives (finding a match where there isn't one) and false negatives (failing to find a match when there is one):

>> **One-to-one matching:** Match a photo to another photo of the same person in a database. Examples: Unlock your smartphone, board an airplane, check a passport.

>> **One-to-many searching:** Determine whether a photo has a match in a database. Example: Identify suspects in an investigation.

For one-to-one matching, most systems reported false positives for Asian and African American faces, with algorithms developed in Asia doing better at matching Asian faces. Algorithms developed in the U.S. consistently registered a high rate of false positives for Asian, African American, and Native American faces. For one-to-many matching, African American females had the highest rates of false positives.

Essentially, facial recognition works best for people with the same phenotype, or observable characteristics of an individual based on their genetic makeup, as the people who developed the algorithm. Those outside the bias of the model will experience problems with determining their identity for travel and law enforcement purposes, or with being falsely accused of a crime when law enforcement gets a false positive in one-to-many matching.

False positives

At the June 3, 2017 UEFA Champions League Final in Cardiff, Wales, the South Wales Police used facial recognition to scan the crowd for known criminals. The system flagged 2,470 potential matches with custody pictures, but 92 percent of those matches were false positives.

In 2018, the American Civil Liberties Union (ACLU) used Amazon's Rekognition face recognition software with default settings to search a publicly available arrest-photo database using the headshot photos of all 535 members of the U.S. Congress. The software incorrectly matched 28 of them with a criminal in the database. In 2019, the ACLU ran the same exercise for the California legislature and got 26 false positives out of 120 legislators.

For now, it seems that you can't turn over identifying a person to the facial recognition algorithms. Human intervention is still required.

Reducing bias

Because AI systems are designed by humans, it is not a surprise that they would have bias in them. It can start at the very beginning when the problem is framed, in data collection, data preparation, or in all three.

As Microsoft's experiment with Twitter revealed, an algorithm maximizes success as defined by the designers. Solon Barocas, an assistant professor at Cornell University who specializes in fairness in machine learning, pointed out that an issue arises while framing the problem when "those decisions are made for various business reasons other than fairness or discrimination. If the algorithm discovered that giving out subprime loans was an effective way to maximize profit, it would end up engaging in predatory behavior even if that wasn't the company's intention."

Increasingly, social media has become a textbook case of algorithmically-enforced confirmation bias, or emergent bias. Emergent bias isn't based on the source data, but rather on how the algorithm interacts with the user. For example, if a user likes, favorites, or subscribes to content with a certain viewpoint, such as articles about vaccinations, vegan diets, politics, or even exotic coffee, the algorithm feeds that user more content with the same viewpoint and excludes content from an opposing viewpoint. For example, coffee lovers get more content about the positive effects of coffee consumption and less content about the negative effects of excessive caffeine intake. Over time, the platform magnifies the echo-chamber effect of self-validation, amplifying the person's inherent bias.

As of this writing, automated and human-in-the-loop tools to address bias, security, compliance, and transparency are appearing in the marketplace.

TIP

When determining a specific use case for AI, consider these guidelines:

1. Create a process that guides the development of trustworthy AI aligned with human values.

2. When framing the problem, seek a wide consensus of people to assure that the rewards are neutral and non-discriminatory.

3. Select people with a diverse set of perspectives to build the models.

4. Use diverse and high-quality relevant data.

5. Scrub your sources for bad data or hidden bias, such as race, gender, ideological differences, and the like. For example, a bank might remove gender and race from its loan-processing AI model, but U.S. ZIP codes can often serve as a proxy for race. Their inclusion could still lead to biased predictions that discriminate against historically underprivileged neighborhoods.

6. Rigorously examine the criteria for identifying selection variables.

7. Test machines for sources of bias and evidence of bias, and remedy any problems discovered.

Choosing a Model

Although you might hear the term "artificial intelligence" bandied about as if it were a single thing, the reality is that it is an umbrella term for a vast discipline covering countless models or algorithms of varying complexity and rigor. Even within machine learning, dozens of methods can help you accomplish your goal, each used for a specific type of problem.

Unsupervised learning

This method of ML recognizes patterns in a dataset and infers the structure or identifies correlations between data elements. You use unsupervised learning when you want to discover relationships, such as between account activity and fraud or an attack on the system. Table 3-4 lists AI project goals and the appropriate algorithms used for that task.

TABLE 3-4   **Unsupervised Learning Algorithms**

Goal	Algorithm
Organize data in clusters or trees, such as evaluating investments according to volatility or return	Hierarchical cluster analysis
Recommend a product or service based on the choices of similar customers	Recommendation engine
Optimize delivery routes by identifying proximate destinations	K-means clustering
Identify risk of heart disease based on heart sounds	Gaussian mixture

Supervised learning

You use supervised learning when you want to classify new data based on known relationships in historical data, such as labeling incoming documents or screening job applications. Table 3-5 lists AI project goals and the appropriate algorithms used for that task.

TABLE 3-5   **Supervised Learning Algorithms**

Goal	Algorithm
Detect fraud in financial transactions	Random forest
Forecast for supply chain management	Regression
Forecast sales	Neural network
Underwrite loans	Decision tree

Deep learning

This method of ML requires massive amounts of data, but typically with more accuracy and efficiency than other methods. You use deep learning when you want to solve complex problems such as image classification, natural-language processing, and speech recognition. Table 3-6 lists AI project goals and the appropriate algorithms used for that task.

TABLE 3-6   **Deep Learning Algorithms**

Goal	Algorithm
Train smarter chatbots, perform language translation	Recurrent neural network
Make medical diagnoses using computer vision	Convolutional neural network

Reinforcement learning

This method of ML learns a task through trial and error based on preferring actions that are rewarded and avoiding actions that are not. You use reinforcement learning when you need to find the optimum way of interacting with an environment, such as to automate stock trading or to teach a robot to perform a physical task.

IN THIS CHAPTER

» Climbing the AI competency pyramid

» Doing things in the right order

» Building a data science team

» Finding the right partners

» Weighing your options

Chapter **4**

Implementing Practical AI

Before you jump into the deep end, take some time to test the water.

The AI Competency Hierarchy

The high-value applications of AI are built upon a hierarchy of competencies. Figure 4-1 shows the hierarchy of competencies required to use artificial intelligence.

Data collection

Data collection is the foundation of the pyramid, the stage where you identify what data you need and what is available. If the goal is a user-facing product, are all relevant interactions logged? If it is a sensor, what data is coming through and how? Without data, no machine learning or AI solution can learn or predict outcomes.

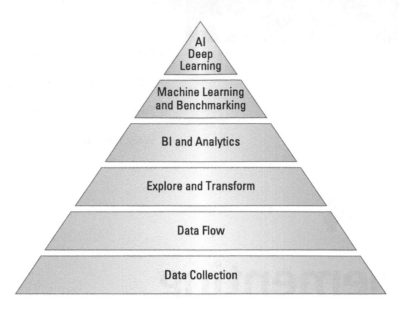

FIGURE 4-1:
Hierarchy of AI
competencies.

Data flow

Identify how the data flows through the system. Is there a reliable stream or extract, transform, and load (ETL) process established? Where is the data stored, and how easy is it to access and analyze?

Explore and transform

This is a time-consuming and underestimated stage of the data science project life cycle. At this point, you realize you are missing data, your machine sensors are unreliable, or you are not tracking relevant information about customers. You may be forced to return to data collection and ensure the foundation is solid before moving forward.

Business intelligence and analytics

After you can reliably explore and clean data, you can start building what is traditionally thought of as business intelligence or analytics, such as defining key metrics to track, identifying how seasonality impacts product sales and operations, segmenting users based on demographic factors, and the like.

Now is the time to determine:

>> The features or attributes to include in machine-learning models

>> The training data the machine will need to learn

>> What you want to predict and automate

>> How to create the labels from which the machine will learn

TIP

You can create labels automatically, such as the system logging a machine event in the backend system, or through a manual process, such as when an engineer reports an issue during a routine inspection and the result is manually added to the data.

Machine learning and benchmarking

To avoid real-world disasters, before the sample data is used to make predictions, create a framework for A/B testing or experimentation and deploy models incrementally. Model validation and experimentation can provide a rough estimate of the effects of changes before you implement them. Establish a very simple baseline or benchmark for performance tracking. For example, if you are building a credit card fraud detection system, create test data by monitoring known fraudulent credit card transactions and compare them to the results of your model to verify it accurately detects fraud.

Artificial intelligence

After you reach this stage, you can improve processes, predictions, outcomes, and insights by expanding your knowledge, understanding, and experience with new methods and techniques in machine learning and deep learning.

Scoping, Setting Up, and Running an Enterprise AI Project

Recently Gartner analyst Nick Heudecker generated a firestorm of debate when he said a previous Gartner statistic that reported 60 percent of big-data projects fail was too conservative and that an 85 percent failure rate is more accurate. Either way, it's a daunting statistic.

One way to avoid becoming a statistic is to approach your AI journey using an industry-proven model — the Machine Learning Development life cycle. Figure 4-2 shows the seven elements of the methodology. This methodology is based on the cross-industry standard process for data mining (CRISP-DM), a widely used open standard process model that describes common approaches used by data mining experts.

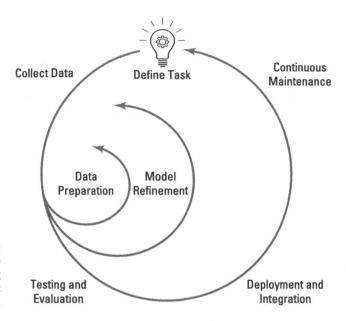

FIGURE 4-2:
The Machine
Learning
Development
life cycle.

Table 4-1 shows the questions that must be answered for each element.

TABLE 4-1 ### The Machine Learning Development Life Cycle: Elements and Questions

Element	Question
Define the task	What problem or question do you want to address with data?
Collect data	What data do you have that could answer our questions?
Prepare the data	What do you need to do to prepare the data for mining?
Build the model	How can you mimic or enhance the human's knowledge or actions through technology?
Test and evaluate the model	What new information do you know now?
Deploy and integrate the model	What actions should you trigger with the new information? What needs human validation?
Maintain the model	How has the data changed over time? Do the results reflect current reality?

The process of developing a machine-learning model is highly iterative. Often, you will find yourself returning to previous steps before proceeding to a subsequent one. A machine-learning project is not considered complete after the first version has been deployed. Instead, the feedback you collect after the initial version helps you shape new goals and improvements for the next iteration.

In the light of this feedback-and-iterate practice, the model is more a life cycle than a process, largely because, for the most part, in the model, data drives the process, not a hunch or policy or committee or some immutable principle. You start with a hypothesis or a burning question, such as "What do all our loyal customers have in common?" or flip it to ask "What do all our cancellations have in common?" Then you gather the required data, train a model with historical data, run current data to answer that question, and then act on the answer. The steering group provides input along the way, but the data reflects the actual, not the hypothetical.

This principle of data-driven discovery and action is an important part of the life cycle because it assures that the process is defensible and auditable. It keeps the project from going off the rails and down a rabbit hole.

TIP

Using the life cycle, you will always be able to answer questions such as how and why you created a particular model, how you will assess its accuracy and effectiveness, how you will use it in a production environment, and how it will evolve over time. You will also be able to identify model drift and determine whether changes to the model based on incoming data are pointing you toward new insights or diverting you toward undesired changes in scope.

Of the seven steps in the methodology, the first three take up the most time. You may recall that cleaning and organizing data takes up to 60 percent of the time of a data scientist. There's a good reason for that. Bad data can cost up to 25 percent of revenue.

However, all that time spent preparing the data will be wasted if you don't really know what you want out of the data.

Define the task

What problem or question do you want to address with data? Follow these steps:

1. Determine your business objectives.

2. Assess the situation.

3. Determine your data mining goals.

4. Produce a project plan.

REMEMBER

Some people think of AI as a magic machine where you pour data into the hopper, turn the crank, and brilliance comes out the other end. The reality is that a data science project is the process of actually building the machine, not turning the crank. And before you build a machine, you must have a very clear picture of what you want the machine to do.

Even though the process is data-driven, you don't start with data. You start with questions. You may have a wealth of pristine data nicely tailored to databases, but if you don't know what you're trying to do, when you turn the crank, the stuff that comes out the other end might be interesting, but it won't be actionable.

That's why you start with questions. If you ask the right questions, you will know what kind of data you need. And if you get the right data, at the end you will get the answers — and likely more questions as well.

TIP

During the business understanding step, you establish a picture of what success will look like by determining the criteria for success. This step starts with a question. In the course of determining what you need to answer the question, you explore the terminology, assumptions, requirements, constraints, risks, contingencies, costs, and benefits related to the question and assemble an inventory of available resources.

For example, your initial question might be "What is causing an increase in customer churn?" This question could be expanded to ask "Can you pinpoint specific sources of friction in the customer journey that are leading to churn?"

Pursuing that question may lead you to brainstorming and research, such as documenting the touchpoints in the current customer journey, analyzing the revenue impact of churn, and listing suspected candidates for friction.

Moreover, it can be advisable to outline what outputs or range of outputs will make the solution valuable to the business. If at any time during the project it appears something is going to get in the way of this outcome — for example, not having enough data — a decision can be made to address that shortcoming or put the project on hold until the issue can be addressed. Ultimately, you want the output to deliver the value sought in the organization. Great organizations maintain a list of AI/ML tasks and projects, prioritized by their likelihood to succeed and the degree of business value if successful. This way, if a project hits a hiccup, you can move to the next project on the list until the kinks are worked out.

Collect the data

What data do you have that may be able to answer your questions? Follow these steps:

1. Collect initial data.

2. Describe the data.

3. Explore the data.

4. Verify data quality.

To get to where you're going, first you must know where you are.

Remember that moment in *The Princess Bride* when Westley, Inigo, and Fezzik list their assets and liabilities before storming the castle and determine that they will need a wheelbarrow and that a holocaust cloak would come in handy? That was data understanding.

TIP

During the data understanding step, you establish the type of data you need, how you will acquire it, and how much data you need. You may source your data internally, from second parties such as solution partners, or from third-party providers.

For example, if you are considering a solution for predictive maintenance on a train, you might pull information from Internet of Things (IoT) sensors, weather patterns, and passenger travel patterns.

To make sure you have the data required to answer your questions, you must first ask questions. What data do you have now? Are you using all the data you have? Maybe you're collecting lots of data, but you use only three out of ten fields.

This step takes time, but it is an essential exercise that will increase the likelihood that you can trust the results and that you aren't misled by the outcomes.

Prepare the data

What do you need to do to prepare the data for mining? Follow these steps:

1. Select the data.

2. Clean the data.

3. Construct the data.

4. Integrate the data.

5. Format the data.

Select the data: In this current data-rich environment, narrowing the options to identify the exact data you need can pose a challenge. Factors to consider are relevance and quality. In cases that might be sensitive to bias, you must pay close attention to seemingly unrelated fields that might serve as a proxy. In a classic example, a loan approval process excluded race from its model, but included ZIP code, which often correlates directly with race, so the process retained the same level of bias as before.

Clean the data: The available data for your project may have issues, such as missing or invalid values or inconsistent formatting. Cleaning the data involves establishing a uniform notation to express each value and setting default values or using a modeling technique to estimate suitable values for empty fields.

Construct the data: In some cases, you might need a field that can be calculated or inferred from other fields in the data. For example, if you are doing analysis by sales region, detailed order records may not include the region, but that information can be derived from the address. You might even need to create new records to indicate the absence of an activity, such as creating a record with a value of zero to indicate the lack of sales for a product in a region.

Integrate the data: You might encounter a situation where you need to combine information from different data sources that store the data in different ways. For example, suppose you are analyzing store sales by region; if you don't have a table for store-level data, you need to aggregate the order information for each store from individual orders to create store-level data. Or you may need to merge data from multiple tables. For example, in the store sales by region analysis, you may combine regional information such as manager and sales team from one source with store information from another source into one table.

Format the data: The data you need might be trapped in an image, such as a presentation or graphic, in which case you would have to extract it through some method, such as optical character recognition, and then store the information as structured data.

Build the model

How can you mimic or enhance the human's knowledge or actions through technology? Follow these steps:

1. Select an algorithm and modeling techniques.
2. Test the fit.
3. Build the model.
4. Assess the model.

This step represents the primary role of a data scientist. Based on the data and likely best fit, the data scientist selects what should be the most promising algorithm, often from an open source library like MLlib. Then, the data scientist uses techniques like those available in popular programming languages like R or Python to build a usable ML model based on the algorithm and the data. The process can take some time based on peculiarities in the data or the nuances of your business. In the end, however, based on training the algorithm using the sanitized historical data, you get actionable information such as a prediction or a next best action.

By now, the modeling technique to use should be an obvious choice based on the questions you developed at the beginning and the data you have to work with. See Chapter 3 for a review of modeling techniques.

TIP

After you have trained the model using the source dataset, test its accuracy with the test dataset. One way of evaluating test results for a classification model is to use a confusion matrix, which is a simple classification quadrant, also known as Pasteur's quadrant.

For a simple example, consider a binary classifier that produces a yes-or-no answer. There are two ways of getting it right (to correctly predict yes or no) and two ways of getting it wrong (to incorrectly predict yes or no). In this case, imagine a recommendation engine offering a yes-or-no prediction for a specific customer regarding 100 items compared to the customer's actual responses. Table 4-2 shows a set of possible results.

TABLE 4-2 ## Example of Binary Classifier Results

Iterations=100		AI (Predicted)	
		No	Yes
Customer (Actual)	No	35	10
	Yes	5	50

A result can be true or false and positive or negative, giving four possibilities as shown in Table 4-3.

TABLE 4-3 ## Example Results Categories

Prediction	Actual	Category	Percent
Yes	Yes	True positive	50
No	No	True negative	35
Yes	No	False positive	10
No	Yes	False negative	5

In this case, the model has an accuracy rate of 0.85. That number may be good or bad, depending on your requirements. You may move forward, or you may refine the model and try again.

Test and evaluate the model

What new information do you know now? Follow these steps:

1. Evaluate the results.
2. Review the process.
3. Determine the next steps.

In the penultimate step, you go back to the beginning and compare your goals with the results to determine if they provided enough of the right kind of insight to allow you to answer your questions.

Deploy and integrate the model

What actions should you trigger with the new information? What needs human validation? Follow these steps:

1. Plan the deployment.
2. Plan monitoring and maintenance.
3. Produce the final report and presentation.
4. Review the project.

After you have an acceptable model, it's time to roll out the information using the plan developed during the business understanding stage so your teams can execute on the insight the project has produced. Look for game-changing insights that will alter how you do business. You might change workflows, introduce automation at some points, and establish touchpoints for human intervention. You might introduce confidence scoring, with automated actions for outcomes above or below a window and human review for the middle ground.

Maintain the model

Because data has a shelf-life, no data science project can run under the set-and-forget philosophy. In the maintenance stage, your model must regularly retrain on fresh data so the answers reflect the new reality of now.

The final report can be as simple as a summary of the life of the project and the outcomes, or it can be an exhaustive analysis of the results, their implications, and your plans for implementing the insights.

TIP

It's always a good idea to have a lessons-learned session after any significant effort, particularly if you plan to continue using it. This meeting can cover rabbit trails you followed and insights into best practices.

Creating a High-Performing Data Science Team

AI projects are not solo sports. They require the ongoing contributions and collaboration from a number of key team members. Because data science is an intersection of various functions, including math and statistics, computer science, and business knowledge, you need a dynamic group of individuals to form a high-performing machine-learning team.

Typically, teams involve individuals from data science and data engineering, as well as subject matter experts. Here is more detail on the people you need:

>> **Data engineers:** These specialists are typically tasked with building the data infrastructure of an organization. They have strong programming and hardware skills, are familiar with big-data technologies, and excel in building data pipelines. They are not necessarily experts in analyzing and modeling data, but they should be able to work with relevant business divisions to determine the data characteristics for each use case.

>> **Data scientists:** After you have built your data infrastructure, you need people who can take that data, clean it, analyze it, apply algorithms, run experiments, and communicate results effectively. These professionals typically use tools (such as Jupyter notebook and RStudio), have knowledge of programming languages (such as R and Python), and have experience working with big-data technologies (such as Apache Hadoop and Apache Spark). In addition, they have a strong background in statistics, programming, and machine learning.

>> **Subject matter experts:** These experts help cultivate strategies, generate ideas, and examine factors necessary for supporting different use cases. They understand the key business problem, processes, and challenges. Their input and knowledge are crucial in helping the team develop meaningful solutions that provide business value and overcome challenges.

>> **Data science manager:** These experts are hands-on leaders who help build the foundation of an organization's data science strategy, recruit and create talent teams, ensure effective communication among members, and develop processes for the team to follow. They are in charge of connecting the data science and analytics team with the rest of the organization, other divisions, and executives. One of their core responsibilities is to translate complex AI and ML terminology to non-experts and make sure the team works in alignment with the strategy of the overall organization.

TIP

You will find other auxiliary roles that come on board in certain situations. Titles might vary for the same role. For applications involving unstructured data and language applications, a computation linguist is an important member of the team. In the past, a business intelligence programmer played an essential role, although now they may go under different titles, such as software developer, technical lead, or enterprise application architect.

The Critical Role of Internal and External Partnerships

For effective execution, AI must be built on strong partnerships, both internally and externally. Each party involved must be aligned with the overarching data strategy to keep all efforts focused on the same goal. When everyone is aligned and knows their role, they can achieve real, measurable results from the AI practice.

Internal partnerships

Having the right people on your team is important, and so is ensuring they have the resources needed to adopt AI technology and to collaborate. To facilitate broad AI training, make sure you have input from an AI expert who can guide your organization. They can work with your chief learning officer (CLO) to find or develop training materials, including video tutorials and courses. The organization should then develop procedures for each role involved with AI, including executive leaders, business unit managers, and data scientists.

TIP

Before, during, and after deployment, there must be constant communication between the AI team and the business unit. Each specialist has strengths and boundaries to their skillsets, so working with others is an essential aspect of project success. Typically, data scientists or data science managers ensure cross-functional collaboration to create business value and ensure complex AI terms are being translated into usable insights. These individuals must also ensure that their work is aligned with the organization's overarching goal. This is where AI systems empower teams to break down silos and communicate insights across teams.

External partnerships

Finding the right AI partner for your organization is another component integral to the success of your AI practice. A trusted AI partner should allow you to leverage underused yet valuable data, allow data scientists to work in their familiar environments, such as Jupyter Notebook and R, and provide the ability to operationalize models in business-friendly interfaces. Establishing a project manager who can collaborate with your AI partner will also be critical to success.

The importance of executive buy-in

One common cause of failure among AI projects is lack of buy-in. While data scientists and subject matter experts may be able to see the value of AI in the enterprise, support must start at the top. Communicating how an AI investment can help the company save money and piloting solutions can help teams establish credibility and attract support from leadership. Moreover, explaining model outputs in concise and tangible terms can help accelerate adoption and build trust among stakeholders.

Weighing Your Options: Build versus Buy

This always comes up when an IT project requiring a large capital outlay is under consideration.

"I could do that in-house for a lot less."

It's a reasonable point, especially if you have the expertise to do it.

When you should do it yourself

There are situations where building an in-house solution is the better option:

>> **You need a point solution.** If you have a challenge that is specific to your business and internal processes and the solution doesn't have to be integrated with other departments, an in-house solution might be the best alternative.

>> **No off-the-shelf solution exists.** You may have found a hole in the market. An in-house solution is your only alternative.

>> **Available solutions lack customization.** A solution may be available, but it fails to address your use case. It's time for a cost-benefit analysis to determine the value of the feature you need.

In all cases, the project must be subjected to a full business review before you decide to build in-house. You are taking resources away from your core business to build out your own AI department.

TIP

Many managers underestimate the infrastructure, resources, and commitment required to build, maintain, and support a solution. They tag a team to take it on, ignoring the fact that the team already has a job with performance targets. Either someone else will have to pick up that slack, or those deliverables will have to be put on hold. Indefinitely.

Typically, when the "I can do it for less" argument comes up, nobody is considering the fact that any business-critical solution must be maintained for the life of the solution. This is especially true with artificial intelligence, where maintenance accounts for 60 percent or more of the total headcount.

Table 4-4 lists the pros and cons of the build-or-buy options.

TABLE 4-4   **Build versus Buy Pros and Cons**

Option	Pros	Cons
Build	Most control Built to specific features	Longer time to market High resource cost up front Higher development and testing cost Higher infrastructure cost Lower reliability Fewer features Fewer integrations with other platforms and data Infrastructure
Buy	Shorter time to market Lower resource cost More features Fewer software bugs Higher reliability Integration capability	Up-front acquisition cost

When you should partner with a provider

Organizations look to an artificial intelligence solution to accomplish significant goals, such as increasing engagement, optimizing inefficient processes, and detecting and preventing negative outcomes such as fraud, service interruption, and network intrusion. AI is targeted at mission-critical initiatives with much at stake:

» **When time-to-benefit is important:** The time to implement a system from a provider is typically 6 months, while a development project for AI runs 18 to 24 months.

» **When you want to optimize your budget:** The cost to build in-house is from four to eight times as much as a comparable solution from a provider. For example, building a moderate team (four backend engineers, four data scientists, and three operations engineers) that can accommodate 1 billion data points per year will cost around $1.75 million annually. A larger team (six backend engineers, six data scientists, and four operations engineers) that can accommodate 10 billion data points per year would cost around $6 million annually.

TIP

Ultimately, in the build-versus-buy scenario, buying allows you to focus on your core competency while reducing the time-to-benefit and minimizing costs for initial development and ongoing costs for maintenance, support, and training.

Hosting in the Cloud versus On Premises

After you have identified why you want to use AI, the next question is where to do it.

You have three options — on premises, in the cloud, or a hybrid approach:

» **On premises:** You locate the hardware, the application, and all the data onsite, secure behind your corporate firewall. This approach gives you complete control over all aspects of your system, including security, access, and data integrity. On the other hand, you are responsible for maintaining and managing the system, which means hiring in-house resources with the appropriate hosting skills and expertise and expanding the budget to maintain and upgrade your software and hardware.

» **In the cloud:** You contract with a third-party cloud provider to host and manage the system, accessing it securely from your facility. The advantage of a cloud-based solution is scalability and repeatable, predictable billing. However, some companies fear losing some control over data access and security.

>> **Hybrid:** A hybrid solution takes advantage of both on-premises and cloud-based benefits. Most processing is done on your premises to take advantage of lower latencies and processing costs, but for spikes in workload you can seamlessly scale to the cloud. In fact, some cloud services providers now offer on-premises options.

What the cloud providers say

The argument for the cloud comes down to the twin pillars of the cloud model — scalability and affordability. You can deploy quickly, scale up or down instantly, and take advantage of powerful processors while keeping your overhead under control. You can customize your environment based on your business needs.

The cloud gives you access to AI capabilities without requiring you to have advanced skills in artificial intelligence or data science. Cloud service providers continue to expand services, allowing you to take advantage of recent advances in the technology without the research and development costs. Ultimately, the cloud offers the benefits of flexibility and savings, while providing the infrastructure required to support transformation.

What the hardware vendors say

At low utilization rates, the cost-per-hour advantage varies based on performance tier. On-premises solutions typically (but not always) offer a price advantage over cloud, but at higher utilization rates, cloud cost-per-hour can be five to ten times higher than on premises.

Some government regulations specify that sensitive data must remain on premises and cannot be moved to the cloud.

The truth in the middle

In many ways, the cloud versus on-premises decision comes down to a simple equation. Time and money are interchangeable. You can always save one by spending more of the other, and you prize most the one you feel to be in short supply.

When deploying AI, sometimes you spend money to save time, and other times you spend time to save money.

You should consider five key areas as you make your decision: scalability, affordability, gravity, security, and regulatory compliance.

Scalability

One of the twin pillars of the cloud model business case, the ability to scale in response to increased demand automatically and instantly, can be more important than affordability. The cloud supports a flexible hardware infrastructure with state-of-the-art processors to accelerate the training and inference processes. You don't need to deal with complex hardware configuration and purchase decisions.

In the on-premises model, scaling up may involve ordering and installing new hardware, and then loading and configuring a deep learning platform, hardly an agile process. In this case, you spend money on the cloud to save time in scaling up.

If you have regular and predictable demand, it comes down to a cost-benefit analysis. If your demand is unpredictable and you need to scale up or down quickly, then the cloud or a hybrid approach will give you the flexibility to respond quickly by outsourcing what you can't support internally.

Affordability

The other pillar of the cloud model business case, affordability, comes into play for small- to medium-sized applications. Using a cloud-based service saves you from large IT-related capital expenditures and in-house staff. However, to some degree, you are just trading capital costs for operational costs. You pay as you go. This means the lower your demand, the greater your savings. However, if you scale up, you may tip the scales in favor of the on-premises model. In this case, you take the time to build out the infrastructure onsite to save money in operations.

TIP

As you decide whether to move on premises, carefully consider your current and future needs and calculate how much you would be paying if your requirements grew by 10, 20, or 30 percent.

Gravity

What weighs more — your data, your services, or your apps? Data gravity might pull your AI out of the cloud or into it. In 2010, Dave McCrory developed the concept of *data gravity.*

McCrory's model visualizes the elements of AI — apps, services, and data — as planets. For the most part, the mass of apps and services remains relatively constant, but the mass of data continually grows. Because data has the greatest mass, it eventually becomes difficult to move easily. The desire to minimize latency and maximize throughput acts on these virtual planets like gravity. The planet with the greatest mass pulls the other planets to it.

What does this mean for the cloud versus on-premises model? Eventually apps and services will migrate to the platform storing the data. For example, suppose you are using the cloud model, but you have an existing data lake onsite housing petabytes of information that you want to use. It would likely be cost-prohibitive to pull the data into the cloud, process it, and then pull it back down.

This means that whatever model you choose for AI services, you will eventually have to house your data in the same environment.

Security

Security is the most often cited reservation when considering the cloud model. Is your data safer behind your corporate firewall or in the cloud? This is a straw man argument. Security is not a matter of the corporate network versus the cloud. It's a matter of corporate security policies and control of the technology. Gartner noted that, "in nearly all cases, it is the user — not the cloud provider — who fails to manage the controls used to protect an organization's data. Through 2022, at least 95 percent of cloud security failures will be the customer's fault."

If your business model moves you toward on-premises, make sure your IT department places security at the highest priority. If you go with the cloud, verify that the service provider offers guarantees on data protection and integrity that are backed by SLAs.

Regulatory requirements

Both on-premises and cloud-based systems can deliver effective compliance. In some cases, government regulations specify that sensitive data must remain on premises or be air-gapped, meaning the server has no network interfaces connected to other networks.

Regulatory and compliance requirements change frequently. For example, if your organization does business with or in the European Union, the General Data Protection Regulation (GDPR) likely kept you on your toes. For companies with rapidly expanding markets or territories, a provider with robust customer support service can take those issues off your plate.

REMEMBER

Prevailing wisdom says to start in the cloud and migrate onsite if you grow big enough. Starting in the cloud may make sense for an organization that wants to experiment with AI or do a proof-of-concept project. However, at some point after those initial forays, the shift to on-premises infrastructure may be the logical route forward to operate economically at higher scales due to the data transfer and throughput fees incurred with cloud providers on the top end of the spectrum.

2

Exploring Vertical Market Applications

IN THIS PART . . .

Identify the challenges in your market.

Discover the value that AI can bring to your organization.

Connect AI techniques with practical applications in your organization.

Explore use cases for your organization.

Chapter **5**

Healthcare/HMOs: Streamlining Operations

I n the last five decades, public and private healthcare spending in the U.S. has risen from 6.9 percent of the gross domestic product (GDP) in 1970 to 17.9 percent of GDP in 2017, according to data from the Centers for Medicare and Medicaid Services. But that increase pales in comparison to the growth of healthcare data. In 2013, the healthcare system produced 153 exabytes of new data. IDC estimates that by 2020, healthcare will generate 2,314 exabytes of data, a compound annual growth rate (CAGR) of 48 percent, effectively doubling every two years.

Fortunately, AI-powered healthcare projects have made great advances in increasing access to healthcare, decreasing costs, and improving quality.

Surfing the Data Tsunami

The explosive growth of data in healthcare poses a significant challenge for all those involved, from primary care workers to lab technicians, insurance providers, and facility administrators, right down to the patient. These areas are among the challenges of the data:

>> Intake of data (patient forms, medical history, examination room notes, lab results, suggested treatment and medication)

>> Storage and retrieval (availability, accessibility, searchability)

>> Sharing it with others (referrals, consultation, billing, insurance)

>> Acting on the information (diagnosis, prognosis)

But it also opens new opportunities to improve the quality of healthcare at every level, from the medical to the clerical and beyond.

Breaking the Iron Triangle with Data

Data is one of the building blocks of artificial intelligence, and healthcare is a remarkably data-rich environment. In addition to optimizing the areas cited in the previous section, AI enables healthcare workers to derive insights from the data to analyze trends, detect anomalies, and think strategically rather than reactively.

The University of Southern California is using a virtual reality chatbot named Ellie to help identify veterans who might be suffering from depression or PTSD. Looking out from the monitor, Ellie makes eye contact and uses common gestures such as nodding to encourage students to say more. She can detect subtle signs, such as tone of voice or shifting gaze using a microphone, a webcam, and a motion sensor. Doctors review recordings of the sessions to determine if they should follow up.

In his 1994 book, *Medicine's Dilemmas: Infinite Needs Versus Finite Resources*, William Kissick propounded the concept of the Iron Triangle of Medicine — access, cost, and quality. The goal is low-cost, high-access and high-availability health care, but there are always tradeoffs. A change in one of the values will affect one or both of the others. For example, if you cut costs, then either quality or access will suffer. Or both.

REMEMBER

The triangle is a dynamic model. Values for the three legs are in constant flux. In the U.S., cost has been the most active element, on a consistent upward trajectory. However, AI is poised to defy the model of the Iron Triangle. By delegating strategic tasks to machines, AI can simultaneously improve quality and availability while lowering costs.

IMPROVING QUALITY OF LIFE

For example, Intermountain Healthcare, a nonprofit hospital system serving Utah and Idaho, used machine learning and natural language processing to save $90 million in costs over four years while significantly improving patient outcomes and quality of life.

Over the past decade, the model for healthcare delivery has trended from a fee-for-service, volume-based approach to pay-for-performance, value-based care. Instead of being paid based on the amount of healthcare services they deliver, providers are paid based on patient health outcomes, such as helping patients improve their health and to reduce the effects and incidence of chronic disease.

Intermountain adopted value-based care in 2011 and quickly realized that it could reduce cost and improve outcomes by optimizing surgical services, which accounts for 55 to 65 percent of their profit margins. The organization started with the mountains of clinical data going back to the 1950s available in its medical records system and data warehouse and used ML and NLP to extract targeted, high-value information from the data, such as a risk score for each type of procedure.

The IT group developed a dashboard for each surgeon that enabled them to compare their performance on cost and medical outcomes with the other surgeons and with historical trends. Using that information, the surgeons reviewed the results and shared best outcomes. In these weekly meetings, the surgeons used the information to develop new protocols that reduced occurrences of post-operative complications and also lowered the cost of replacement surgery. They also used the data to reduce the cost of supplies.

Regarding patient outcomes and improved quality of life, the AI initiative and the decisions made based on the insights from the data were responsible for reducing hospital readmission rates for total hip and knee replacements by 43 percent, complication rates by 50 percent, the length of a hospital stay for total-joint-replacement by 35 percent, and the number of opioid pills prescribed at discharge by 44 percent.

Matching Algorithms to Benefits

AI can quickly and economically acquire, classify, process, and route unstructured text to everyone in the information pipeline, increasing accessibility while lowering costs. Here are some of the ways AI can help:

» **Natural language processing** can extract targeted information from unstructured text such as faxes, clinical notes, intake forms, and medical histories, to improve end-to-end workflow. The process starts with data capture and classification, and then routes data and documents to the appropriate backend systems, spotting exceptions, validating edge cases, and creating action items.

» **Data mining** can accelerate medical diagnosis. In a 2017 Neurology Journal study, AI diagnosed a glioblastoma tumor specimen with actionable recommendations within 10 minutes, while human analysis took an estimated 160 hours of person-time. A 2020 Nature Medicine study involved a test that helps brain surgeons make critical decisions during surgery. Typically, pathologists receive a tissue sample from the operating room, freeze it, stain it, and then study it through a microscope. The AI diagnostic tool uses lasers to study the tissue sample in a non-destructive process. The study covered samples from 278 patients. Accuracy between humans and the AI tool were similar, 83.9 percent versus 94.6 percent. But pathologists took 30 minutes or longer for each sample, as opposed to less than 3 minutes for the AI tool. That makes a big difference for the patient because the surgeon may send five or six samples to be analyzed during the course of a single surgery, which can extend the duration of the surgery by several hours.

» **Entity and concept extraction** can identify and automatically redact sensitive information in individual documents or across entire datasets.

» **Artificial neural networks** can successfully triage X-rays. In a 2019 Neurology Journal study, the team trained an artificial neural network model with 470,300 adult chest X-rays and then tested the model with 15,887 chest X-rays. The model was highly accurate, and the average reporting delay was reduced from 11.2 days to 2.7 days for critical imaging findings and from 7.6 days to 4.1 days for urgent imaging findings compared with historical data.

» **Speech analytics** can identify, from how someone speaks, a traumatic brain injury, depression, PTSD, or even heart disease.

Examining the Use Cases

While healthcare is a major presence in big data, it also has an outsized presence in "big paper." AI can liberate that data from its paper prison to revolutionize the way healthcare touches the lives of millions.

Delivering lab documents electronically

When it comes to lab test results, you want accurate results and you want them quickly, but which is more important? Surprisingly, a 2014 report showed that failure to deliver an accurate result to the right place on time caused twice as much harm as getting an inaccurate result.

As the demand for clinical lab tests continues to grow, so does the need for timely delivery. Add to that a downward cost pressure due in part to cuts in Medicare reimbursement of 40 to 50 percent for laboratory tests, and you have a good candidate for process optimization. AI can automate the delivery of lab tests, eliminating the manual steps in the process that are time-consuming and susceptible to error.

TIP

An AI-assisted document delivery process can accommodate a wide variety of file types and deliver them securely to any connected device at the destination, such as a printer, fax machine, mobile phone, or EMR system, performing file conversions on the fly as required. In addition, it can select the optimum delivery channel and switch to a backup channel if the primary channel is unavailable.

Taming fax

I hear you. Who faxes anymore? The healthcare industry, that's who. A 2019 IDG survey found that 50 percent of all medical communications were done via paper (44 percent) or digital (56 percent) fax.

And it isn't just healthcare. According to a 2017 Spiceworks poll, 89 percent of small- to medium-sized organizations use fax (paper or digital), and 62 percent of IT departments support physical fax machines. And the use of fax is growing.

Yes, I hear you again. Why? Turns out it's cheaper than deploying secure email and is considered compliant to security requirements for many government agencies. And if you have a stack of paper, you can just put it in the fax tray, hit a button, and walk away, as opposed to a more "modern" process where you scan with the copier, find the file on your computer, rename it, create an email, attach it, and send it.

That being said, paper-based faxing is a labor-intensive, inefficient process that creates barriers to patient information availability at the point of care and introduces friction when coordinating between providers. It actually degrades all three legs of the triangle. It increases labor cost, decreases access, and thus compromises the quality of care. The seamless alternative is paperless fax, also known as digital fax or e-fax.

TIP

Unlike paper fax, digital fax integrates with electronic health record systems, document management systems, and desktop applications. It reduces the time it takes to get patient information to the right provider and provides faster access to critical information at the point of care.

Automating redaction

Healthcare and the law are both paper-heavy. When their paths cross, the need for redaction on a large scale can crop up in a heartbeat. Take the example of a 2017 false claims case where the plaintiff filed a discovery order to show the volume of falsified records the hospital submitted to get higher Medicare and Medicaid payments. The defendant determined that the order covered 15,574 patient files, and that satisfying the order would take 7,787 working hours and cost $196,933.

In addition, the court issued a protective order that bound the parties to de-identify the contents of the medical records. The defendant determined that redacting the records would take 10 reviewers 14 days at a cost of $37,260.

The problem is that, in addition to being costly, manual redaction is a tedious process that is liable to human error. One mistake can incur legal issues, large fines, and potentially a damaged reputation.

AI uses natural language processing in an integrated workflow to automatically redact personal information, such as names, credit card numbers, and account numbers, without altering the source data.

Improving patient outcomes

One medical research agency uses AI to compare clinician performance and patient experiences and outcomes across 90 hospitals. For colon cancer surgical procedures, they track more than 100 quality metrics in each of the hospitals, observing strict data privacy regulations, and compare the performance of the individuals and the institutions. Not only can individuals measure their performance against their peers and identify areas for improvement, but over the span of four years the system has helped reduce complications after colon cancer surgeries by more than half.

When the hospital authorizes these indicators to be sent to insurance companies, they can use the data when selecting where and from whom to buy medical services. The government also uses the service for reporting and analysis.

Optimizing for a consumer mindset

These days, patients have little patience for interacting at the glacial speeds of bureaucracy-laden paper-heavy infrastructure. Their experience in online retail interactions are bleeding over into their interactions with healthcare. Before scheduling an appointment, they look to social media for reviews and recommendations.

Your patients may not have the expertise to judge your medical competence, but they will judge your consumer friendliness.

This expectation has implications for front-office technology, such as online appointment scheduling, bill pay, messaging, and test results delivery. But that's just the tip of the iceberg. Optimizing back-office technology can also impact the quality of customer service.

AI can use natural language processing and supervised learning to digitize a paper-heavy process to improve the patient experience, such as when a major national healthcare system used AI-assisted document management to reduce a 13-step manual, paper-based financial aid application process to just five steps.

Another example is when organizations improve the data collection process from paper to digital. How many times have you gone to the doctor's office or hospital and been asked to fill out pages and pages of input forms, just to get to the back and get asked the same questions again for the technician to input digitally? Fixing this problem often comes down to requiring front-line professionals to switch to digital entry or employing a staffer to do the manual transfer from paper to digital, although that can be met with resistance or additional costs. Alternatively, augmenting the document digitization process with machine reading and routing or mapping of information based on the contents of the documents, through AI, can help more effectively and efficiently improve this process and provide a better patient experience.

Another major children's healthcare facility used AI for peer reviews and rehab scheduling, reducing the average time to deliver treatment plans from days to minutes. By giving hospitals a better understanding of financial outcomes and how they can improve processes across the organization, AI helps put proper checks and balances in place to lower costs.

Chapter **6**

Biotech/Pharma: Taming the Complexity

The life sciences sector is in a season of transformation. On one hand, price pressure and regulatory requirements place great demands on corporations. Some studies show that the cost of drug development has exploded over the last 20 years while patient outcomes have worsened. Governments around the world are focused on driving down what they perceive as an unacceptably high cost of medicines. The sector is increasingly moving to a value-based pricing model, where payment is determined by demonstrable results. Achieving innovation and outcomes at a lower cost is imperative.

On the other hand, like many other disciplines, biotech and pharmaceuticals have access to a massive wealth of information of all kinds and increased volume, including scientific research, clinical trials data, patient profiling, regulatory requirements, sales training, and other product-centric assets. However, as the data sources increase in speed and size, so do the challenges of managing and analyzing that data for maximum business advantage.

To add to this complexity, the industry is highly regulated, and the cost of non-compliance can be significant, almost three times as much as the cost of compliance, according to a recent Ponemon Institute study.

AI is taking on drug development, rising costs, patient outcomes, and regulatory compliance with solutions in product discovery and development, trials, quality control, and many other applications.

Navigating the Compliance Minefield

It sometimes seems that the pharma marketplace can be a minefield of regulatory "gotchas," and a single misstep can be very costly. For example:

>> In 2017, Amerisourcebergen paid $260 million for distributing drugs from a facility that was not registered with the Food and Drug Administration. A year later, Amerisourcebergen again paid $625 million for improperly repackaging injectable drugs into pre-filled syringes and improperly distributing those syringes to physicians treating cancer patients.

>> In 2018, Actelion Pharmaceuticals settled False Claims Act copay allegations by paying $360 million.

>> In 2019, Insys Therapeutics paid $255 million to settle a case regarding payment of kickbacks and other unlawful marketing practices in connection with the marketing of Subsys, a sublingual fentanyl spray that is a powerful, but highly addictive, opioid painkiller.

>> In 2019, Purdue Pharma agreed to pay Oklahoma $270 million rather than face trial on charges of misleading marketing practices and misrepresentation regarding Oxycontin. In a different suit representing more than 2,000 local and state governments, the Sackler family offered to pay $3 billion and relinquish control of Purdue Pharma. Also in 2019, an Oklahoma judge ordered Johnson & Johnson to pay $572 million for its role in the opioid crisis.

REMEMBER

The operating environment for life sciences companies has become more complex. The costs of research and development have grown while the window to break even has shrunk. The increasing use of generic drugs is undermining the profit of branded medicines, and personalized and patient-centric approaches require new business models.

Is it all starting to sound pretty grim? Look up, because the clouds are parting.

Weaponizing the Medical, Legal, and Regulatory Review

Remember all that data? The real-world-outcomes data, clinical data, genetic data, demographic data, and patient sentiment data? You can leverage all that data to stage more efficient clinical trials, accelerate discovery and approval of new medicines, improve production and supply chain operations, and do more targeted sales and marketing.

Consider some of the tedious and sometimes chaotic processes that artificial intelligence can automate and optimize, such as medical, legal, and regulatory (MLR) review.

MLR review for product development

The product life cycle for a medication includes discovery and development, pre-clinical research, clinical research, FDA review, and FDA post-market safety monitoring. Each step is highly detailed and highly regulated, and for good reason. Lives are at stake. As the data flows through the whole life cycle, it passes through many departments, sometimes onsite, sometimes offsite, and is generated, modified, consumed, reviewed, and assessed by many teams.

Given the number of hands the data passes through, the question arises of how to establish a single source of truth that is common to the entire organization. And more importantly, how to gain visibility into deeper insights locked up in that data.

The process of achieving that single source of truth is complicated by the inherently siloed nature of organizations in the medical sector. There are strict boundaries between the medical side and the commercial side of any organization due to stringent regulations published by the U.S. Food and Drug Administration (FDA) and the European Medicines Agency (EMA), and due to laws, such as the Health Insurance Portability and Accountability Act (HIPAA), the General Data Protection Regulation (GDRP), and the Personal Information Protection and Electronic Documents Act (PIPEDA), passed by various legislatures around the world. Additionally, information silos continue to proliferate due to frequent mergers and acquisitions.

TIP

People at all levels of the organization are overwhelmed by the maelstrom of data, from the technician who needs to access the most recent specifications to the executive who must access the most recent and reliable information possible for strategic planning. They both need data that is secure, compliant, and actionable.

If a regulatory body requests an audit tomorrow, would your organization be ready with the whole process validated?

MLR review for sales and marketing

In 2019, the top ten drugs falling off the patent cliff, the date when the patent expires and generic brands hit the market, had a combined 2018 sales revenue of $21 billion.

You are challenged more than ever to extract value from existing products on the market and to launch new products. For highly regulated organizations, this means efficiently using and managing digital media assets while avoiding possible fines and other punitive measures. It's an uphill battle with increasing regulatory compliance and new laws constantly coming into play, nationally and internationally. Punitive measures can include production stoppage, inability to sell into drug markets, loss of revenue, and high fines. The goal is to manage brands better while reducing regulatory risk and improving quality control.

However, in many organizations, MLR review is a complicated manual process hampered by information silos, especially in international offices because policies aren't aligned across locations. Each division or country has their own version of the processes.

AI-assisted marketing content management (MCM) solutions are now helping with the MLR process challenges by centralizing MLR data sources and organizing the process in a workflow. By incorporating digital asset management, analytics, and automation into an orchestration process, they can assure nothing is missed, everything is accounted for, and help bring order to the chaos. Table 6-1 shows the marketing content management workflow. Each phase consists of a five-step cycle. The phases provide bilateral feedback by capturing and integrating the results of adjacent phases.

TABLE 6-1 **Marketing Content Management Workflow**

Plan	Build	Deploy
1. Budget	1. Channel Analytics	1. Medical review
2. Concept	2. Platform build/optimize	2. Legal review
3. Design	3. Content build/optimize	3. Regulatory review
4. Build	4. Deploy	4. Distribution/Retrieval
5. Integrate results	5. Integrate results	5. Capture results

MCM for life sciences automates the regulated marketing asset life cycle for faster innovation, better brand consistency, and regulatory compliance through process harmonization.

AI-assisted MCM platforms support digital asset management with machine-learning techniques to identify and categorize digital assets end-to-end as they are acquired, created, managed, and deployed. Regulatory requirements, approval status, claims, and related information can be maintained at every step in the process.

TIP

Breaking down internal silos with a shared single source of truth allows the right information to be quickly searched, retrieved, shared, and centrally managed.

By streamlining a tedious and error-prone manual process, you can accelerate asset delivery, improve brand consistency, and control costs. The real value comes when you use the data not only to address compliance and reduce risk, but also as a key business enabler. By analyzing the vast amounts of data acquired for MLR review, you can answer these types of questions:

>> How long does it take a piece of collateral to reach its target audience?

>> How much does an individual item cost and how often is it used?

>> Where are the major throttle points in our marketing production processes?

Enlisting Algorithms for the Cause

AI uses machine learning, text mining, and natural-language processing to process content, extracting concepts and entities, such as names, places, dates, and customized elements relevant to the business. AI then uses that information to create metadata and import it into a digital asset management platform, accelerating searches and data analysis. At the same time, the system automatically classifies the document based on its type and content and either assigns it to the next step in an automated workflow or flags it for review. Here's how these capabilities help:

>> **AI uses text mining** to gather real-time data from Internet of Things (IoT) devices and historical data (structured and unstructured, machine-based and non-machine-based) and regression techniques to predict when to perform maintenance or replace equipment to avoid unplanned downtime.

>> **AI uses IoT sensor data and machine learning** to monitor emissions to alert you when your plant is out of compliance or nearing compliance limits so you can take corrective action.

>> **AI uses data pooled from multiple sites** and regression analysis to reveal best practices to assist in developing good practices (GxP) compliant environments and optimizing processes.

Examining the Use Cases

In addition to optimizing MLR review, you can use AI in several points in the product life cycle, such as in the plant to reduce waste and downtime, increase yield and equipment life, and stay in compliance with regulations.

Product discovery

Developing a new drug is a very expensive and time-consuming process. Extensive up-front research is essential to identify appropriate drug targets and shut down non-performing projects quickly. Fortunately, there is a wealth of data touching all aspects of drug development, production, commercialization, and use, both on-label and off-label.

That's where AI comes in. When it comes to ingesting, processing, categorizing, and establishing relevance and connections, AI can do in hours or days what it would take humans months or years to achieve, working through disparate datasets across multiple domains, such as biochemical, genomic, academic, commercial, and many others, to predict the likelihood of success.

Clinical trials

You can use AI to streamline clinical trial planning and design, especially trial recruitment and enrollment. Using patient electronic health records (EHR) and data from comparable trials, you can more accurately profile and identify candidates and better estimate the time needed to recruit trial subjects. You can also refine resource and planning estimates while automating the process, so you are notified before delays or problems arise.

Product development

You can use AI to analyze the results of clinical trials and patient records to identify follow-on indications and discover adverse effects before products reach the market. AI can infer relationships between biological entities that were previously hidden to accelerate innovation and discovery while shortening the product development process.

Quality control

You can use AI to reduce your discard rate and increase production yield by compiling and processing data from multiple sources such as IoT sensors and devices, manufacturing execution systems, quality management systems, and enterprise resource planning systems.

AI-powered analytics allow you to closely manage the production process and reduce risk to minimize the chance of impurities in a formulated drug product.

TIP

Applying AI to root-cause analysis allows you to efficiently identify the main causes for reported product defects to understand the impact and manage the overall defect count. You can also correlate data from previous production runs with capacity and operational data to improve resource planning and management.

One company responded to a drop in quality in production by gathering data from IoT devices and other sources and applied machine learning to detect a correlation between fermentation performance traits and yield.

Predictive maintenance

You can use AI and IoT sensor data to monitor the condition of production equipment, performing just-in-time maintenance instead of preventative maintenance, which results in wasted parts and labor spent on machines that are in perfect working order, or reactive maintenance, which adds downtime to maintenance costs.

Manufacturing logistics

Life sciences companies are increasingly involved in extended partner ecosystems, working closely with contract research organizations, suppliers, customers, academic bodies, and regulators. Managing the supply chain becomes more important as companies rely more heavily on a wide range of suppliers.

TIP

You can use AI to improve supply chain automation and visibility by managing supplier relationships and performance in real time. By processing a combination of internal and external data, AI-powered analytics can help you reduce unforeseen shortages and supply chain disruptions that would affect customer service levels and sales revenues. You can also use AI to improve contingency planning for situations like power failures, natural disasters, or cyber attacks to ensure business continuity.

Regulatory compliance

In recent years, regulatory requirements and penalties have expanded to the point that compliance and legal departments must reach out across the entire organization and work with data from all business functions to demonstrate compliance.

TIP

You can use AI to streamline the discovery and retrieval process by mining all data, structured and unstructured, to quickly detect anomalies and exceptions that could place your organization at risk. Within pharmacovigilance, for example, real-world patient data can be integrated with EHR data to minimize risk and improve drug safety.

In a real-life example, one company found that its plant was exceeding limits for volatile organic compound emissions, resulting in fines and environmental impact. Using AI and the cloud to monitor its reactors, the company gained insight into how to reconfigure the production process to stay in compliance. As a bonus, cooling costs decreased significantly.

Product commercialization

You can use AI to improve sales forecasting by analyzing previous sales activity, customer purchasing patterns, market sentiment, competitor pricing, and demographic sales trends to provide highly accurate pictures of future sales opportunities. In sales negotiations, company representatives can apply machine learning to reveal insights from contracts and related documents, customer and competitor behaviors, and market analysis that can help close the sale — including through avoiding poison clauses, deviations from standard or approved language, and costing outside of approved ranges for the goods being procured.

TIP

You can also use AI to more fully understand customer perceptions about your products, which channels are most likely to convert, and which marketing campaigns deliver the most return.

Accounting and finance

You can use AI in your accounting and finance departments to improve your cash-based processes by automating invoice processing. AI can help you gain insight into your accounts receivables, which you can use to secure financing options. In addition, you can accelerate payments by using AI to automatically validate and process invoices to take advantage of early payment discounts. When errors occur, the system can react automatically or suggest resolution options to accounts payable staff.

Chapter 7

Manufacturing: Maximizing Visibility

I f you look at the greatest hits of challenges for manufacturing in the twenty-first century, you see some issues consistently bubbling to the top:

» How can I maintain the right inventory levels?

» How do I deal with inefficient manual processes?

» How do I reduce downtime?

» How can I keep up with all the new technology?

» How can I get better visibility and transparency in my supply chain?

Lurking just beneath the surface of these questions is a common theme: How can I improve margins?

The relationship between manufacturing and AI goes back for decades. Long before the emergence of the term Internet of Things (IoT), manufacturing plants were using feedback from sensors to optimize performance and efficiency. The business case for integrating AI and analytics into your manufacturing processes kind of writes itself.

Peering through the Data Fog

A recent KRC Research study showed that the top challenges to maximizing revenue included unscheduled downtime (40 percent), supply chain management issues (39 percent), and equipment breakdown (32 percent). The cost of manually managing and using information along the supply chain (suppliers, third-party logistics providers, and customers) is estimated at 5 to 10 percent of revenue, according to an NIST study.

Historically, cost containment was the primary driver for offshoring manufacturing, but recent developments are prompting businesses to re-evaluate. In response to trends such as the rising cost of shipping and growing economies that increase the wages in the offshore factory, businesses are looking at reshoring — returning to domestic manufacturing to shrink the supply chain, reduce shipping costs, and be closer to customers and suppliers.

Finding ways to reduce costs

As companies examine the alternatives for reducing costs, they often focus on three areas: inventory, processes, and the supply chain.

>> Optimize inventory

>> Optimize operations

>> Globalize the supply chain

Inventory is a significant asset on the balance sheet of most companies, ranging from 15 percent to as high as 40 percent of total assets. Holding too much inventory affects your cash flow and having too little inventory loses you sales.

The recent emergence of technologies pulled together under designations such as Industry 4.0, Manufacturing 4.0, and the like provides the infrastructure to address these challenges.

Handling zettabytes of data

As it always does, it comes down to data — how to get it and what to do with it. That's where IoT comes in.

The first device connected to the "Internet" was a Coke machine in the computer science department at Carnegie Mellon University in the mid-1970s. The department installed microswitches in the machine that tracked the stocking and dispensing of bottles and reported the status to a mainframe computer. That computer was connected to ARPANET, a network created in 1969 by the Advanced Research Projects Agency, which later became the foundation for the Internet. Before they made the long trek to the third-floor vending machine, faculty and students used the system to determine whether the machine was stocked and whether the bottles were cold.

Today, all sorts of things are connected to the Internet — security cameras, domestic appliances, utility thermostats, automobiles, and ultimately industrial devices. With sensors in the plant, the supply chain, and the warehouse, manufacturers have unparalleled access to incredibly valuable data. However, the volume is staggering.

A single autonomous vehicle can generate 4TB of data per day. The performance logs from a single machine on the manufacturing floor may dispense around 5GB of data per week. Multiply that by the number of machines on your floor, and you can see why, for IoT, you have to talk in terms of zettabytes (abbreviated *ZB*), which is 1,000,000,000,000,000,000,000 bytes. According to IDC, the data generated from IoT devices per year is growing from 0.1ZB in 2013 to 4.4ZBs in 2020.

How do you process that much data without overwhelming your network? And once you have it, what can you do with it?

A recent Manufacturing Leadership Council survey found that only 7 percent of companies felt that they were prepared to use the volumes of data from IoT devices to drive decision-making. More than 80 percent of respondents said they were either moderately or poorly prepared.

Clearing the Fog

All that data being collected in manufacturing from IoT devices at unprecedented volume and velocity is driving the fourth industrial revolution. The first industrial revolution was powered by steam. The second was powered by electricity. The third was powered by silicon, which enabled unprecedented computing power. And the fourth industrial revolution is being powered by data.

In fact, in the last decade, data has emerged as the new currency that operates across all levels of commerce, right down to the consumer, who pays for the use of "free" social media platforms with their personal data, which those platforms exchange with their clients.

The combination of AI and analytics can help manufacturers optimize the use of their IoT data for many applications. Taking the three challenges mentioned earlier in this chapter, consider three related strategies: proactive replenishment, predictive maintenance, and pervasive visibility.

Figure 7-1 shows the relationship between the method of controlling costs and the AI technique used to accomplish it.

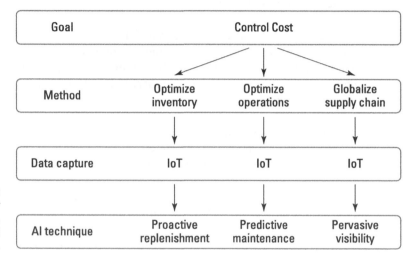

FIGURE 7-1: Using AI for inventory, operations, and the supply chain.

Connected supply chain

A *supply chain* connects a customer to the raw materials required to produce the product. It can be as simple as a single link, such as when the customer stops at a roadside stand to buy tomatoes directly from the farmer. Or it can be very complex and involve dozens of links, such as all the steps between a customer driving a car off the lot back to mining the iron ore or bauxite for the steel or aluminum engine block.

In a traditional supply chain, each link operates as a black box, connected to each other by a paper-thin link made up of documents such as purchase orders, shipping manifests, invoices, and the like. Each entity does its own planning, forecasting, and ordering while being blind to conditions on either side of it in the chain.

You could think of the links in the traditional supply chain as separate continents, each with its own ecosystem but largely isolated and insulated from the ecosystems of other continents. A connected supply chain brings those continents together like the supercontinent Pangea in the Paleozoic era, forming one interconnected ecosystem of partners, suppliers, and customers.

REMEMBER

In the connected supply chain, the paper-thin connection of the traditional model is replaced with a digital connection that provides full visibility in all directions.

A 2017 McKinsey study suggests that companies that aggressively digitize their supply chains can expect to boost annual growth of earnings by an average of 3.2 percent — the largest increase from digitizing any business area — and annual revenue growth by 2.3 percent.

In a recent KRC Research survey of manufacturing executives, 46 percent indicated that big-data analytics and IoT are essential for improving supply chain performance. They identified the two areas where big-data analytics can have the greatest impact on manufacturing to be improving supply chain performance (32 percent) and enabling real-time decisions and avoiding unplanned downtime (32 percent).

The study also identified the top three benefits of big data for manufacturers:

>> Enabling well-informed decisions in real time (63 percent)

>> Reducing wasted resources (57 percent)

>> Predicting the risks of downtime (56 percent)

REMEMBER

The connected supply chain enables you to react to changing market needs by sharing insights between every node in the value chain. There are many other applications for AI in manufacturing, some of which I address later, but the three elements of connected supply chain — proactive replenishment, predictive maintenance, and pervasive visibility — provide an intuitive case for using AI to revolutionize your business.

Proactive replenishment

Optimizing inventory levels while improving customer experience requires the ability to automate much of the replenishment process. Proactive replenishment leverages analytics to monitor inventory consumption and initiate a purchase order on the business network to the supplier to replenish the stock before an out-of-stock situation occurs. The intelligent and connected supply chain provides real-time inventory visibility. In addition to reporting stock levels, it can indicate the condition of each item — such as the temperature at which it is stored — to ensure the quality of those items. Manufacturers can automate the replenishment of parts from the supplier before they are needed in the production process. And, query between suppliers to procure from which has availability, the best rates, and taking into account shipping times required for in-time delivery.

Predictive maintenance

The ability to predict when a part of a sub-system of a serviceable product is likely to fail and intervene can save a manufacturer millions of dollars, and thus predictive maintenance is a key investment area for the supply chain. Whether that part is within the production process, within the warehousing environment, or part of a connected vehicle, an IoT network automatically monitors and analyzes performance to boost operating capacity and lifespan. This system intelligently decides whether the part needs to be replaced or repaired and can automatically trigger the correct process, typically reducing machine downtime by 30 to 50 percent and increasing machine life by 20 to 40 percent. Studies by the Federal Energy Management Program of the U.S. Department of Energy found that predictive maintenance provides a 30 to 40 percent spending reduction compared to reactive maintenance, and an 8 to 12 percent spending reduction compared to preventative maintenance.

Organizations often make incremental progress toward predictive maintenance, starting with monitoring IoT data in the control room and reacting to problematic readings. In the next stage, they run reports to view recommendations for maintenance. In the final stage, they remove the requirement for human interaction to initiate maintenance by automating the creation of repair tickets.

TIP

To read a real-life use case of a steel mill using production line predictive failure and corrective action to reduce scrap and maximize uptime, check the "Examining the Use Cases" section of Chapter 19, "Asset Performance Optimization."

Pervasive visibility

Pervasive visibility is the ability to see exactly where goods are during their life cycle, providing a view of the current state of all assets across the entire organization and beyond to partners, customers, competitors, and even the impact of the weather on operations and fulfillment. IoT plays a key role in providing that visibility.

Current estimates predict that there will be 75 billion connected devices by 2025, ten connected devices for every human on the planet. Most of those devices will be in the manufacturing sector. When you consider that a single device can produce gigabytes of information each minute, the volume and velocity of data within production and operations can easily spiral out of control — or, more often, simply be ignored.

While 60 percent of executives that McKinsey surveyed said that IoT data yielded significant insights, 54 percent admitted that they used less than 10 percent of that IoT information.

Making sense of that data is where AI comes in. By combining AI and analytics, you can bring together information from a variety of data sources, identify patterns and trends, and provide recommendations for future actions. It provides the basis for new levels of production and business process automation, as well as improved support for employees in their daily roles and in their decision-making.

REMEMBER

To achieve these gains in the supply chain, AI has the potential to bring together both structured and unstructured data from a wide range of sources, including IoT devices, plant operations, and external partners to identify patterns linking factors such as demand, location, socioeconomic conditions, weather, and political status. This information forms a basis for a new level of supply chain optimization spanning raw materials, logistics, inventory control, and supplier performance and helps anticipate and react to market changes.

DELIVERING VALUE FROM DATA

For an example of making use of pervasive visibility, consider a steel manufacturer that has been rated a leader in its industry sector for well over a decade for having the safest plant, highest quality, best on-time delivery, and great customer service. It has achieved this position through a focus on delivering the most value from its data.

The company manager identifies pervasive visibility as a key benefit. "If you look at how our company operates, we source our raw materials from many places around the globe. The geopolitical environment can have a major effect on our business. How are prices and quality going up and down from our different global suppliers? How easy is it for us to switch supply and when should we do it?

"Weather patterns are a great example of where AI can help. Shipping our raw materials to our plants can be hugely affected by weather patterns. We need to work out quickly how the weather is going to affect us and whether we need to change our point of supply to ensure business continuity and that we're not introducing delays to the final delivery to customers."

Clarifying the Connection to the Code

Technologies that underpin Industry 4.0 include advanced manufacturing systems, extensive IoT deployments, and AI for fully automated production processes, but the challenge lies in collecting, processing, and using the masses of data available to enable the smart factory. The key is the move from big-data analytics to AI-assisted analytics, placing the focus firmly on enterprise information management as a means to ensure information is properly captured, manipulated, managed, and made available where needed.

Optimize inventory

AI uses decision trees and neural networks to establish baseline requirements and then uses real-time data to tease out patterns and relationships to determine demand behavior, which drives optimized inventory levels and replenishment plans.

Optimize maintenance

AI uses text mining to gather real-time data from IoT devices and historical data (structured and unstructured, machine-based and non-machine-based) to enhance a digital representation of a device. AI then uses regression techniques to analyze the IoT data to predict when maintenance should be performed or when equipment should be replaced to avoid unplanned downtime.

Optimize supply chain

AI uses text mining, data mining, and optimization planning techniques to help you understand your current business, address issues, and formulate strategies for improved performance. You can use supply chain analytics to compare the performance of trading partners to operational and business metrics to make better decisions about your partnerships. For example, you can identify high-performing suppliers, discover which suppliers consistently deliver on time and which are consistently late, or which make the most mistakes on orders.

Improve quality

AI uses analytics to improve product quality. Quality defects in production can eat as much as 40 percent of a manufacturer's annual revenue. Analytics can help improve product quality by capturing machine-level information to boost production yield and throughput. Data that shows the cost and effort involved in developing products helps quickly identify problem areas and predict issues.

Automate repetitive tasks

AI uses reinforcement learning to automate repetitive human processes. In addition to improving production, companies also use analytics to revolutionize back-end processes. Robotic process automation (RPA) combines analytics, rules-based software, and occasionally machine learning to capture and interpret existing data-input streams to process a transaction, manipulate data, trigger responses, and communicate with other enterprise applications.

TIP

Most repetitive, data-intensive tasks and workflows, previously handled manually, can be conducted more efficiently and accurately by analytics-enabled robots. Industrial robots significantly improve the production line, and RPA can bring similar benefits to business areas such as accounting, human resources, and customer service.

Examining the Use Cases

All manufacturers have a focus on optimizing production and many have invested in technologies to increase productivity and efficiency, boost quality, and control costs. As Manufacturing 4.0 becomes more established, AI offers improvements in a wide range of applications.

Minimize risk

Some materials, such as certain paints or glazing, must be stored at specific temperature ranges to prevent explosions. One chemical plant has a substance that must be stored at temperatures below 40°F (4°C). The company has combined IoT sensors with machine learning to anticipate temperature fluctuations and maintain the warehouse at proper levels.

Maintain product quality

In time-sensitive continuous production processes, you want to be able to check the quality at each step so you can make corrections before it's too late, and brewing beer is one of those processes. One brewery decided to gain better control over the final product by installing IoT sensors at every point during the brewing process to monitor quality. In addition to introducing decision points at which they can intervene to keep the process on track, the AI-enabled process gave them the ability to simulate changes in the remaining steps in the brewing process, to predict how they would affect the beer quality and recommend the best actions in each scenario.

Streamline database queries

In this real-life example, a manufacturer relied on spreadsheets to do sales forecasting and track the status of orders. Because the spreadsheets had to be manually updated from the output of internal management systems, the sales team rarely had access to real-time information, and meeting deadlines became problematic.

Using AI, the technology team created a report that the sales team could use to extract information in real time without having to rely on IT to generate it. In addition to getting up-to-the-minute order status, the sales team used the report to identify high margin items. Armed with this information, they adapted their sales strategies, adjusting what they sold and how they sold it to increase margins.

The technology team further enhanced the solution to incorporate the use of a digital assistant to take requests via voice command and return results via voice response. This enabled the sales team to ask for current information just before a customer meeting or even while in a meeting and get instant results.

When the finance department got wind of the project, they identified areas where the application could streamline their work; for example, while in the process of paying an invoice, they could research the invoice and purchase order without switching applications or interrupting their workflow.

Outsource predictive maintenance

You need not restrict predictive maintenance to your manufacturing facilities. If you build IoT sensors into your product, you can monetize the data it produces to create a new revenue stream by offering your customers the increased value of improved productivity and minimal downtime.

In Finland, elevator and escalator manufacturer KONE did that very thing, providing their customers with the visibility required to perform predictive maintenance while also giving KONE visibility into the typical usage of their product and to allow their technicians to arrive at a service call prepared with everything they need to resolve the problem in one visit.

This use case demonstrates the power of combining big data with AI to transform a business model. Many manufacturers are moving away from the traditional model of selling a product packaged with a maintenance plan to selling the product as a service. For example, companies no longer buy photocopiers; they buy an always-up service that provides a certain number of copies per billing period, including consumables.

In this model, you collect performance data from your customer site and sell that information to them, helping them optimize operations. In like manner, your customer can sell valuable data services to their clients, such as information on the transportation logistics of their cargo.

Customize products

For every one-thousand feet of elevation, your car engine loses 3 percent of its power. So, if you move from San Francisco (52 feet) to Santa Fe (7,200 feet), your car's performance will be cut by 21 percent. It's one thing if you're just driving to the office or school. It's another if you're driving a delivery truck all over town every day.

One manufacturer uses AI to optimize vehicles for specific elevations and markets them accordingly as the most efficient vehicle available, customized for the region.

Expand revenue streams

When human creativity collaborates with machine efficiency, innovation can't be far behind.

One manufacturer wanted to increase global distribution but found that the retailers in regions with a financially depressed economy lacked the cash to increase inventory. Using machine learning, they created a financing program that processes data for each merchant, such as age of the account, aggregate purchase data, location, and neighborhood demographics, including average household income.

The system provides better scoring data than the third-party underwriters the company had engaged. The pilot currently finances inventory buys for 13,000 retailers, and they are expanding into other regions.

Save the planet

As long as you're putting IoT sensors into your product to optimize productivity, why not also use the data to minimize emissions? The Manufacturing Leadership Council identified sustainability as a key element of its 2020 Critical Issues agenda.

Delegate design

Everybody knows design starts at the drawing board and often requires that you go back to the drawing board for each iteration. In modern times, the drawing board has been replaced by computer-aided design, the most modern of which uses AI algorithms to support generative design techniques to optimize designs.

REMEMBER

Through the process of generative design, AI takes your requirements, such as which materials are available, dimensions, weight, strength, and other constraints, and uses reinforcement learning to cycle through thousands of possible designs, testing each one against your metrics to converge on the best design.

Chapter **8**

Oil and Gas: Finding Opportunity in Chaos

Although the first oil wells are said to have been drilled by the Chinese using bamboo poles thousands of years ago, modern oil production started with the discovery of oil in Pennsylvania in 1859. In the 160 years since then, the industry has seen many ups and downs. Today, oil is credited for powering half the world's energy and most vehicles. It's also a base ingredient for many chemicals, and is necessary for manufacturing, the production of plastics, and countless other industrial activities.

To address the volatility of the industry, producers are turning to AI and a wealth of data from Internet of Things (IoT) sensors to introduce predictability and optimization.

Wrestling with Volatility

Oil is an industry characterized by extreme volatility. Despite the steady rise of crude oil prices in recent years, factors such as regulatory challenges and technological disruption have led to a 60 percent reduction in the global profit pool.

Natural gas also faces rapid changes and increased complexity. As production in the U.S. grew by nearly 50 percent, over the last decade, prices were slashed in half. Several nations, including the U.S., Australia, and Qatar, are well-positioned to become the biggest exporters of natural gas in the coming years, but quick changes in demand and infrastructure challenges pose a threat to an otherwise thriving industry.

The inherent volatility of supply and demand, evolving regulatory changes, and a largely negative public perception continue to plague the sector.

On the other hand, demand may plateau within a decade or two. Some industry pundits suggest that although the demand for oil and gas will continue to rise over the short term, renewable energy will likely outpace fossil fuels in the next two decades. In fact, 40 percent of the increase in primary energy is already accounted for by renewable sources, and by 2040 the energy mix is projected to be the most differentiated ever seen.

The public seems to favor renewable energy over sources like crude oil. Forbes reported that more than 75 percent of adults reported having a positive perception to wind, solar, and other forms of renewable energy, but positive perceptions of natural gas and oil were rated at just 60 percent and 35 percent, respectively.

TIP

In addition to navigating the difficulties of volatile supply and demand, regulatory changes, and a negative public perception, in the oil and gas industry you must juggle the ongoing priorities of maintaining safe operations and reducing costs to stay competitive. To keep operating costs down, many companies have scaled back on their maintenance activities, but assets across the industry are largely past their prime. Safety continues to be a pressing issue both on a small scale and the global scale. Navigating new territories to search for new supplies is risky for employees, and you must also prioritize the safety of your customers and the environment. Preventing and minimizing the impact of spills remains critical, as does the effort to prevent other unforeseen events that disrupt operations, including shutdowns.

While the list of challenges is certainly daunting, the good news is that the oil and gas industry is one of the best candidates for AI-powered solutions. Many companies have already begun leveraging intelligent technology to propel their operations toward greater efficiency, safety, and productivity.

Pouring Data on Troubled Waters

The good news is that your production process generates a significant volume of data, especially if you are using IoT devices.

TIP

Sensors can produce tens of thousands of data points, not to mention the many other sources in use. With advances such as seismic software, logging tools, and IoT sensors, wells across the globe generate a massive amount of data.

And that data volume is only growing. In March 2019, the U.K. launched an oil and gas National Data Repository (NDR), which houses 130TB of data. Comprising information from thousands of pipelines, seismic surveys, and wellbores, the NDR's expansive dataset is equivalent to roughly eight years' worth of HD movies.

Deriving meaningful insights

Yet, even as you keep producing data, you probably struggle to derive meaningful insights from all this information. Most data in the oil and gas industry is under-utilized. In fact, of all data coming from hundreds of rigs around the world generating data from more than 30,000 sensors, only 1 percent of that data is used for decision-making. Without cognitive technology to collect, sort, analyze, and derive key insights from this data, you can't use all this information to your advantage. After all, the value of data lies in the interpretation.

Fortunately, AI is the perfect tool to take advantage of this wealth of data. While the AI of yesteryear could provide only retrospective insights, advising you on how you could have prevented an outage or improved past actions, today's systems are forward-thinking, using predictive insights to help you determine the best course of action for the future. They're intelligent enough to not only collect and sort both hard numerical data and textual information, but also contextualize it for increasingly accurate analyses and predictions.

While the industry will likely remain inherently volatile, AI can help you address the many challenges, drive efficiency, and explore new opportunities.

TIP

AI can help you make sense of a massive collection of data points to better predict demand. It can help you take a cost-effective approach to asset management, extending the lifespan of equipment pushed harder to produce more and keeping the overall infrastructure in good working order. And you can use it in customer-facing applications to provide better service and a greater presence with consumers.

Regaining control over your data

Currently, most oil and gas companies use legacy systems with disparate datasets, thereby hindering enterprise-wide visibility.

TIP

Automated assessment can help you regain control over your data and content. AI-powered solutions use advanced text analytics to capture content in documents and route it appropriately. By reducing manual processing, you can reduce errors, gain better insight into your data, and increase overall efficiency. Plus, when all data sources are connected in a single, unified platform, you have better access to accurate information to help you make better decisions.

Plenty of opportunities exist for enormous improvement in the sector. Analytics alone can improve production efficiency by ten percentage points, resulting in a $220 million to $260 million bottom-line impact on a brownfield asset. In 2017, industry analysts from Ernst and Young said that introducing AI to drive operational excellence could lead to a 29 percent increase in oil and gas production and reduce costs by 43 percent for a savings over a five-year period of $30 billion across the industry.

Wrangling Algorithms for Fun and Profit

The opportunities for AI in the oil and gas sector are vast and extend across upstream, midstream, and downstream processes. From the exploration and production sides, you can use AI features such as machine-learning algorithms and text mining to accomplish these tasks:

>> Minimize risk and increase speed to production in well-site development by collecting, combining, and assessing data for informed decision-making.

>> Enhance well-site development strategies through predictive insights.

>> Improve operational performance and reduce costs.

>> Boost health and safety and improve environmental performance.

>> Achieve optimum uptime with predictive maintenance.

AI uses IoT sensors and machine-learning algorithms to enhance midstream processes, such as storing and transporting oil and gas, to make data-driven decisions and achieve operational excellence.

The downstream sector, which includes refineries, plants, and distribution companies, can streamline internal processes and lower operational costs by breaking down data silos.

Examining the Use Cases

Now that you have the necessary foundation, it's time to look at how people are using AI right now to cut costs, increase revenue, and open new lines of businesses in oil and gas.

Achieving predictive maintenance

Maintenance is important throughout the oil and gas sector in general, but in areas with aging infrastructure, it's especially critical. Almost half of all offshore equipment is at least 15 years old with a collective downtime of 13 percent, but outliers exist, such as the North Sea Forties pipeline.

The pipeline, which carries 150 thousand barrels per day, experienced a hairline crack in December 2017, resulting in halted production and a loss of an estimated $25 million per day. Although the pipeline was designed to last approximately 25 years, it has been in operation for more than 40 years. Such issues highlight the pressing need to gain visibility into your high-value assets to predict problems and address them before they arise — which is precisely where AI comes in.

Digital twins support predictive maintenance for rigs and other high-value equipment. A digital twin is a virtual simulation of an asset, which operators use to monitor performance while performing stress testing to predict when and where failures might occur. Running simulations enables you to pinpoint potential areas of improvement without having to stop operations. One company used predictive maintenance and early detection to avoid two malfunctions, saving an estimated $2 million in maintenance costs and downtime. The use of this technology is predicted to triple by 2022.

TIP

Machine-learning algorithms analyze actual sensor data, which further helps you to determine when assets are underperforming or at risk for failure. IoT data from a single sensor can be combined with information from other equipment to create predictive models. Some companies have even begun collecting data from drill bits, including pressure and temperature information, and are comparing it to historical data that brackets past malfunctions to assess equipment and make targeted maintenance decisions. To further drive efficiency, AI-powered solutions can even order required parts and schedule maintenance as needed.

Enhancing maintenance instructions

Clearly, maintenance is critical to your success, but most maintenance activities in this sector are inherently complex. You can't simply replace a pump, for instance. Many preliminary steps are involved, including shutting down part of the pump, draining the pipes, and verifying that the system has been depressurized. Each step is governed by written procedures, which are essential to preventing injuries and accidents.

Because countless maintenance activities are performed each year, you may be challenged to understand why some instances are successful while others result in problems. One company is using AI to answer this question. Using machine learning and text mining, they're correlating maintenance successes — including those that were completed on time and without issues — with written maintenance instructions. By analyzing the language inside documents, they can pinpoint specific terms that are associated with better outcomes. For example, one company found that using the words "warning" and "critical" interchangeably in maintenance instructions led to several preventable incidents. These findings can help you clarify the language in your manuals to better communicate the information to your operators to improve maintenance outcomes and decrease the risk of injury or accidents.

Optimizing asset performance

While predictive maintenance helps to prevent downtime, using AI to optimize the performance of high-value machinery allows you to analyze and make better use of your operations. Oil and gas companies have been generating huge lakes of unstructured performance data for years, but until now, they haven't been able to dig deep into the data to make sense of it. AI capabilities such as text mining and machine learning can be used to detect patterns in this data, helping to pinpoint the variables that lead to the best performance.

TIP

Oil companies often find that despite having many wells in the same geographical area, certain wells consistently perform better than others. AI can help you find out why some wells are able to extract more oil. For instance, you might suspect that drilling at a specific rpm or pressure would lead to greater success, but AI takes the guesswork out of the equation and provides recommendations based on hard facts derived from historical data. And AI-powered solutions can analyze all this data to deliver clear, impactful insights, as well as automatically adjust assets as needed to optimize performance.

Exploring new projects

Exploration spending has stagnated in recent years and is expected to have a modest growth rate over the short term. Yet, to meet supply-related challenges in the midst of an oil and gas renaissance, you must continue to look for stores in new territories. And because most destinations have already been explored, those remaining are likely to be challenging to access.

With a wealth of geophysical data already collected and the potential to gather more through drones, you can discover and exploit new territories with the help of AI. Intelligent technology brings data together more cohesively to link key information together, helping you identify new potential production opportunities to drive growth.

One company used machine learning to filter out noise produced by underwater currents and other factors in seismic surveys, reducing the time to clean up the data by 80 percent.

TIP

You can also use AI-driven insights to shape decisions for acquisition and divestment. Oil companies are constantly buying and selling wells, but the analysis derived by one company is often vastly different from the next. With the ability to analyze a robust collection of data, you can more accurately pinpoint which areas, whether offshore or onshore, have the greatest potential for yielding significant volumes of oil. As such, you'll be able to make more strategic investment decisions and drill in better places to further enhance overall performance.

Chapter **9**

Government and Nonprofits: Doing Well by Doing Good

This book is about AI projects for the enterprise, or more specifically, corporations, which are primarily focused on profit. Consequently, you might think it strange to find a chapter focusing on organizations that aren't focused on profits. Consider, though, that on dictionary.com, defining enterprise as a company is way down the list at number five.

The first definition is:

enterprise [en-ter-prahyz] noun, a project undertaken or to be undertaken, especially one that is important or difficult or that requires boldness or energy

If anything requires boldness and energy, it is working for the betterment of the human condition. And if you're intent on doing good, you best do it well. Thus, if you aren't concerned with profits but with reducing costs, AI offers a wealth of solutions.

The challenges can be daunting, including budget constraints, outdated infrastructure, inadequate security, and propensity for fraud. The good news is that in the era of big data, solutions are available to increase efficiency, consolidate data, and protect the organization from hackers and fraudsters.

Battling the Budget

In addition to not pursuing profit, government agencies and nonprofit organizations often work with constrained budgets and limited resources.

Government

In 2002, the world generated 5EB (exabytes) of data. That is the equivalent of a 4-quadrillion (18 zeroes) page text document or 5 billion hours of high-definition YouTube videos. Ten years later, the world was generating that much data every week. Now, the world churns out more data than that every day. Figure 9-1 gives you an idea of how quickly data generation has ramped up since the commercialization of the Internet.

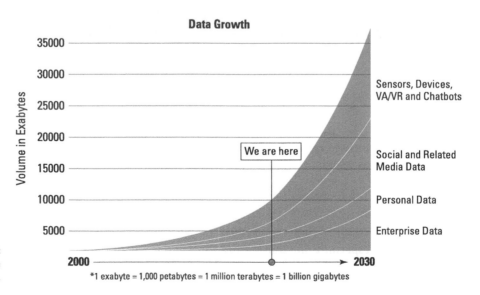

FIGURE 9-1: Volume of data growth.

The data tsunami touches everyone, but it particularly hits government, the ultimate bastion of paperwork. Government offices and officials have been swamped by numbers and paperwork for centuries.

For the 1880 U.S. census, it took eight years to process 50 million responses by hand. To address this problem, inventor Herman Hollerith took a hint from Joseph Marie Jacquard's automated loom, which created sophisticated weaving patterns controlled by punched cards. Hollerith developed a punched card-driven electronic calculating machine. As a result, even though the population grew 25 percent to 62 million, the 1890 census took only six years to process, saving the government $5 million.

Legacy IT systems

For 2022, Gartner has projected the global government and education IT budget will hit $634 billion. Unfortunately, most government IT departments spend nearly 75 percent of their budgets on maintaining legacy systems.

Seventy percent of U.S. government workers are over 40 years old, matching the age of many of the IT systems they use to do their jobs. For example, until July 2019, the Strategic Automated Command and Control System that controls the U.S. nuclear arsenal ran on a computer system that requires eight-inch floppy disks. In July, the U.S. Department of Defense upgraded the system to highly secure solid-state digital storage.

Citizens routinely encounter twentieth-century systems when renewing a driver's license, engaging with elected representatives, or applying for benefits, an experience that can be underwhelming at the least, if not frustrating.

Data silos

Typically, every agency has its own intake process with its own forms and its own databases, which severely hampers any attempt to deliver a seamless experience to the user of government services. In addition, the silos expand across domains, preventing agencies from acting on the valuable information available in social media, websites, forums, and email. This vast pool of unstructured data can provide significant insights into the people that government agencies serve and could significantly enhance the quality of services provided.

Data security

Budget cuts are also having an impact on security. A recent Thales Security report revealed that 70 percent of U.S. government agencies have experienced a data breach, 57 percent in 2018 alone.

Nonprofit

Nonprofits also suffer their share of data breaches. Approximately 15 percent of breaches reported in *CyberCrime Magazine's* "Cybercrime Diary" target nonprofit and government organizations. Some of these breaches compromise millions of accounts, exposing personally identifiable information, such as names, addresses, tax ID numbers, electronic medical records, and financial information such as bank and credit card numbers.

Consequently, it's not surprising that in a recent CohnReznick survey 89 percent of nonprofits placed cybersecurity in their top three (37 percent) or top ten (52 percent) concerns. However, only 32 percent of the surveyed organizations had performed a cybersecurity assessment that included penetration testing.

A Salesforce survey found that 74 percent of nonprofits list among their top challenges capturing and managing accurate donor data. In addition, 37 percent said their priority was to reduce the costs of program execution, but only 16 percent prioritized reducing manual tasks, a significant contributor to cost reduction.

Fraud

A global Association of Certified Fraud Examiners report on fraud across all sectors indicated that 25 percent of fraud cases occur in government agencies (16 percent) and nonprofit organizations (9 percent). The study also showed that although the risk stays fairly constant regardless of the size of an organization (between 22 and 28 percent), the median financial loss from organizations with fewer than 100 employees ($200,000) is twice as much as for larger organizations.

A McKinsey study found that government programs detect less than half of the losses due to fraud, waste, and abuse, which amounted to $57 billion detected out of $148 billion lost in 2017.

Nonprofits had the smallest median loss of $75,000, but given the limited resources of most nonprofits, this amount can deal a death blow to the organization. In fact, another study showed that 25 percent of nonprofits that experienced a publicized fraud incident shut down within three years, with the mortality rate focused on smaller and newer organizations.

TIP

Artificial intelligence is uniquely suited to address these challenges that nonprofits and government agencies face.

Optimizing Past the Obstacles

Applications that leverage AI can help organizations handle many tasks that humans can't easily do alone, including these:

>> Reduce backlogs

>> Cut costs

>> Overcome resource constraints

>> Free workers from mundane tasks

>> Improve the accuracy of projections

>> Inject intelligence into scores of processes and systems

REMEMBER

AI presents organizations with new choices regarding how to get work done — automate work, divide it among people and machines, or enhance what people already do.

Digital transformation

For a growing segment of the population, if it's not online, it doesn't exist, and that segment isn't restricted to the millennials and younger populations. Regarding adults over 60 years old, 90 percent own a computer or laptop, 70 percent have a smartphone, and 40 percent have a tablet. Startups have been launching boomer-centric apps for years, such as OurTime.com, Stitch.com, Honor.com, and HomeTeamHealth.com, not to mention all the finance apps targeted to the market segment that still retains the most buying power.

Across all ages, citizens expect their interactions with government to mirror the consumer apps they use every day, and artificial intelligence plays a major role in supporting a digital user-support platform.

TIP

A 2017 Infosys survey found that the average amount of time managers spent executing day-to-day activities in the organization at the end of an AI-supported digital transformation was 84 percent less than for individuals at organizations beginning their digital transformation. Just think of what your organization could do with that kind of time savings.

TRANSFORMING THE POSTAL SERVICE

For an early example of digital transformation in government, look at the U.S. Postal Service (USPS). Yes, you read that correctly: the Postal Service. In the last two decades, they reduced their headcount from 797,795 to 497,157, a 38 percent drop since 1999, all while adding more than 4,000 addresses to their network every day and delivering 187.8 million pieces of mail daily. Surprising, isn't it? How did they do it?

In 1998, the USPS partnered with the State University of New York and other federal agencies to fund the Center of Excellence for Document Analysis and Recognition (CEDAR). Their mission was to develop the technology to digitize handwritten and typed text using machine learning. The USPS uses this technology to read addresses, and then each item is encoded and automatically sorted and routed. Within two years, they were reducing headcount while maintaining the same level of service.

That was more than 20 years ago. Imagine how much more you can do with AI today.

The future of work

Digital transformation extends beyond the transformation of data and systems to encompass the workforce. The future of work changes what employees do, how they do it, and where they do it. In the public sector, it shifts the focus from tasks and compliance to results and the customer experience by improving service delivery, streamlining operations, and optimizing productivity in a culture that works seamlessly with technology.

The transformation includes automating routine tasks, optimizing other tasks through human-machine collaboration, and focusing employees on high-value, customer-centric tasks. It also includes a transition to a blend of permanent and contingent workers.

In fact, the gig economy has already come to the government of Canada, which spends $12.9 billion annually on contract workers and typically takes 197 working days to hire a new employee. A group of renegades inside the system envisioned a third option beyond the typical permanent or contract position: "a project-based employee on a self-directed career path with high mobility but with the rights and benefits that have traditionally been restricted to permanent employees." Workers build a profile on the website and browse the job postings.

Data security

TIP

You can use AI to quickly and efficiently detect threats, including non-human patterns, spikes of activity outside normal business hours, and other red flags for a more robust and fast-acting response to data security risks. Using AI to detect and reduce risk can automate data validation and ensure compliance to avoid regulation-related penalties.

Operational costs

Data from the Office of Personnel Management and the Labor Department estimate that federal employees spend 4.3 billion hours per year on routine tasks such as documenting and recording information and monitoring and controlling resources. Deloitte's Center for Government Insights indicates that those agencies could offload up to 25 percent of that time, or 1.1 billion hours per year, by using AI to automate tedious, repetitive processes, granting employees what is essentially an extra day per week to focus on high-value tasks requiring a human touch.

Fraud

Internal fraud typically happens so slowly and comes from the person you least suspect. Most perpetrators of fraud have no previous criminal record. Many are trusted, long-tenured employees. And it can take from 12 to 24 months to detect the fraud, depending on their position — employee, manager, owner, or executive.

Nonprofits can be particularly vulnerable because they assume everyone is committed to the mission and they place more faith in their coworkers than for-profit organizations. Also, nonprofits typically lack the resources, internal controls, and training to spot the telltale signs of fraud.

Fraud in government often comes from outside the organization, such as doctors filing fraudulent claims, though AI offers solutions:

>> The Centers for Medicare and Medicaid Services saved more than $7 billion in inappropriate payments. By employing data analytics to examine fraudulent claims made by patients and/or physicians, it was able to proactively prevent more than $4.5 billion in false claims. Data mining allowed the agencies to recover another $2.5 billion in improper payments.

» In 2018, the U.S. Internal Revenue Service used AI to prevent $10 billion in fraudulent tax refund claims.

» Also in 2018, the U.K. Department for Work and Pensions reported that an AI-based program enabled them to recover an estimated £1.1 billion in overpaid benefits for the fiscal year.

Engagement

Whether donor or constituent, people respond when they engage on their own terms. This principle worked well for Amazon, but Jeff Bezos doesn't have a monopoly on consumer analytics.

Nonprofit

Most successful nonprofits have a donor database, but many don't realize the wealth of insights locked up in that data — insights that can help you find and intelligently engage new donors and improve your relationship with existing donors. AI-powered analytics can answer questions such as these: What do donors who donate $1,000 or more have in common? Is the average gift size for a donor increasing, decreasing, or holding steady?

TIP

Using data analytics to target donors may sound cold and calculating, but in reality, it empowers you to engage with each donor on a personal level to give them an individualized journey rather than shuffle them through the same pipeline of letters and emails that everyone goes through, treating them as just another donor ID number in the database, like a visitor in a theme park shuffling through the line to the roller coaster along with everyone else.

TIP

Starting with a pool of potential donors, you can use data about your existing donors to predict the behavior of prospects, identify those with the capacity to give, and segment them based on similarities, such as preferences in method of contact or giving. As you expand your knowledge and understanding of donors through analytics, you can create increasingly personalized interactions that focus on the mission, not the money, to prioritize their values and goals and help them make a difference.

Government

Twenty-first century commerce has raised consumer expectations by showing what is possible. Consequently, constituents have diminishing patience when they encounter the inefficiencies of the one-size-fits-all processes and services at their local, state, or national government.

But the difference hasn't gone unnoticed. Government is responding. Ten years ago, it would have been unthinkable nirvana to bypass the interminable line at the Department of Motor Vehicles to renew your license. Countless comedy sketches milked the frustration of these encounters. These days, in most, if not all, states, you can renew your license online or reserve a time slot if you don't qualify for online renewal.

TIP

Online registration is a simple innovation that has an outsized impact on the life of the average driver, but AI-powered analytics goes beyond a simple online scheduling system to bring the power behind the recommendation engine to the public sector. Now agencies can take advantage of all the internal and external data, structured and unstructured, to learn the preference of the constituent and adapt their services accordingly, providing visibility into timelines and milestones for approval or fulfillment of services.

Front-end processes such as streamlining the citizen touchpoint, mobile 311 apps, and 24-hour access to services via websites are typically what people think of when discussing digital transformation and the customer experience. However, a correlation exists between citizen satisfaction and how long it takes to get a response or resolution, and the factor that most affects time-to-resolution is the back-office system, not the customer-facing system. One study found that 20 percent of customer service calls were initiated because of back-office issues.

IMPROVING URBAN LIFE WITH AI

In the public sector, the cities of Chicago and Washington D.C. have applied predictive analytics to the problem of rat infestations by using 311 call data to identify leading indicators of conditions that could support rodent infestations and predict where those populations could spike, resulting in inspectors spending less time finding infestations and 20 percent more time treating infestations.

Chicago also uses predictive analytics to determine which of 15,000 food establishments their three dozen health inspectors should visit, resulting in finding critical violations sooner, before many diners are exposed. Las Vegas used natural-language processing and machine learning to mine live Twitter data for mentions of nausea and geotagged the user's location to mark likely destinations for their health inspectors. The tweet-based system scanned 16,000 tweets from 3,600 users each day. The hits led to citations for health violations in 15 percent of inspections, compared to citing 9 percent when performing random inspections.

TIP

AI can automate and streamline front- and back-office processes to maximize resources, reduce costs, and accelerate the delivery of services. To borrow an example from another back-office-heavy environment, one bank optimized the customer journey to open an account and reduced the time from sign-up to working account from two weeks to ten minutes.

Connecting the Tools to the Job

At the federal level, agencies are beginning to deploy AI-powered interfaces for customer service and are using AI applications to automate simple tasks. AI investments in infrastructure planning, legal adjudication, fraud detection, and citizen response systems are also underway.

To reduce fraud, AI uses supervised machine learning, neural networks, Bayesian classifiers, regression, and decision trees to train a machine-learning model based on historical data. It then processes real-time data such as fraud alerts, chargebacks, and complaints to label transactions as fraud and not fraud. Alternatively, AI can also use unsupervised machine learning, clustering, peer group analysis, and breakpoint analysis to determine the characteristics of common behavior ("most transactions look like this") and anomalous behavior ("this transaction looks different") without labeling them beforehand. Supervised methods can efficiently isolate incidents of known fraud tactics, while unsupervised methods detect unusual activity that may not fit a known pattern but should be investigated.

AI uses unsupervised machine learning and clustering to increase the efficiency and impact of compliance and quality inspections. For example, the U.K. Ministry of Transportation used three months of auto service test data broken down by garage to train a clustering model that, when combined with historical violations data, generated a risk score for each garage. They focused their efforts on high-risk garages, increasing enforcement of standards and reducing examiner preparation time by 50 percent.

Here are some additional ways agencies are applying AI:

>> **AI uses supervised machine learning and natural-language processing (NLP)** to tag documents at speeds beyond human capabilities to optimize time and budget. For example, the U.K. Government Digital Service used an existing taxonomy and samples of previously tagged documents to train a model, and then used NLP to process document content and metadata and properly classify and tag 96 percent of the 100,000 pages. The effort was projected to take years, but using AI, the project was completed in less than six months.

>> **AI uses handwritten text recognition, neural networks, and NLP** to enable organizations to make handwritten documents machine searchable to accelerate processing requests. For example, the Swedish Land Registry contains handwritten property records dating back to the mid-nineteenth century. To fulfill requests, case workers spent approximately 48,000 hours per year manually processing the records, the cost being passed on to the citizen submitting the request. The land registry office used handwritten text recognition to digitize the documents, a neural network to correct inaccuracies in scanning and to complete sentences, and NLP to highlight key features in the document, such as location, names, and summary.

>> **AI uses regression** to reduce public transit delays and optimize routes. For example, one transit system wanted to improve their on-time arrivals from 82 percent to 90 percent. They built a model based on historical data such as the timetable, train arrival times, positions, and lateness. Then they used unsupervised machine learning to find patterns in live data to reveal causes of delay. Finally, they trained a recommendation engine to suggest alternative destination platforms during conditions that create delays. Now the system notifies operators about potential delays up to an hour in advance with a 50 percent improvement in accuracy over the former system, reducing cumulative lateness by up to 200 minutes per day.

Examining the Use Cases

The opportunities for improving the constituent journey for government and nonprofit organizations are limited only by your imagination. Here are a few examples of what other people are doing now.

Enhance citizen services

You can use AI to allow citizens to bypass long hold times on telephone calls, waiting in a queue during in-person visits, or searching antiquated websites for answers by employing AI-powered chatbots and assisting users when filling out documents.

The U.S. Citizenship and Immigration Services responds to more than 8 million applications each year, answers 13.9 million telephone calls, and hosts 193 million visits to their website. In 2015, they launched Emma, a virtual assistant that answers questions from visitors to the website. In 2018, Emma responded to

9 million inquiries in English and 2 million inquiries in Spanish. Emma has a success rate of 91 percent for answering questions posed in English and 89 percent for answering questions posed in Spanish.

But AI really reaches its potential when it is seamlessly integrated with systems to provide employees with contextual information to adapt the process to the individual rather than forcing them into a one-size-fits-all service, making operations smarter and more cost-effective.

AI solutions are well suited for handling simple requests, automating conversations, and routing people and information, while human agents are still excellent at understanding customer emotions, building trust, and handling more complex requests.

Provide a global voice of the citizen

Traditional surveys force respondents to choose among fixed options. You can use AI to get a direct link to what people think, need, and want, spending less money and time while gaining more insight. Whether by tracking opinions about a new emergency system, gathering indirect input into proposed policies or identifying strengths and weaknesses of an infrastructure plan, you can use AI to read through massive amounts of unstructured data, transform it to structured data, and then ingest it to monitor email, voicemail, website feedback, and social media, using sentiment analysis. You gain a wider and deeper understanding of your constituents, measuring satisfaction and improving the perception of your organization.

Make your city smarter

The smart city recently overtook connected industry in terms of the number of Internet of Things (IoT) projects worldwide and is doing its part to contribute to the data tsunami while using AI to reduce operation costs, increase revenues, and improve public safety. Many cities are already using IoT projects to improve parking, traffic monitoring and control, bike sharing, and environmental monitoring. All kinds of things are getting smarter, including bus lanes, bus shelters, ferries, utilities, and lighting.

In 2012, the City of Pittsburgh piloted an automated traffic optimization and control system on nine traffic signals in three major roads. The system reduced travel time by 25 percent, traffic stops by 30 percent, wait time by 40 percent, and overall emissions by 21 percent. By 2018, the city expanded coverage to 50 signals.

Boost employee productivity and engagement

You can use AI to process massive amounts of content, allowing employees to focus on higher-value work. For example, document intake requires workers to wade through thousands of forms and emails. With the power of AI, this process can be automated and optimized to ensure thorough and efficient discovery and delivery.

A team of students at Ben-Gurion University developed TradeMarker, a machine-learning model that uses similarity matching, string matching, and computational neural networks to match trademark applications with existing trademarks. It achieves an immediate successful match rate of almost 80 percent, finding similarities that older systems don't detect and producing results five times faster. The tool liberates IP examiners, leaving the tedious part of the job to AI so they can focus on critical tasks that are more nuanced than pattern matching. Trade-Marker is also available on the team's website to allow citizens to do their own research to verify that their idea is unique before submitting an application.

Find the right employees (and volunteers)

The average job opening attracts 250 resumes. You can use AI to make your recruiting and hiring more efficient. Scanning resumes into an applicant tracking system can reduce the time to screen from 15 minutes per resume to 1 minute. Natural-language processing and intent analysis go beyond keyword searches to find qualified candidates whose wording doesn't exactly match the job posting. Virtual assistants interact with candidates to schedule meetings, an otherwise time-consuming and tedious task. By automating these and similar tasks, HR personnel have more time to focus on strategic tasks that require an interpersonal approach.

But you don't have to stop with employees. A 2018 U.S. study determined that a volunteer is worth $25.43 per hour. That can make a big difference, especially for large organizations that use lots of volunteers to not only increase manpower for events and special projects, but to expand the skill sets of the organization.

TIP

The benefit depends on the quality of the volunteer. A good volunteer can add value beyond that dollar amount to help your organization focus on the mission and improve outcomes. A bad volunteer can not only slow things down, but can also disrupt operations and degrade your effectiveness, costing you much more than the estimated hourly value. You can use your HR system to get the same insight and efficiency gains when on-boarding volunteers.

Improve cybersecurity

AI-assisted threat intelligence collects threat information from a diverse set of sources, such as network logs, incident response records, threat databases, and the like. It then processes the information to assign risk scores to behavioral patterns based on information such as time of login and geolocation. Supervised learning allows the security team to label past events for future reference, while unsupervised learning detects anomalies and new behaviors. The system uses the combined intelligence to create counter measures and mitigate the risk of a breach. When an alert is triggered, security engineers can use advanced analytics and machine learning to identify the root causes and even address vulnerabilities before they are exploited.

Chapter **10**

Utilities: Renewing the Business

The energy and utilities industry has undergone a significant transformation in recent years. Prompted by evolving customer expectations, increased competition, regulatory change, and an increasing availability of new technology, this shift drove the industry into a new era in which better customer-facing support, back-office operations, and overall performance are constantly evolving targets. According to Deloitte research, the U.S. electricity industry is characterized by low load growth, so asset utilization is also an increasingly important area of focus. Of course, there is an increasing push toward renewable energy sources, characterized by rapid growth in areas such as solar power.

To take advantage of time and cost savings from automation, many utilities are turning to AI and big data to drive the smart grid and streamline back-office operations.

Coping with the Consumer Mindset

Changing customer expectations have affected nearly every industry, and the utilities sector is no exception. The modern, smartphone-equipped customer demands more choices in rate plans, a greater level of control over electricity purchasing, and the ability to interact with providers directly. Their 24/7 connectivity calls for an entirely new customer experience with utilities — an industry that has traditionally had limited interaction with consumers.

And because some areas have become deregulated, consumers now hold more power than ever. In regulated markets, customers purchase electricity and natural gas from local utility companies at state- and federally-regulated prices at a time when deregulation is offering consumers far more choice and flexibility. In the U.S., regulation has become a state-by-state issue. While consumers in Texas and Ohio can change providers as they please, Californians don't have that option, because their state is completely regulated. The issue isn't concentrated just in the U.S. In Europe and Canada, deregulation is also forcing utility companies to take a greater interest in appealing to their existing and potential customers to improve competitiveness.

In addition, the rise of net metering, an arrangement in which customers with solar or wind installations can sell electricity back to the power company, has complicated things. In the U.S., net metering regulation has expanded beyond a handful of states in the 1980s to 44 states, with most of the customers located in California.

All things considered, traditional utilities like electricity and oil are even more pressed to drive improvements.

TIP

In this new market landscape, you are faced with reducing outages, targeting maintenance, and improving network reliability and safety. Making the power grid more intelligent can boost your competitiveness. The U.S. Department of Energy developed a Multi-Year Program Plan for fiscal years 2016-2020 to drive energy savings by leveraging emerging technologies.

Regulations are requiring utilities to move away from a standalone risk management program to making it an integral component of operations. Self-assessments and detailed recordkeeping will continue to be important as regulators seek to minimize the risk of incidents across the industry.

As with virtually all other industries, energy and utilities have an opportunity to streamline their back-office systems and processes. Although digitization is a good place to start, it may not be enough to remain competitive in the face of mounting external pressures. For this reason, intelligent solutions that leverage technology such as text mining and machine learning will empower this sector to improve across all facets of operations.

REMEMBER

Ultimately, technology, specifically AI, is an area of huge opportunity to help companies deliver energy more efficiently and dependably.

Utilizing Big Data

As a part of the energy and utilities sector, you face the challenge of staying competitive and keeping pace with the modern consumer without increasing costs or manpower. Fortunately, to increase overall efficiency and service, you can use a tool you already have in your toolbox: your enterprise data.

Historically, the energy sector has been slow to embrace digital transformation. Yet, as AI continues to reduce costs and increase revenues across industries, machine learning, text mining, and other intelligent technologies will be key assets to support innovation and growth.

While less than 10 percent of IoT projects were powered by AI as of 2018, Gartner predicts that more than 80 percent will include an AI component by 2022. Gartner also revealed that AI deployments were rare in 2015, with just 10 percent of CIOs across major industries leveraging this technology in their organizations. By 2019, that figure had increased by 270 percent.

The smart grid

Your operations produce an abundance of structured and unstructured data every day. Yet, that data is likely underused due to technological limitations and lack of resources. From grid performance metrics and outage data to customer complaints, countless pieces of information must be tracked.

Beyond simply tracking this data, you can use it to forecast usage patterns, provide a better customer experience, make informed and targeted maintenance decisions, and predict and respond to outages promptly. Historically, compiling, analyzing, and drawing insights from this data has been too tedious and time-consuming for humans to do alone, but AI solutions such as text mining and machine-learning algorithms are a perfect match for the rapid proliferation of big data in the utilities sector.

TIP

You can collect and analyze data points such as usage patterns, outage times, and maintenance schedules to gain predictive insights with the help of AI. Machine-learning algorithms can help forecast demand to optimize economic load dispatch, while IoT sensors and AI can work together to detect grid issues automatically and minimize the need for hazardous manual inspections.

Empowering the organization

In the back office, AI can help you manage everything from sensitive customer data to incoming requests through email and customer service chats, streamlining operations and extracting insights into your customer base without increasing their administrative burden. You can also monitor payment history and consumption patterns to identify irregularities that could point to energy theft, which is an ongoing problem in many developing nations. On the retail side, AI helps you navigate the changing market by allowing you to access insights such as customer profiles to identify the most profitable accounts, which can help you make more tailored offers for improved retention and satisfaction.

Connecting Algorithms to Goals

From text mining and natural-language processing to IoT sensors and machine learning, a wide range of algorithms are useful in utilities. Here are some of the ways they work:

>> **AI uses IoT sensors and analytics** to support predictive asset management, giving you visibility into every measurable aspect of the grid status in real time.

>> **AI uses machine-learning algorithms** to make predictions based on historical data to help you predict how much energy will be needed to meet short-term or long-term needs, pinpoint which areas of the plant or grid truly need maintenance or repairs, and reduce waste by uncovering inefficiencies.

>> **AI uses text mining, natural-language processing, and machine learning** to analyze enterprise content based on its context and route it to the appropriate workflow, thereby streamlining repetitive and tedious administrative processes to save time and money.

>> **AI uses text mining, natural-language processing, and sentiment detection** to tap into customer insights across a wide range of sources, from social media to customer service chats, to better identify the needs and expectations of your customers, which you can use to improve the overall customer experience.

Examining the Use Cases

The opportunities for improving operations are limited only by your imagination. Here are a few examples of what people are doing now.

Optimizing equipment performance and maintenance

You can use AI to run operations more intelligently and efficiently by operating on a predictive — instead of reactive — basis. Your grid already reroutes power in the event of an outage, but AI takes grid efficiency a step further. Using machine-learning algorithms and historical data, AI predicts failures and outages in grids, power plants, and other high-value assets by using digital twins.

TIP

Digital twins enable you to assess the performance of an asset, such as a trans-former, in real time. This digitized model of the equipment represents the ideal performance under actual in-the-field conditions for that asset, such as amperage load on a transformer. The system uses the digital twin as a basis of comparison to real IoT data from the actual asset. AI-powered solutions trigger alerts when the results don't match the twin, indicating a need for repairs or maintenance. This process avoids unnecessary maintenance so technicians can focus on the assets that truly need their attention. In doing so, AI helps you run more efficient grids and plants that are less likely to experience unforeseen outages.

Enhancing the customer experience

In an industry that has traditionally kept customers at a distance, increasing competition and the demand for interactions across a variety of channels are forcing companies to reevaluate their approach. AI can help you improve customer satisfaction while reducing costs.

Consumers now expect a multichannel platform linking interactions across mobile and web-based channels where they can interact with a chatbot when they're experiencing an issue, pay their bills, look at usage data, and customize their products or services to fit their needs. Machine learning can analyze historical usage trends and trigger personalized high-usage alerts for customers based on these patterns to avoid the surprise of an unexpected high bill.

TIP

You can use insights provided by AI to offer tailored energy-saving tips to help customers keep their energy bills down. These solutions significantly reduce the administrative burden on utilities while giving customers access to the information they want and need in the channel they prefer.

Of course, providing a multichannel platform for customers has another benefit. By tracking behaviors and actions through the customer journey and identifying sentiment in emails, social media platforms, and other sources, you can use AI tools including text mining to learn more about your customers and their expectations.

REMEMBER

AI-enhanced analytics provides deeper insights into what customers want and need, as well as how they feel about existing products and services. You can then use these insights to answer questions about pricing, demographics, and supply and demand. With this information, you can make data-driven decisions to tailor offerings more appropriately, optimize the customer journey, and improve customers' overall experience and satisfaction.

Providing better support

The modern, informed customer expects support staff to be available for immediate answers around the clock, but with shrinking budgets and a need to focus on more demanding challenges, customer-facing roles are often low on the list of priorities for energy and utility companies. Yet, providing timely support is growing more important to public perception and brand image, which is why many companies use AI-powered assistants to answer questions promptly.

Chatbots are available 24/7 to answer multiple inquiries at once and are knowledgeable across a wide variety of topics. Customers get technical expertise in just a few clicks while the support teams focus on outlier cases and other pressing issues that truly require human input. Providing the assistance customers need when they need it can go a long way in strengthening customer loyalty, which is especially important for utility companies in areas affected by deregulation.

Streamlining back-office operations

The ability to automate standard processes can free up time for administrative staff. For example, a regional power company might have a "Contact Us" feature on its website, along with the ability to send messages through social channels. Sorting through hundreds of incoming messages daily can be daunting for employees. An AI system with text mining can quickly process incoming messages; determine the context, sentiment, and content; and prioritize those that need to be addressed first. Complaints about outages, for example, might get priority over billing questions. The system can even trigger actions and route workflows appropriately to ensure issues are addressed promptly, improving the customer experience.

TIP

You can use AI to read meters without rolling a truck. Some utility companies use robotic process automation to automate meter reading, eliminating travel costs, freeing up employees for higher-value tasks, and reducing the rate of human error — typically by more than 60 percent.

Across the U.S., utilities have installed nearly 80 million smart meters. These modern systems generate 1 billion customer data points — 3,000 times more than traditional meters. They can provide deeper insights into energy usage, which, when combined with data such as customer interactions and payment history, offer a deeper understanding of consumer behavior.

Managing demand

Although 82 percent of consumers across the globe believe that it's important to create a world powered by renewable energy, you need to know who wants the option of renewable energy and who realistically will pay for it. Predicting usage by region and other key demographics is, therefore, an essential preliminary step to pursuing energy projects.

TIP

AI can help you sort through massive stores of data to derive meaningful insights, including demand forecasting. IoT-enabled appliances and devices such as smart refrigerators are now able to feed the smart grid information about power usage, which helps ensure that you are generating the optimum amount of power.

Mismatching demand on the low side can result in blackouts or brownouts that can infuriate customers — if not risk their lives. Mismatching demand on the high side results in expensive storage costs if not outright waste in financial and environmental terms. As such, even marginal improvements in demand forecasting by detecting patterns through machine learning can quickly pay for themselves. Additionally, this information comes into play when you are planning for new infrastructure, ensuring that you will have the bandwidth to meet customer demand without over-building.

Chapter **11**

Banking and Financial Services: Making It Personal

The financial services industry has been shaken up by several factors in recent years. Since the 2008 financial crisis, consumer banks, corporate banks, and wealth management firms alike have been forced to adapt to increased regulations such as the Dodd-Frank Act. Dodd-Frank is 2,300 pages long, but wait, there's more. The Home Mortgage Disclosure Act requires an improvement in the quality of data reported by financial institutions. With an abundance of regulations to satisfy, the costs of compliance are rising rapidly.

Traditional banks can use AI and big data to gain a competitive advantage over financial technology (fintech) companies through the level of personalization and customer experience they offer, while reducing their risk of fraud and cyber attack.

Finding the Bottom Line in the Data

If you're in the financial marketplace, I don't need to tell you about managing massive amounts of sensitive data. Although data privacy laws like the General Data Protection Regulation (GDPR) are already in place in certain parts of the world, banks everywhere must be especially careful in how they collect, store, and use personally identifiable information (PII). Taking a defensible approach to data privacy isn't just important from a compliance perspective. It's also a matter of strengthening security to prevent against hacks, fraud, and identity theft.

Traditional financial services companies are also facing mounting competitive pressure from fintech companies, who provide financial services as an end-to-end process on the Internet. Payment websites and apps like PayPal and Venmo blend financial services with the newest technology to make banking simpler than ever for individuals and businesses alike. Goldman Sachs has predicted that this new wave of banking could divert $4.7 trillion or more in annual revenue away from traditional banks. The gravitation of app-based banking is largely due to the desire for a simpler and more intuitive customer experience.

TIP

Customers expect a more personalized experience across all industries, and your organization is no exception. Although today's consumers anticipate sharing more data with their service providers, they expect it to pay off. In an Accenture survey, roughly 66 percent of consumers believe sharing their information should result in personalized product and service advice. For example, a high schooler opening a student savings account doesn't want to get email offers for low mortgage rates.

Moving to "open banking"

Recognizing the need for a more personalized customer experience while also putting pressure on big banks to level the playing field, some nations have rolled out a new wave of banking. This move is called "open banking," "platformification," or "the platform economy." This approach enables the electronic sharing of financial information under conditions approved by customers. It is supported by application programming interfaces (APIs) that allow third parties to access customers' financial data more efficiently, prompting incumbent banks to engage with digital banks.

Open banking is meant to create a frictionless, personalized experience for customers. Instead of having to log into different provider apps or websites, open banking creates a single source of truth, providing a comprehensive view of all accounts through one platform. As a result, customers can compare offers more easily to make informed decisions that meet their needs. They can also achieve greater clarity when budgeting, because all their spending and savings activity is aggregated in one place. Plus, customers can make quicker payments and take out loans with less time and effort, because financial institutions already have the necessary information needed to make approvals.

Dealing with regulation and privacy

Of course, with this evolution in banking comes a new set of regulations. The European Commission unveiled regulations for open banking under its Second Payment Services Directive (PSD2) in 2018. The Australian parliament introduced Consumer Data Right (CDR) legislation allowing bank customers to direct banks to share their information with fintech services and other third parties. These regulations also drive financial institutions to become more transparent, requiring banks to publish unbiased and accurate information to help customers make more informed decisions. The U.S. and Canada do not yet have legislation for open banking in place, but some banks have already begun implementing it.

Although 94 percent of banks EY surveyed in the U.K. believe that open banking represents a major area of opportunity, it also introduces new challenges for financial institutions. With customer data becoming readily available to banks and third-party providers, it is more important than ever to anticipate customers' wants and needs. Staying competitive in the face of these changes requires you to harness customer data in meaningful ways. The speed with which you leverage customer information to make tailored offers and provide a seamless, personalized banking experience significantly impacts your success in this new era of banking.

TIP

You must be poised to respond to a certain level of pushback from customers, who may be reluctant to share their financial data with third parties. After customers establish enough trust in banks, which could be facilitated through transparent data-sharing policies and with the help of regulations like GDPR, they will begin to think of open banking as less of a means of sharing personal data and more of a solution to make their day-to-day lives simpler.

You see the need to acquire and retain customers through more personalized offerings across all areas of financial services. Both financial institutions and wealth management firms need to provide a customizable, self-service customer experience that's available around the clock and accessible from anywhere. And, to make targeted offers, you must also be able to access and understand customer preferences through relevant insights and recommendations in real time. You must be able to forecast trends with increasing accuracy to gain a competitive edge and respond quickly to market changes, even amidst unpredictable times.

While thinking that all banking customers want the same offerings is a dangerous assumption to make, it's equally dangerous to assume that they all seek the same banking experience. Although it's true that 50 percent of customers now use mobile banking primarily, PwC found that 65 percent consider a local branch an important feature to have when choosing a bank, and 25 percent wouldn't consider a bank without one. Thus, understanding the wants and needs of various customer segments is critical to achieving long-term success in banking.

Offering speedier service

Not only do customers expect their banking experience to be personalized to fit their needs, they also expect service to be faster than ever. Most banking customers say that opening a bank account should take an hour at most, while nearly half think a mortgage application shouldn't take more than a day to process. American Banker found that the largest source of frustration, according to younger generations of banking customers, is the need to resubmit information, especially when opening bank accounts or applying for credit cards.

TIP

Although complaints on social media and a declining brand image are potential consequences to bear in mind, the greater threat is that these customers won't wait for you to respond to their needs and desires. With so many options to choose from, there's a high risk that they'll take their business elsewhere upon their first bad experience. It's therefore more important than ever for you to be nimble and anticipate changes in customer expectations.

You are expected to do all this despite shrinking IT budgets. Like many industries, companies in this sector are being pressured to reduce operating costs while improving business outcomes.

Leveraging Big Data

Because the industry is characterized by the collection and management of large stores of data, especially on the cusp of open banking, financial services are well-positioned to embrace AI solutions. In particular, traditional banks have one advantage over fintech companies: They tend to have more data on their customers than web-based banking solutions. Soon, however, the dynamics are likely to shift as more nations embrace open banking, and fintech companies pursue partnerships with financial institutions to access customer data. The key to staying competitive lies in using data to drive an improved customer experience. This includes making services more relevant and appealing to customers — an initiative for which AI is perfectly suited.

AI takes what would be overwhelming amounts of data for a human (including both hard, numerical data and textual content), analyzes it, and delivers relevant insights that trigger workflows or provide recommendations for next best actions.

TIP

AI can help you pinpoint which products are cooling off, such as holiday savings clubs, and which are becoming more popular. It can also uncover specific customer preferences by drilling down into usage patterns as specific as preferred ATM locations and high-traffic times for online banking.

That's certainly not where the value of AI for financial services ends, however. From automating tasks to strengthening security and boosting compliance, there are many other viable applications for AI in the industry. According to Business Insider, the majority of banks — 80 percent — are well aware of the potential benefits of AI. And most banking industry professionals are optimistic about implementing AI.

Most executives believe that AI will lead to cost savings, while employees believe AI will create — not take away — opportunities for them. And they're right. Accenture found that AI/human collaboration could drive revenue by 34 percent within four years. Forbes reports that top-performing financial services that have already deployed AI projects attribute 19 percent of their revenue growth to AI.

Clearly, AI is positioned to help financial institutions accelerate business on several levels. In fact, the area of opportunity for AI in financial services spans so far and wide that it can be challenging for a business to know where to start.

Restructuring with Algorithms

Although each business will develop an AI strategy unique to its overarching business goals, you should consider some especially promising applications. AI helps you manage massive stores of data more efficiently, while also uncovering patterns of customer activity to identify preferences and spot potentially fraudulent activity. It can therefore increase personalization, strengthen security, and improve the customer experience, all of which can support a successful entry into open banking. AI also automates tasks, such as customer service interactions, to reduce costs and free up employee time.

REMEMBER

Machine learning, natural-language processing, and chatbots are among the most popular AI-powered solutions already deployed throughout financial services. For companies that haven't already implemented these tools, in most cases they are either scheduled for deployment, budgeted, or on the roadmap. Clearly, AI isn't just nice to have in financial services. It's becoming integral to success.

Examining the Use Cases

Now that the foundation has been laid, it's time to look at specific ways you can use AI to address your challenges.

Improving personalization

AI's powerful pattern-recognition capabilities allow for comprehensive insight into consumer preferences and buying trends, which supports more accurate predictions to help them outperform competitors. With the ability to forecast customer wants, goals, and needs, you can make more accurately targeted offers, thereby achieving boosted sales and profits.

TIP

You can use customer data to make your services more relevant. Collecting, analyzing, and acting on huge stores of customer data as rapidly as possible is integral to success. AI can uncover patterns in data and make increasingly accurate recommendations based on the insights it gathers, making it an invaluable tool for adapting to and excelling in this new frontier.

In addition to product and investment recommendations, AI supports a more personalized customer experience. Machine-learning algorithms can identify which users do most of their banking online and trigger interactions such as options to receive paperless statements. AI can also alert customers when automatic payment due dates are approaching or when a checking or savings account balance is at risk of dipping too low. It can help customers monitor monthly spending behaviors and suggest real-time adjustments based on patterns — a feature that 59 percent of customers want, according to Accenture.

TIP

Ultimately, AI can enable a more intuitive, streamlined experience for banking customers, which can have a significant impact on retention. Customers look to you to partner with them and look out for their best interests through personalization. Thus, by offering personalization, you can achieve increased loyalty and wallet share.

Enhancing customer service

Accenture found that for nearly half of banking customers, customer service is a key driver of loyalty. And, while many customers rely on self-service banking, they still expect service to be available when and where they need it. Issues such as fraudulent activity can happen at any time, day or night, and customers feel more secure when they know that they can get in touch with someone from their bank when an issue occurs.

TIP

Customer service automation is a simple way you can provide an enhanced experience without increasing costs. In particular, many banks are already using chatbots on the front end to provide humanlike support quickly and efficiently. Less than a decade ago, the main use for chatbots was to respond to repetitive or simple customer queries. They can now analyze a high volume of structured and textual data, determining context to recommend solutions and next best actions.

Chatbots can answer questions such as, "Where is my nearest ATM," but they can also automate several day-to-day tasks. For example, in some financial institutions, they're being used as virtual assistants, taking instructions from customers to transfer certain amounts of money to vendors on demand. They can even recommend investment options, provide market-related insights, and offer options for using credit card points. Most importantly, virtual assistants can provide timely resolutions for key issues or direct inquiries to human agents for outlier cases that need further intervention.

Strengthening compliance and security

One of the most important uses for AI in banking is strengthening compliance and security. AI technologies can collect and mine data, perform comprehensive analyses, and deliver insightful reports to identify and reduce compliance risks. For example, GDPR requires companies in Europe to disclose the type of consumer information they collected and how they use it. Pinpointing all PII in vast pools of historical data would ordinarily be time-consuming and cumbersome for a human, but with AI capabilities such as text mining, personal data is quickly recognized. AI solutions can then trigger actions to store, destroy, or otherwise process this information as needed to support a robust compliance program across the enterprise.

TIP

You can use AI to standardize processes and ensure procedures are consistently followed. As you face new regulatory or policy changes, this technology will help you keep pace.

You can also use AI to detect spending anomalies and alert customers when purchases exceed a certain threshold or even block certain purchases based on amount or geographical location to prevent fraud and theft. McAfee reports that cybercrime is responsible for a loss of $600 billion worldwide, and AI can help bring this figure down with intuitive fraud protection technology. Yet, while machine-learning algorithms can be used to detect patterns and pinpoint anomalies, they can also reduce the amount of legitimate activity flagged as fraudulent, which inconveniences real customers. By deploying AI, MasterCard has been able to reduce its rate of false declines by 80 percent. Of all the business outcomes made possible by AI, banking professionals believe the technology has the greatest potential to impact fraud reduction.

Chapter **12**

Retail: Reading the Customer's Mind

I f you were shopping for a new television, where would you go? Would you start online, scouring reviews to find out which store has the best features for the most reasonable price? Or would you head to your closest big box store to compare picture quality firsthand and scout out any in-store specials? Chances are good that if you're like most modern consumers, your purchase will ultimately combine both.

And maybe your interaction won't stop there. Perhaps you'll sign up for the store's mailing list or loyalty card to get an additional discount on your purchase. Or maybe your new TV will come with a store gift card, which you could use toward accessories or a future purchase. You might even wind up leaving a review based on an especially pleasant (or poor) experience.

If you're in retail, then you know more than most that the marketplace can sometimes feel like a funhouse mirror maze. Consumers often think about the frustrations that come with a challenging shopping experience: long checkout lines, depleted inventory, extended shipping times, and high prices, sometimes, with no discount code in sight.

But it's not one-sided. As a retailer, you face significant challenges as well. Each customer has his or her own unique preferences and expectations. With more shopping options available, a truly outstanding customer experience is the key factor that can make or break a brand.

REMEMBER

Successful retailers have discovered the secret sauce of delivering that outstanding experience: the killer one-two combination of AI and big data, which you can use to create a streamlined customer experience through personalization and inventory optimization.

Looking for a Crystal Ball

Many retailers haven't been able to keep up. Store closings continue to show up in headlines, and while the pace has slowed a bit since the record 8,000-plus closings in 2017, figures for the following years improved little. This is despite the fact that the global retail market continues to grow, with experts expecting it to surpass $31.8 trillion by 2023. While several challenges have led retailers to suffer in spite of overall industry growth, a few issues present the biggest hurdles.

Omnichanneling

Do you have the omnichannel thing figured out yet? In today's connected world, retail is now everywhere — as are consumers. Understanding where and when each customer prefers to shop is key to offering the experience shoppers want, but with so much information to track, many retailers find it difficult to discern the insight buried in the information. In the U.S., 96 percent of consumers shop online, but still spend 65 percent of their budget in bricks-and-mortar stores.

Bridging online and in-store channels

To capture market share, you must provide a seamless omnichannel shopping experience by breaking down the internal silos between channels.

For example, suppose a consumer wants to make a same-day purchase at one of your stores. They first check the website, and the item shows in stock. If the customer visits the store only to discover it's sold out, this discontinuity introduces frustration and friction into the experience, creating a negative brand perception.

Now consider a different experience. The customer checks the website, sees the item is in stock at your store, clicks the BOPIS (buy online, pickup in store) button, and goes in and out of the store without having to wait in a single line. How many stars is that customer experience worth? Even better, after the customer is your store, she decides to browse and ends up in a checkout line with a real, physical shopping cart. Retail Dive found that 85 percent of BOPIS shoppers made additional in-store purchases during pickup.

Many retailers are still struggling to create this important seamless bridge between the bricks-and-mortar and online experiences.

Then there's the issue of showrooming, a phenomenon that you probably are all too familiar with, in which shoppers test the physical qualities of products showcased in-store before looking for a better price online. Forward-thinking retailers have turned showrooming on its head, using it as an opportunity to drive sales instead. For example, Best Buy offers side-by-side price comparisons against other major retailers, including Amazon. Nordstrom makes in-store purchases more convenient with roving cashiers, who provide on-the-spot checkout services to eliminate lines.

REMEMBER

A fair amount of thought goes into many purchasing decisions today, and the most successful retailers use data from historical sales and consumer preferences to give customers what they want, when they want it, in the most convenient way possible.

Offering a consistently positive experience

When it comes to purchasing options, more is better, but only if the experience is positive across all channels.

Bad shopping experiences on your website can affect both in-store and online sales. Bad in-store shopping experiences might drive shoppers online to find a wider product mix or increased inventory with other retailers.

A PwC study found that a single poor experience in a store can deter up to 33 percent of customers, while two or three negative interactions can almost triple the reaction, causing 92 percent of customers to leave a brand for good.

For these reasons, you must be able to support a seamless experience across all channels, because shoppers are likely to explore more than one.

Personalizing

Shoppers increasingly suffer from offer fatigue, with dozens of promotions flooding their inboxes daily. Customers don't want irrelevant offers clogging their inboxes, especially from their favorite retailers who should know what they want by now. In fact, a bombardment of poorly targeted marketing messages can backfire, sending shoppers away to competitors who are willing to get to know them better.

Customers expect you to pay attention to their preferences. While most companies have access to a wealth of purchase and customer interaction data, few leverage this information to provide personalized content through their customers' preferred contact methods.

TIP

If you aren't personalizing content and channel preference, you are missing out on a huge area of opportunity. Research shows that 75 percent of shoppers are more likely to make a purchase from a company that recommends options based on their purchase history or knows them by name.

For online retailers like Amazon, enhanced personalization is facilitated through complex yet increasingly accurate algorithms that provide detailed recommendations based on a shopper's purchasing and browsing history. Of course, retailers with multiple shopping platforms have to work a bit harder to connect all of their disparate data points for a clear picture of customer preferences.

Yet, both enhancing the customer experience and learning to navigate the omnichannel environment more effectively will do little good if you aren't offering the products customers want. The third challenge, therefore, is the ability to accurately forecast buying trends. While this skill has always been an integral component to a brand's success, shoppers have many more choices now, so it's more important than ever to anticipate trends and consumer demand, and on a more granular level. You must go beyond predicting sales, to estimate store-level demand. After all, a customer who needs the hottest Christmas toy now will go to great lengths to get it, and if a store is sold out, they're more likely to search through other local or online retailers to find it than they are to wait for inventory replenishment.

REMEMBER

While it may seem that these challenges paint a dismal picture for the future of retail, plenty of companies are thriving in this changing environment. And, in most cases, they're doing so with the help of AI.

Reading the Customer's Mail

Technology and retail have had a strained relationship in recent years. Many people have cast blame on the Digital Age for the surge in store closures. Yet, it's clear that some retailers aren't just surviving, but are actually excelling in this climate. The difference is that they know their customers exceptionally well and are catering to them appropriately.

Customers aren't shy about what they want, but to truly listen across all channels, you need a robust tool that takes data from all points of sale and customer interactions. With its ability to deliver meaningful insights from massive stores of data, AI can solve the major challenges you face in retail.

A fluid omnichannel experience

TIP

AI allows you to recognize which product categories are best suited for each type of shopping. With these insights, you can provide the most relevant offers and positive experiences for your customers.

For instance, grocery stores and big box retailers can use AI to recognize which items are commonly purchased by specific customer segments in-store versus online. They can then use these insights to suggest options that most appropriately fit their customers' needs, such as automated shipping for household products like paper towels and laundry detergent. Or, for the shopper who tends to do most of their purchasing in-store, convenient site-to-store shipping options can be recommended for items that are sold online only. You can also pull data from both online and in-store sales for each customer to ensure loyalty points are maintained across all channels.

Enhanced personalization

AI can compile data from a customer's historical in-store and online purchases, along with any interactions they've had with your customer service teams or social media accounts. You can use this data to formulate targeted offers both in the store and online. For instance, a shopping app can detect when the customer is near or enters the store, and trigger a personalized, one-day-only offer. Likewise, AI can recognize the intervals at which shoppers typically make online purchases and automate personalized offers when it comes time to reorder.

TIP

Personalization isn't just about triggering offers, however. You can also use it to make shoppers aware of new inventory. For instance, retailers often use AI to analyze historical shopping data and trigger emails alerting customers of other products they might be interested in, based on algorithms that assess similar purchasing patterns. They can even trigger smartphone alerts through geolocation when a customer walks in or near a store, or even by a specific in-store display, to point out a new or recommended product. These tailored notifications should be reserved only for customers who have opted in to receive offers. This will help your brand stay on the right side of the "creepy versus cool" factor.

Accurate forecasting

While retailers of yesteryear had only historical sales to use as a basis for their future inventory decisions, you can now use a wealth of additional data for demand forecasting. AI can pull data from sources such as social media mentions and web searches, and then perform advanced analysis and use machine-learning algorithms to provide forecasts with increasing accuracy.

With all these impressive capabilities, it's no surprise that retailers who leverage AI may save more than $340 billion by 2022, and the global AI market for retailers is projected to reach 4.4 billion by 2024.

Looking Behind the Curtain

Initiatives such as enhancing personalization, improving the omnichannel experience, and accurate forecasting can sound a bit daunting. While these pursuits certainly hold the key to success in retail, the question remains: How can you actually use AI capabilities in a practical sense to make both short- and long-term progress? Here are some of the ways AI can help:

>> **AI uses advanced analytics and machine-learning capabilities** to answer these types of questions:

- How can I enhance the customer experience? What do I need to do to get the right offer to the customer's device or shelf at the right time?

- What, exactly, do my customers want? When I track preferences across various touchpoints, including bricks-and-mortar stores, mobile, and online, what do I learn about customer behaviors?

- How well do I know my customers? Which offers appeal best to which customer segments?

- How can I use our inventory more strategically?

>> **AI uses machine-learning algorithms and Internet of Things (IoT) devices** to track customer interactions with products in-store. You can make data-driven decisions that help you provide the best experiences and offers across every channel. With the right technology, you can combine all your segmented data to get your entire marketing team on the same page, ensuring your tools work together instead of against each other. Using this information, you can begin to understand the key customer attributes that drive sales, including how, when, and what they purchase. And, using these analytics, you can then begin to make more informed decisions about product assortment and pricing, promotions, and optimal use of retail space.

>> **AI uses natural-language processing and machine learning** to increase the power and effectiveness of AI-powered chatbots that help answer questions about coupon codes, shipping options, and other common inquiries. In stores, robot assistants have been shown to increase foot traffic by as much as 70 percent. Aside from offering directions and answering common questions, some of these AI-powered assistants can blush and play music and have become popular props for selfies. Thus, these innovative solutions don't just free up time

for workers to focus on customers who need more attention and collect data from customer interactions; they also offer an engaging experience — something today's consumers seek out continuously.

Examining the Use Cases

Now that you have peeked under the hood to get a glimpse of several AI techniques that are useful in retail, it's time to dig deeper into practical ways to use AI to increase your engagement and revenues.

Voice of the customer

Customers want retailers to listen, but without the proper tools, it's impossible to derive meaning from all the noise. Social media, email interactions, customer service chats (whether with human representatives or AI-powered chatbots), surveys, and phone calls all provide insights into a customer's satisfaction with their experience, including the service they received and the quality of products. Sifting through all these granular insights is impossible for humans to do, but it's exactly where AI excels.

AI-powered solutions use techniques such as text mining to collect and analyze customer feedback and provide a single comprehensive view of their opinions. These systems are even intelligent enough to recognize sentiment through tone detection, so you can grasp the true nature of your customers' thoughts and feelings.

TIP

Tracking the customers' voice is essential for several retail initiatives. Finding out what customers have to say about online or in-store experiences (or both) lets you know where you need to improve. You can pick up insights from every stage of the buying journey to understand what compels shoppers to make a purchase and what might cause them to abandon their cart or look elsewhere for a product. These insights can factor into several different retail decisions, from purchasing to pricing to product mix.

Personalized recommendations

Pinpointing which offers customers want, when they want them, and through which channel they hope to receive them might be one of your biggest challenges. Yet, addressing them is also one of the most important things you can do to improve personalization, and ultimately, customer loyalty.

TIP

With AI, you can leverage features such as text mining and advanced machine-learning algorithms to extract data from every channel in real time. Marketing teams can use these insights to make timely offers or generate future campaigns. You can also automate offers to save you time and hassle and to avoid missing out on the key window of opportunity when shoppers are most likely to make a purchase.

AI-powered inventory

AI can help you pull data from a broad range of sources to predict demand on both a global and local level, and then manage your inventory in each location more effectively. For example, Walgreens uses predictive analytics to gauge appropriate inventory levels for their flu vaccines. Using data from recent antiviral prescriptions across their 8,000 locations, they perform a geospatial analysis to determine which areas are likely to be hit with the flu the hardest. This not only helps them decide which stores should receive flu shots in higher quantities, but it's also a clever marketing strategy. Using an interactive map that they update weekly, they show consumers which locations are experiencing flu outbreaks in the highest number, encouraging them to get vaccinated.

Walmart uses AI to refine their inventory strategy. Called the Intelligent Retail Lab, or IRL, their AI-powered system uses IoT devices to track purchasing patterns. The system can track inventory levels on the shelf and compare quantities against predicted demand. This allows associates to restock with greater precision and provides a better shopping experience for customers. They're even using the data to determine when perishable products need to be removed. Together, these capabilities help them manage their inventory of more than 30,000 in-store products more efficiently.

TIP

AI is also helping retailers manage their return rates through more accurate product descriptions. Online retailers, in particular, must verify that descriptions are accurate in terms of size, color, material, texture, and other key features, because inaccurate descriptions lead to large return volumes. With capabilities such as text mining, AI solutions can peruse manufacturer descriptions and customer reviews to generate detailed product information. One example is the "fits as expected" scale many clothing retailers now include in product descriptions. They may offer sizing information based on aggregate reviews, such as "80 percent of customers say this sweater runs large" or "Based on customer reviews, we recommend ordering these sneakers a half-size up from your normal shoe size." With this level of detail, customers can make the right selection from the start to help reduce returns.

Chapter **13**

Transportation and Travel: Tuning Up Your Ride

Transportation has evolved rapidly in just a few short years. While in the past you might have expected to wait a week or more to get the stuff you ordered online, now you're probably getting things the next day or even the same day. Public transportation and traditional taxi services are giving way to rideshare apps and autonomous vehicles. Shipping companies are looking for ways to extend the life of their fleets and drive maintenance costs down. Airlines seek to address the dilemma of balancing market-driven pricing and services with passenger comfort and amenities.

From long- and short-haul drivers to public transportation to airlines, AI-enhanced solutions help organizations improve the passenger experience.

Avoiding the Bumps in the Road

With an increased need for both long-distance and local drivers, it's no surprise that you're likely to find a "drivers wanted" sticker plastered across the back of most delivery and freight trucks. The truck driver shortage is predicted to double across the U.S. within the next ten years. It has become more difficult to replace aging drivers as individuals entering the workforce seek more flexible career options. Without a major shift, this shortage won't just cause a major headache for logistics; it will significantly affect the convenience of rapid delivery services to which we've grown so accustomed.

Options for catching a ride are also changing. In urban areas, public transportation and taxis were once the only alternatives to getting around by your own means. Now, ride-hailing or ridesharing apps have shaken up the industry and are providing more freedom for passengers. And, by the looks of it, they're here to stay. The number of U.S. adults who use ride-hailing services such as Lyft or Uber more than doubled from 2015 to 2018.

REMEMBER

The proliferation of ridesharing has put pressure on automakers. According to a Lyft study, nearly 250,000 of its passengers sold their vehicles or decided not to replace their current one, thanks to their app. While companies such as Tesla are already leveraging technology to provide a unique driving experience, others are just now catching on to the trend. To keep the interest of existing drivers and attract new ones, automakers must provide a new wave of innovative features that make transportation a more enjoyable experience. By incorporating built-in infotainment and safety features, auto manufacturers can create a superior driving experience that keeps motorists interested, even in an age with numerous other transportation options.

Public transportation must also go to greater lengths to compete. While it's often a more affordable option than ridesharing, many people in the U.S. still avoid public transit when possible. Roughly 75 percent of professionals drive to and from work alone, and in Dallas, where a $5 billion light-rail network was installed in the 1990s, commuters using city transit still hovered at a dismal 6 percent over the last few decades.

Why is it that so few city dwellers use a seemingly affordable and convenient option to get around, an option that could help to reduce roadway congestion and emissions? Clearly, there's a disconnect between what passengers need and expect and the level of service offered by public transportation.

As with any industry, consumers of transportation also expect an improved experience, especially for high-cost industries such as air travel. While the airline industry is strong overall, due to ridership increasing in recent years, it faces several challenges. Although the market has favored cheaper fares and the accompanying effect of maximizing flight capacity, it has come at the cost of passenger comfort. In addition, flight delays cost up to roughly $32 billion per year, half of which is passed on to the passenger. It's therefore no surprise that only 40 percent of people in the U.S. have a positive view of the industry.

The rail industry has its own obstacles. Safety continues to be a challenge for both freight and passenger trains. On the heels of the Positive Train Control (PTC) Enforcement and Implementation Act of 2015, railroads in the U.S. face pressure to implement full PTC systems before 2021. PTC systems combine real-time IoT device monitoring with AI to make real-time recommendations or adjustments to control speed as trains approach stations. These automatic adjustments have the potential to drastically improve safety across railways, but they also require major investments.

Many organizations have turned to AI to address these issues.

Planning the Route

In the U.S., trucks transport more freight than water, rail, and air combined. In fact, trucking is responsible for roughly two-thirds of all goods shipped throughout the country. So you won't be surprised to learn that if you want to maximize the impact of your investment in AI, your best bet is to focus on supply chain logistics. For the automotive OEM supply chain alone, AI is projected to yield $173 billion in savings by 2025 through self-driving technology and other initiatives.

Experts predict the full roll-out will take at least a decade, but it has already begun. In December 2019, an autonomous truck drove 2,800 miles in less than three days to deliver 40,000 pounds of butter from California to Pennsylvania, with a driver along to assist getting on and off the interstate for fueling and rest stops, but otherwise navigating on its own.

REMEMBER

Table 13-1 describes the levels of autonomous driving defined by the J3016 standard from the Society of Automotive Engineers (SAE).

The platooning technique, a Level 3 (conditional automation) implementation, involves a lead truck with a human driver connected wirelessly to one or more following autonomous trucks.

According to a recent McKinsey report, AI in general could reduce operating costs by 45 percent to save the for-hire trucking industry up to $125 billion.

TABLE 13-1 **SAE J3016 Level of Driving Automation**

Level	Description
0	No automation.
1	Driver assistance. Vehicle controls either the steering or the vehicle speed, but not both simultaneously.
2	Partial automation. Vehicle can steer, accelerate, and brake in certain circumstances.
3	Conditional automation. Vehicle can manage most aspects of driving under certain conditions, including monitoring the environment.
4	High automation. Vehicle can operate without human input or oversight, but only under select conditions defined by factors such as road type or geographic area.
5	Full automation. Vehicle can operate on any road and in any conditions that a human driver could negotiate.

TIP

To further maximize profits, you can deploy AI-powered features such as predictive maintenance and asset performance optimization (APO) to better manage your fleets. APO can save you 15 to 20 percent on maintenance costs due to improved productivity, reduced downtime, and more predictable operations.

In private vehicles, at the time of writing, some manufacturers have released vehicles that implement Level 2 (partial automation), which helps with braking and steering but requires full human attention, but research and development continues. A recent Kenneth Research report estimates the self-driving car market will reach a global revenue of $173 billion by 2023.

Applications for AI in vehicles go beyond autonomous driving. Studies estimate that motorist fatigue causes 20 to 35 percent of serious crashes. In response, auto manufacturers such as Lexus and Mercedes-Benz use sensor systems to detect drowsiness and erratic driving behaviors. Other manufacturers are developing seatbelt sensors to detect heart attacks.

AI technology is also enabling drivers to pay for fuel without leaving their vehicles, schedule and receive discounts on maintenance at nearby auto shops, and access phone and messaging systems more easily than ever through speech and gesture recognition.

In the public sector, AI-powered traffic control systems can time lights at intersections based on vehicle flows. In Europe, driverless buses powered by AI-enhanced GPS and sensors help passengers get to their destinations safely.

A new model for urban transportation is emerging, known as Transportation-as-a-Service (TaaS) or Mobility-as-a-Service (MaaS). It leverages app-based systems and AI to allow passengers to set up trips spanning multiple transportation methods and to pay and manage their account details in real time. AI can also help municipalities to better pinpoint what passengers want and expect, allowing public transport departments to provide desired features.

AI manages routes for drivers using real-time traffic updates. In Tokyo, autonomous taxis reduce costs for taxi services and increase transportation options for passengers.

Airlines use AI-enhanced analytics to analyze flier spending habits, demographics, and other data to achieve dynamic pricing, thereby offering the best value to prospective fliers at the best time. They can also use AI to analyze passenger sentiment across channels such as social media, email, and customer service chats. In doing so, airlines can assess which areas of the customer experience may need attention to serve as the basis for making decisions to improve.

Some airports use facial recognition instead of manual ID checks to verify identities. This practice can streamline the security process to reduce congestion at busy airports. AI can also automate messages to give passengers up-to-the-moment information about flight delays.

Checking Your Tools

Several AI techniques work together to power solutions for transportation applications.

Autonomous vehicles use machine learning to process data from a complex system of sensors, cameras, and communications systems to see the environment and react as a human driver would.

AI-powered solutions use a technique known as *digital twins* to predict breakdowns, optimize maintenance schedules, and maximize performance. These solutions use machine-learning algorithms to make maintenance recommendations based on historical data under a set of given circumstances. With geolocation, AI systems can then automatically trigger deals at nearby maintenance shops that have partnered with the auto manufacturer, offering deals on oil changes and other forms of preventive maintenance. For more information on digital twins, see Chapter 19, "Asset Performance Optimization."

AI uses text mining, sentiment analysis, and machine-learning algorithms to gather passenger sentiment by collecting data from a wide range of sources, contextualizing it, and analyzing it to achieve a comprehensive picture of what passengers want and need. You may have had the experience of a streaming music app suggest music for your commute just before you typically leave. Or an offer or a coupon pop up on your dash screen as you approach a store you frequent. All applications of AI in mobility.

Examining the Use Cases

The variety of transportation-specific AI application areas give you many opportunities to improve products and services to increase your competitive edge.

Autonomous vehicles

While years will pass before you see a Level 5 autonomous vehicle pull up beside you at a stoplight, pre-AI driving automation has been in place for decades. Cruise control, invented in the 1940s, maintains the speed of a vehicle without driver intervention by engaging the throttle valve through a cable connected to an actuator. AI-assisted autonomous driving uses more advanced technology. In addition to actuators, they employ complex algorithms, sensors, and machine learning.

Multiple sensors map the vehicle's surroundings, while radar detects the position of nearby vehicles and video cameras capture the presence of pedestrians, traffic lights, and road signs. Light detection and ranging sensors (LIDAR) help to measure distances to surrounding objects. Ultrasonic sensors detect nearby curbs and other parked vehicles.

These days, cars can parallel park on their own, alert you to a blind spot obstruction when you're changing lanes, and even brake when obstacles are detected.

REMEMBER

AI-powered systems analyze data from multiple sources to recommend actions. For example, an autonomous truck might use real-time weather data to slow down during heavy rains or avoid bridge travel during high wind advisories. Advances in autonomous vehicles reduce costs, streamline deliveries, increase safety, and perhaps even fuel sales for the automotive industry.

Predictive maintenance

Downtime is a major barrier to profits in the transportation sector. It's estimated that a single downed truck can cost a fleet up to $760 per day, which can add up quickly when you have multiple trucks down for days at a time. The age of same-day shipping options has no room for unplanned downtime. The cost of downtime varies by industry. Aircraft on-ground-time can cost tens of thousands of dollars, with just one day of not flying costing more than $17,000 on average. The ability to predict and address maintenance issues before they actually happen is therefore critical to helping you reduce downtime to improve profits.

TIP

Through machine learning and digital twins, you can assess the performance of a vehicle, plane, train, or other piece of equipment in real time. By subjecting the digital twin, or digitized model of the machine, to various simulated conditions, you can provide a basis of comparison for the actual asset. Comparing data from the machine's IoT sensors to the status of the digital twin helps you make informed maintenance decisions. AI-powered systems can also trigger notifications or alerts when a vehicle needs repairs or preventive maintenance, and even automate maintenance scheduling or parts ordering. Ultimately, predictive maintenance leads to enhanced efficiency, maximized uptime, reduced downtime, and cost savings — benefits that you can realize across all aspects of transportation and travel, including public transit, logistics, and airline travel.

Asset performance optimization

Predictive maintenance helps to reduce downtime, but you can use AI to take it a step further to optimize your assets by getting the most out of their uptime. Figure 13-1 provides framework of how thinking about asset production has evolved from reactive to proactive to optimization.

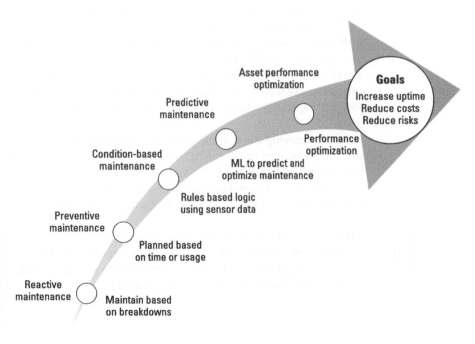

FIGURE 13-1: Evolution from reactive maintenance to asset performance optimization.

You may have been using IoT sensors and historical maintenance data to generate massive amounts of data for years. Yet, like many others in the transportation industry, you may have found that unlocking the value of that data to make better decisions to be tedious and time-consuming. Now you can use AI capabilities such as text mining and machine-learning algorithms to detect patterns in this data and discover which circumstances support the greatest level of performance. As you have probably discovered, trucks of the same make, model, and year can have vastly different levels of performance. While one may need frequent repairs, another may function optimally with just preventive maintenance. AI-powered solutions use data mining and machine learning to look for patterns in data sources such as running hours, mileage, idle times, and even driver behaviors to recommend optimized routes and vehicle usage to ensure you maximize all your assets.

Enhanced driver and passenger experiences

If you work in automotive manufacturing, you know that keeping consumers interested in the driving experience is critical to success. While many manufacturers are naturally focusing on the race toward self-driving vehicles, it isn't the only feature that attracts drivers.

From in-car virtual assistants to driver behavior monitoring, AI is already making the driving experience more interactive and personalized. Infotainment systems with customized settings allow drivers to request podcasts, music, and temperature settings verbally, eliminating the need for removing their hands from the wheel — or their eyes from the road, for that matter. Because your company has a considerable way to go before you achieve full autonomy, you can use other AI-powered capabilities to attract drivers in the near term.

In fact, improving the current passenger experience has become more important since the advent of social media. In recent years, airline passengers have become resigned to the fact that the experience seems to be deteriorating. First-class fliers may still receive on-board meals for certain flights, but more often it appears that passengers riding in coach are lucky to get a soft drink while on board.

REMEMBER

With the rise of social media, passengers have become much more vocal about negative (and, occasionally, positive) flight experiences. From overbooked flights to hours-long delays, factors that contribute to a poor passenger experience are fodder for Twitter rants and scathing reviews that can tarnish your reputation.

On a smaller scale, drivers for ride-hailing services must cater to their passengers to stay in good rankings. A dirty car or risky driving could result in one-star ratings, which can lead to fewer passengers and may even cost a driver their job. While drivers can typically read through reviews on their own to see how they can improve their passengers' experiences, the company as a whole must listen to the voice of their passengers when it comes to repeated occurrences that could compromise convenience, enjoyability, or most importantly, safety. Public transit departments must follow suit if they hope to contend with ride-hailing apps or other alternatives to their services.

TIP

To track the collective sentiment of passengers, you can use AI-powered voice of the customer (VoC) solutions to gather feedback from all available channels. By analyzing comments and opinions, VoC solutions provide recommendations that can improve the passenger experience.

For instance, an airline whose performance is suffering due to complaints about delays might consider offering a simple voucher for a free drink at the airport to improve passenger sentiment. Public transit departments in a busy city can use apps to communicate delays or schedule changes based on a passenger's typical route, leveraging historical data to trigger notifications that make their passengers' lives easier. As the availability of travel options expands, companies must work harder to stay relevant and turn the passenger experience into a competitive advantage.

Chapter **14**

Telecommunications: Connecting with Your Customers

I f you're in telecom, you don't need me to explain how growth has exploded in the past few years. In addition to gaining millions of subscribers within the past few decades, many providers have undergone transformations as consumers increasingly move away from traditional landlines to devices such as smartphones, smart watches, and tablets.

Recent figures show that 37 percent of subscribers now opt in for unlimited data plans, and 85 percent of U.S. consumers have a smartphone. They're also using their devices more than ever, with people viewing their phones 52 times per day on average. You may have also experienced the pressure to increase capacity to handle Internet of Things (IoT) data. Billions and trillions of new data sources are being generated annually, and soon your networks may need to handle zettabytes per year.

Although these shifts have opened tremendous growth opportunities, they come with significant challenges. Increasing demands for data and saturated markets have forced providers to become more competitive in their pricing, which has led to decreases in the average revenue per user (ARPU). Prices of unlimited plans are falling, and consumers are taking advantage of offerings such as bundled services. With recent developments in infrastructure, many subscribers are finding that features such as connection speeds and coverage are becoming commoditized.

REMEMBER

AI and big data can improve customer experience and operations and boost revenue from new products and services.

Listening Past the Static

To reduce churn, maintain market differentiation, and ultimately balance the competitive landscape, you are likely looking for new opportunities and focusing on optimizing the customer experience, such as improving access to support and the quality of that support. Customers also expect uninterrupted service with no outages, the ability to select plans and products from highly personalized offers, and access to emerging solutions such as 5G network coverage.

You're doing all this while keeping an eye on affordability and efficiency. New products, customized solutions, and support in terms of customer care and order fulfillment can be overwhelming. Simply keeping pace with the industry's massive growth is challenging enough. Tapping into customer trends to accurately identify market segments, forecast demands, and improve overall service adds another layer of complexity.

REMEMBER

Fortunately, improving the customer experience to win among top-performing telecoms is possible through the very resources you already have at your disposal: your data. With a little help from AI.

Finding the Signal in the Noise

You are likely dealing with staggering amounts of data. These volumes have increased at an astounding rate within the last decade or so. Consider AT&T: The data volume in their wireless network has increased 470,000 percent since 2007, and not through phones alone. From fitness trackers to smart home devices, today's consumers are creating upwards of 2.5 quintillion bytes of data each day. In addition to the data consumers are actually using, there's also the information your network accumulates through mobile applications, geolocation, service usage, billing histories, IoT sensor data, customer service chat transcripts, and customer profiles.

There's a wealth of value hidden within all that data, but until recently, many telecoms lacked the resources to unearth it. With sophisticated algorithms and machine-learning techniques, however, AI can look for patterns in that data, extract insights for improved customer experience and operations, and boost revenue from new products and services. AI-driven solutions allow you to better understand the health of your network and the behavior of your customers to respond rapidly to emerging trends, reduce churn, improve efficiency, and provide more targeted offerings.

AI doesn't simply aid in data management, however. It can also parse huge volumes of data contextually, offer reports or analysis, and trigger actions. In doing so, it allows you to get the full value of your enterprise data while simultaneously eliminating tedious, repetitive work so your employees can focus on key initiatives, such as handling outlier cases.

Looking Inside the Box

AI implementations hold enormous value for your business by streamlining and automating processes, enhancing customer support, and improving business decisions in these ways, among others:

>> **Text-mining capabilities** allow you to scour textual data, from customer support chats to social media posts, to understand and analyze customer needs, wants, and sentiment. This capability enables you to better identify and profile customer segments, make targeted offers, and ultimately, reduce customer churn. Insights into customer trends can also help you make tailored product recommendations, which is critical in the age of offer fatigue and flooded inboxes.

>> **AI-powered solutions such as digital twins** use advanced machine-learning algorithms to recommend specific maintenance activities by comparing historical trends against real-time operational data collected through IoT devices. This helps you predict and prevent outages, optimize maintenance schedules, and streamline your network.

>> **Capabilities such as machine-learning algorithms and predictive analytics** allow you to better forecast trends, predict churn, and plan for new products and services. AI automates the data crunching to provide the key insights needed for smarter and faster decision-making.

Examining the Use Cases

Now that you have taken a glimpse at how AI can help you tackle your challenges, it's time to look at some specific examples.

Achieve predictive maintenance and network optimization

AI can detect and predict network anomalies and trigger actions to proactively resolve issues before they result in outages or affect customers.

TIP

You can leverage AI to make predictions based on historical trends. In addition, with the help of IoT data, you can monitor the state of high-value assets such as power lines, repeater towers, satellites, and data center servers in real time. By comparing incoming equipment data against historical trends, AI enables you to address issues proactively and keep your assets functioning optimally, thereby reducing downtime.

Beyond preventing issues, however, AI also aids in network optimization. Through incoming traffic data and sophisticated machine-learning algorithms, you can optimize network quality for specific regions, analyzing for inconsistencies in data patterns which can alert you to issues. Nearly two-thirds of telecoms use AI to enhance their infrastructure, relying on the technology for initiatives such as optimized capacity planning and 5G network deployment.

Enhance customer service with chatbots

Chatbots, or virtual assistants, are also a powerful AI solution already being leveraged by many telecoms. With the ability to assist customers through intelligent one-on-one conversations, research from Juniper predicts that by 2022, chatbots may reduce business costs by $8 billion per year. Telecoms in particular are inundated with support requests. Customers regularly need assistance with everything from installing and troubleshooting network routers to adding lines or upgrading their plans. These requests can leave support centers overwhelmed, leading to lengthy wait times that ultimately influence customer experiences and perceptions.

To provide the timely, quality support customers expect, companies like Nokia are investing in virtual assistants, leading to a 20 to 40 percent improvement in resolution rates. Likewise, Vodafone improved customer satisfaction by 68 percent through its chatbot, TOBi.

TIP

You can use chatbots as concierges that apply natural-language processing and machine-learning algorithms to understand and process requests. In many cases, you can resolve support issues by simply providing the right information. Chatbots can provide instructions based on the customer's inquiry, automate actions, escalate requests as needed, and even trigger offers or recommend other products or services that may interest the customer. They make decisions in real time based on historical data, providing the assistance customers need when they want and expect it. These capabilities are achieved without the need for human intervention, which frees up time for your support teams to focus on the requests that truly demand personalized assistance.

Improve business decisions

Navigating the competitive landscape of the telecommunications industry continues to be a significant challenge. You are sitting on a wealth of data from your customers, but you may lack the capabilities to retrieve the insights that matter most from this information. Manually sorting through these vast stores of data to find the pieces that matter most isn't feasible. It would take far too long and use up the valuable manpower that you must use as strategically as possible. Yet, customer data is the very key to helping you make quicker, smarter business decisions.

AI simplifies the gathering and processing of data with advanced capabilities such as machine learning, natural-language processing, and text mining.

TIP

You can use AI to extract sentiment from social media and customer chat transcripts to create both granular and holistic insights of customer opinions. Plus, AI can establish patterns by analyzing data such as purchase history, demographics, customer interactions, customer journey information, usage patterns, and billing information. In doing so, it can uncover the drivers behind purchase decisions to help you shape the best possible offers and overall customer experience. Using both new and historical data, AI can also predict the lifetime value of the customer, provide key churn analytics, and offer information to help you make better decisions for price optimization and product development.

Chapter **15**

Legal Services: Cutting Through the Red Tape

Although at times it may seem like law departments and law firms are two teams separated by a common profession, the two have more similarities than differences, including coping with the tidal wave of data that has hit the legal profession in the last few decades and navigating the emerging alternative fee arrangements that their clients demand.

In a profession mired in paperwork from the beginning of time, many lawyers are turning to AI to tackle overwhelming tasks such as discovery, regulatory compliance, and risk reduction.

Climbing the Paper Mountain

Historically, lawyers have relied on their own expertise, knowledge and instincts when predicting case outcomes or providing advice regarding risk and strategy. But today, the sheer volume of data and the seemingly impossible task of considering every input that could potentially have a significant impact on outcomes require a different strategy. The legal profession is shifting from a reactive stance to proactively using data to drive decisions, service delivery, and internal operations.

Reading and writing

At the risk of being accused of *reductio ad absurdum*, I could characterize the life of a lawyer as reading lots of stuff and then writing lots about what they just read, and mixing in their own thinking along the way. The reading and writing have only increased:

>> In the 1980s, lawyers created, received, or reviewed about 16 documents a day, including letters, contracts, telephone message slips, legal-pad notes, and so on. Those were the days.

>> By 2013, that number was up to 50 documents a day, more than half of which were email. In 2015, only two years later, the total had grown to 70 a day. Does that pace sound more familiar?

>> By now, it may be even higher. Higher, that is, for those who are not using artificial intelligence to hold back the flood.

Of all the legal activities that could use some help in bailing out the flood of information, discovery is in need of the biggest bucket. According to a Rand study of electronic discovery costs, 70 percent of the cost of litigation in the U.S. is consumed by the discovery process, and 70 percent of that budget is consumed by document review.

Discovery used to involve thousands of documents. Now it can involve millions. Here are a few examples of recent discovery challenges:

>> The discovery team on a liability suit had 45 days to process a broad range of data, including 1.2 million emails from 10 custodians over a four-year period.

>> A discovery team of three attorneys on a class-action lawsuit had 1.3 million documents to review.

>> A discovery team of 40 attorneys on an international patent infringement case had one month to review 1.65 million documents and code them for 11 issues and privilege.

With superhuman challenges like these facing the legal profession, it's not surprising that many are looking to automation to stay afloat.

And arithmetic

As you know, a lawyer experiences life in six-minute increments. That is the effect of hourly billing, which divides the hour into tenths. If the lawyer spends any fraction of a six-minute block doing something for a client, that block is billed to the client, which can have the effect of inflating the cost of services without increasing the quality of service. Then there's human nature. When you are paid by the hour, you are incentivized to maximize the hours you devote to that project. As a result, there is growing pressure from clients to transition to alternative fee arrangements (AFAs).

In fact, in 2017, Microsoft announced that it would move 90 percent of its legal spending away from hourly rates to AFAs. This trend puts pressure on you to better understand your actual costs, not just how you spend your time, so that clients can forecast expenses and create a more accurate legal budget in advance.

Foot in mouth disease

An American Bar 2017 survey showed that 77 percent of law firms and 81 percent of lawyers have a presence on social media. However, news stories indicate that a surprising number of lawyers are using social media poorly, to say the least. Lawyers get in trouble for dispensing legal advice online, posting personal opinions on current cases, sharing client stories without consent, getting caught in lies, and sharing private or privileged information. So, while social media can be a very effective marketing tool for law firms, it can also be a source of liability and risk.

Planting Your Flag at the Summit

In what might be considered a case of fighting fire with fire, technology is now solving the problem it was partially responsible for — a super-abundance of documents. For example, in the task of spotting legal issues in five non-disclosure agreement contracts, a 2018 test matched 20 lawyers with decades of experience against an AI agent three years into development and trained on tens of thousands of contracts. The lawyers lost to the AI agent on time (average 92 minutes as opposed to 26 seconds) and accuracy (average of 85 percent as opposed to 94 percent). This translates into faster execution of agreements and increased productivity.

TIP

With machine learning, text mining, and visualization tools, you can apply data models and taxonomies to streamline document intake, accelerate in-depth analysis, and significantly reduce the time and costs associated with discovery. Specifically tackling the mountain of paper, AI can perform document on-boarding and reviews based on continuous active learning to prioritize the most important documents for human review — lowering the total cost of review by up to 80 percent.

Remember those three discovery cases with millions of documents? Here's what happened when they used AI to help with discovery:

>> The team used data visualization to narrow the relevant dataset. AI coded the remaining documents for 20 different issues, and the team of five attorneys completed the review in three weeks instead of 45 days.

>> AI coded 97.7 percent of the 1.3 million documents as non-responsive, leaving fewer than 30,000 documents for the three-attorney team to review.

>> AI culled the corpus from 1.65 million documents to a review set of 800,000 and then further reduced the set to 278,000 requiring human review. The team of 40 attorneys hit the one-month deadline on time and on budget.

Automation and machine learning are also making it possible to handle other mundane and time-consuming tasks more quickly and accurately. This reduces human error, improves consistency, and frees up time so you can focus on more important, value-adding tasks — giving your clients more value for their money.

Speaking of value, law departments are using AI to help contain costs, measure spending, support supplier selection and performance evaluation, and support decisions regarding hiring law firms and which candidates to on-board for specific roles. In-house legal departments use AI to automate tasks and generate reports relating to contract analysis, risk assessments, and case and department budgeting and planning.

As regulated industries strive to enforce rigorous rules and policies, many compliance and legal departments are working together to protect their employer against unnecessary risk, including the conduct of individual employees, executives, and board members. They can also mitigate compliance risks and even prevent improprieties by analyzing and monitoring relevant data and communications to identify and isolate threats.

TIP

With AI, you can aggregate and analyze data for all the cases across a law department for budget predictability, outside counsel and vendor spend analysis, risk analysis, and case trends to facilitate real-time decision-making and reporting.

Law firms are using AI to predict time frames for litigation, estimate staffing requirements for litigation projects, and provide analytics to assist teams in making informed decisions to produce better outcomes.

Linking Algorithms with Results

Data increases in value when it can be used to inform decision-making. According to a recent survey of in-house corporate attorneys, almost two-thirds have access to data regarding outside costs, yet less than half (49 percent) are effectively using this data and only 29 percent of respondents said their legal departments are effectively using their data. The data is there, but it's not being analyzed to find ways to reduce costs, develop business strategy, minimize contract risks, or better deliver legal services. One attorney said, "AI will be able to take over record-keeping roles like entity and document management. I could see some significant AI document preparation as well." Here are some of the ways AI can help:

» **AI uses text mining** to process large pools of unstructured data, such as legal documents, emails, texts, social media, and even voicemail, to identify key concepts, categorize content, detect subjectivity, isolate behavior patterns, discern the sentiment expressed in the content, and extract phrases and entities such as people, places, and things.

» **AI uses supervised and unsupervised learning** based on native or custom taxonomies to classify or characterize documents to support litigation and investigation activities such as early case assessment and privilege detection.

» **AI uses machine learning and natural-language processing** to analyze large amounts of textual content to a degree of understanding and at a large scale not possible using ordinary analytics. AI then distills the information into short summaries and chronologies, which can display entity and concept trends over time, as well as behavioral patterns of people of interest. The results can be integrated with data visualization to display the outcome in a consumable and intuitively understandable structure using interactive reports and dashboards. You can take advantage of these techniques to achieve greater data-driven insights to better understand facts, improve and develop forward-thinking strategies, predict outcomes, mitigate risk, and deliver results faster and more intelligently to support business or matter-specific considerations.

» **AI uses machine learning and predictive analytics** to process enormous amounts of data, including internal and external information, to identify and anticipate compliance risks before they turn into a liability. In the case of insider trading, bribery, theft, fraud, contractual malfeasance, or political corruption, the source data can extend to company communications, which can be correlated with data from emails, news stories, social mentions, and stock prices to spot potentially troubling patterns.

Examining the Use Cases

Now that you have peeked under the hood to get a glimpse of several AI techniques that are useful in optimizing workflow, it's time to dig deeper into practical ways to use AI to turn your practice into a lean machine.

Discovery and review

Searching for relevant information is a core competency of legal practice. And like many things involving the law, it is labor-intensive, time-consuming, error-prone, and costly. Such work can involve activities as diverse as discovery in a case under litigation or performing due diligence for a merger or acquisition. In any case, the end goal is gathering all information pertinent to the case, evaluating it, and then advising the client as to their options and the optimum path forward.

The quality of due diligence has significant implications for the parties involved. For example, in an acquisition, a more thorough search typically benefits the buyer by lowering the price.

Electronic discovery, also called *technology-assisted review,* uses supervised learning to categorize and summarize documents to extract the relevant information in a fraction of the time taken by human reviews — and with higher accuracy.

TIP

You can use AI to analyze data in support of early case assessment activities that drive case strategy, improve document review to support discovery obligations, and enhance post-discovery case preparation. Both law firms and corporate law departments can interact with data in new ways to better understand and unearth investigatory facts without using traditional discovery methods, which are time-consuming and labor-intensive. Recognizing the same opportunity, traditional legal research giants Westlaw and Lexis Nexis have been incorporating same into their product portfolios to capitalize and help maintain their position in the market, and more of this is likely in the future.

Text mining enables you to identify key concepts; extract phrases and entities (people, places, and things); categorize content; and detect subjectivity, behavior patterns, and sentiment in unstructured content such as depositions or court records.

TIP

You can use text mining and natural-language processing to let AI analyze and distill large amounts of textual content into short summaries and chronologies while you focus your efforts on higher-value legal activities such as analyzing data to support legal conclusions. After the summaries are available, you can quickly gain a better understanding of the timeline of the case, including entity and concept trends and the behavioral patterns of people of interest.

In one real-life example, by using AI for discovery, one large law firm was, in their words, "able to leverage a very small team to perform an incredible amount of work that would otherwise require a lot more staff and a larger commitment of resources." They also used machine learning, grouping, and phrase analysis to categorize documents into contextually related subsets to jumpstart fact investigation. By using predictive coding, they accelerated relevancy decisions to prioritize the most probative content for expedited analysis to minimize errors and foster consistency among human reviewers.

Predicting cost and fit

As AI matures, it is emerging as a tool for strategic and tactical planning while preparing court cases. Here are a few examples:

>> A 2004 Washington University test pitted an algorithm against experts in forecasting U.S. Supreme Court decisions. After processing all 628 cases argued before the court in 2002, the algorithm correctly forecasted 75 percent of the outcomes compared to the 59 percent accuracy of the human experts.

>> In a 2017 Michigan State University study, the team performed a similar test to predict U.S. Supreme Court decisions from 1816 to 2015 with 70 percent accuracy on case outcomes.

>> A 2016 University College London study used machine learning to analyze case text to predict European Court of Human Rights decisions with 79 percent accuracy.

TIP

You can use AI to more effectively oversee the time and costs associated with managing cases and legal matters.

In-house law departments use AI to help contain costs, measure spending, and aid in supplier selection and performance evaluation. AI also supports decisions regarding which law firms to hire and which candidates to on-board for specific roles.

Law firms use AI to analyze historical and relevant data they accumulate regarding billing, client service costs, project management, past cases, rulings, win/loss data, attorney efficiency, and other key performance indicators. With this information, they develop predictive models to identify and predict patterns in managing service delivery in terms of profitability, productivity, case resolution, and overall performance. Benefits include understanding the following:

>> The kinds of cases best suited to the firm's strengths — and those it should avoid

>> Likely settlement amounts and billable hours before discovery begins

>> Discovery project burn-rate with respect to staff time and cost

>> The likelihood of litigation and ultimate success based on whether a case goes to trial, is filed in a specific jurisdiction, who the judge is, and historical rulings

Analyzing data to support litigation

You can use AI to classify or characterize documents using native or custom taxonomies to support specific pre- and post-production requirements, such as early case assessment and AI-enabled privilege detection. AI and analytics can also help you understand context and gain insights and communicate those to others via data visualization. Research into past cases, win/loss rates, and past rulings can be used to identify trends and patterns to extract key data points from these documents as you develop and support arguments.

Automating patent and trademark searches

Trademark and patent searches require reviewing hundreds, even thousands, of results, but you never know what you missed. There are spelling errors in patents, so a patent might match your intellectual property, but not your spelling. Or they might have used a different word, such as "vehicle" instead of "truck." Coding the proper Boolean expression to catch all the corner cases is just the start. Then you have to actually read the documents.

You can use AI-enhanced search tools that support semantic search and natural-language processing to get comprehensive results that match all the variations, scan the documents for relevance, and flag documents that warrant pursuing.

Analyzing costs for competitive billing

Law firms that don't understand their true costs will find themselves at serious risk of shrinking or even disappearing margins in the face of the trend of clients wanting to transition from hourly billing to an alternative fee agreement. Analyzing true cost will enhance a competitive stance.

You can use AI to analyze case histories to identify the resources required for different types of litigation; the mean, median, range, and distribution of costs for a type; and circumstances that trigger outlier outcomes. This analysis identifies and reduces risk for all parties.

Chapter **16**

Professional Services: Increasing Value to the Customer

Business organizations look to professional services firms to offload existing processes such as payroll, claims processing, and other clerical tasks. Consequently, rather than push the innovation curve as early adopters of emerging technology, professional services firms have traditionally followed well-established procedures and used conventional tools. However, much of the work they take on involves processes that are well suited for optimization through AI, and many corporations are investigating the benefits of AI for streamlining workflows and cutting operational expenses.

A KPMG report predicts that enterprises will increase their spending on intelligent automation from $12.4 billion in 2019 to $232 billion in 2025, almost 19 times as much in just seven years. A McKinsey report estimates that 20 percent of the cyclical tasks of a typical finance unit can be fully automated and almost 50 percent can be mostly automated.

Exploring the AI Pyramid

From all appearances, the industries typically served by professional services firms are in the early stages of a tectonic shift that will reverberate throughout the professional services industry. The initial shock will involve adopting new ways of organizing and delivering professional services, but the aftershocks could very well challenge the essence of what professional services firms deliver. Figure 16-1 shows the hierarchy of business complexity.

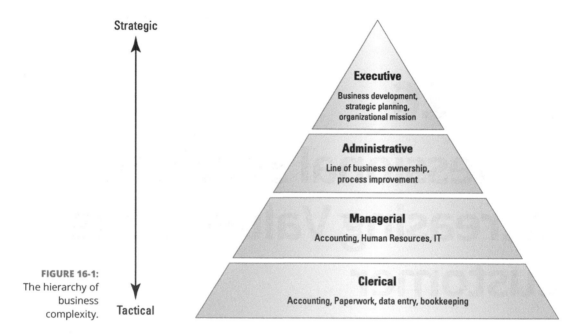

Strategic

Executive

Business development, strategic planning, organizational mission

Administrative

Line of business ownership, process improvement

Managerial

Accounting, Human Resources, IT

Clerical

Accounting, Paperwork, data entry, bookkeeping

Tactical

FIGURE 16-1: The hierarchy of business complexity.

AI projects usually start at the base of the pyramid, where the goal is to save costs by optimizing manual process via human-machine collaboration. As the projects move up the pyramid, they move away from saving costs and focus on increasing revenue by making more informed decisions regarding existing lines of business or launching new lines of business.

In a real-life example, one cookware company uses home demonstrations to sell high-end pots and pans using internal financing. They brought in AI to replace a manual workflow based on rules and decision trees with a semi-automated process that streamlined the underwriting decision and reduced acquisition cost. This project was a tactical move to save money by making the process more efficient.

On the strength of that success, they moved up the pyramid. They used AI to analyze the historical behavior of accounts that underwriting declined and passed on to a third-tier lender. The model looked for common characteristics of borrowers that had been declined but got financing from the third-tier lender and didn't default but paid it in full. They then applied the model to new loan applications to identify candidates who might not meet the traditional requirements for financing but were still a good risk. This project was a strategic move to expand their market to increase revenue.

To begin with, if AI doesn't eventually replace the most fundamental tiers of service delivery, such as paper handling and data entry, it will at the very least optimize them to the point that they can be delivered by a significantly reduced staff through human-machine collaboration.

Or it could lead to an increase in staff by freeing up funds through increased efficiency. An Accenture report indicated that AI could boost employment levels by 10 percent if the rest of the world invested in AI and human-machine collaboration at the same level as the top-performing 20 percent.

Professional services firms touch many of the industries discussed in this book, and just as technology matures and affects all industries, by necessity it affects how professional services firms engage their clients.

TIP

AI won't replace core professional expertise, but it will make you more efficient and thus enable you to increase the value proposition for your clients. However, professionals who do embrace AI will replace those who don't.

Climbing the AI Pyramid

The research tells us that enterprises across the board will increasingly turn to AI and big data to reduce costs and errors while improving efficiency and strategic planning. With a history of anticipating the needs of the market and then providing the services, you can use that knowledge to automate your own back-office processes and build on that experience to offer expanded services that relieve your clients of the heavy lifting of creating the architecture for an in-house or outsourced AI initiative.

Many firms focus on helping their clients automate routine tasks as a low-friction entry point with obvious time and cost savings. This simple application also serves as a platform for educating the client on the principles of AI and evaluating use cases for the best fit and results. With a proven win under their belt, clients are more receptive to expanding the role of AI and machine learning in their organizations, allowing them to introduce innovation and differentiation in their product and service offerings and to use the data to tackle tasks at higher levels of the pyramid.

TIP

By applying AI to your client's environment, you can also increase your value to your clients by weaning them from reactively correcting when unexpected issues arise to forestalling common issues with preventative practices and ultimately to anticipating outcomes with predictive management.

As the application of AI to routine processes relieves employees from attending to mundane tasks, it also frees them to tackle more valuable and interesting tasks, thus enhancing their own career paths and adding more value for the clients.

Another byproduct of the cycle of expanding automation upward through the tiers of the complexity pyramid is that, as the capabilities of artificial intelligence grow, the practices of your firm become more specialized until they are distilled to services that are beyond the touch of AI.

Or the singularity happens, whichever comes first.

TIP

But until that time, those who lean into innovation will gain the competitive advantage, but only if they incorporate continuous learning for their employees as a part of the business model.

Unearthing the Algorithmic Treasures

The uses for AI are as varied as the industries served by professional services firms. For more detail on the vertical markets relevant to your practice, check out the other chapters in Part 2.

Healthcare

AI can quickly and economically acquire, classify, process, and route unstructured text to everyone in the information pipeline, increasing accessibility while lowering costs.

Natural-language processing can extract targeted information from unstructured text such as faxes, clinical notes, intake forms, and medical histories, to improve end-to-end workflow. The process starts with data capture and classification, and then routes data and documents to the appropriate backend systems, spotting exceptions, validating edge cases, and creating action items.

Content management

AI uses machine learning, text mining, and natural-language processing to process content, extracting concepts and entities, such as names, places, dates, and customized elements relevant to the business. AI then uses that information to create metadata and import it into a structured database, accelerating searches and data analysis. At the same time, the system automatically classifies the document based on its type and content and either assigns it to the next step in an automated workflow or flags it for review.

Compliance

AI uses unstructured data mining, robotic process automation, statistical data aggregation, and natural-language processing to read and interpret compliance documents, interpret metadata, and identify roles and relationships, and then uses cognitive-process automation to deliver concise, actionable insights.

AI uses supervised and unsupervised learning, natural-language processing, and intelligent segmentation to capture, analyze, and filter possible compliance violations to discard false positives that waste the time of compliance officers.

AI uses structured and unstructured data mining and natural-language processing to monitor internal and external records, documents, and social media to detect errors, violations, and trends, allowing the compliance department to be proactive and avoid costly penalties.

AI uses robotic-process automation, natural-language processing, and machine learning to identify potential violations of Know Your Customer (KYC) and Anti-Money Laundering (AML) regulations.

Law

AI uses text mining to process large pools of unstructured data, such as legal documents, emails, texts, and social media to identify key concepts, categorize content, detect subjectivity, isolate behavior patterns, discern the sentiment expressed in the content, and extract phrases and entities such as people, places, and things.

AI uses supervised and unsupervised learning based on native or custom taxonomies to classify or characterize large volumes of documents and cull irrelevant documents as required in support of pre- and post-production activities, such as early case assessment and privilege detection.

AI uses machine learning and natural-language processing to analyze large amounts of textual content and distill it into short summaries and chronologies, which can display entity and concept trends over time, as well as behavioral patterns of persons of interest. The results can be integrated with data visualization to display the outcome in a consumable and intuitively understandable structure using interactive reports and dashboards.

Manufacturing

AI uses decision trees and neural networks to establish baseline requirements and then uses real-time data to reveal patterns and relationships to determine demand behavior, which drives optimized inventory levels and replenishment plans.

AI uses text mining, data mining, and optimization planning techniques to integrate suppliers and automate transactions to help clients understand their current business, address issues, and formulate strategies for improved performance. Clients can use supply chain analytics to compare the performance of trading partners to operational and business metrics to make better decisions about their partnerships.

AI uses reinforcement learning to automate repetitive human processes. Robotic process automation (RPA) combines analytics, machine learning and rules-based software to capture and interpret existing data-input streams to process a transaction, manipulate data, trigger responses, and communicate with other enterprise applications.

Oil and gas

AI uses predictive maintenance algorithms to achieve optimum uptime.

AI uses IoT sensors and machine-learning algorithms to support data-driven decision-making and enable operational excellence for midstream processes, such as storing and transporting oil and gas.

AI uses text mining, natural-language processing, and machine learning to read legacy exploration and production data to optimize new construction and development projects.

AI uses text mining and machine learning to collect, combine, and assess data to improve operational performance, reduce cost, minimize risk, and accelerate time-to-production in well-site development. It also uses those techniques to boost health and safety and to improve environmental performance.

Utilities

AI uses machine-learning algorithms and data from IoT devices to help energy and utility companies predict energy demand to assist in meeting short- or long-term needs, pinpointing areas of the plant or grid that need maintenance and reducing waste by uncovering inefficiencies.

Examining the Use Cases

The applications span a wide range of industries. In addition to reading through these horizontal uses cases that have application across multiple industries, you should also investigate the chapters that apply to the vertical markets that are relevant to your practice.

Document intake, acceptance, digitization, maintenance, and management

AI can process large pools of documents, emails, texts, social media, unstructured data, and even voicemail to identify key concepts, categorize content, discern the sentiment expressed in the content, and extract relevant information and entities such as people, places, and things. All this can be done in a fraction of the time taken by human reviews and with higher accuracy.

You can also use AI to automatically find and redact personal information, such as names, credit card numbers, and account numbers, without altering the source data.

Auditing, fraud detection, and prevention

Using predictive analytics, AI can quickly process reams of documents and transactions to recognize patterns of fraud previously unobserved across billions of accounts to detect the subtle telltale markers that flag potential fraud or erratic account movements that could be the early signs of dementia.

Risk analysis and mitigation

Potential violations of regulations, such as KYC and AML often lurk in internal and external records, documents, and social media. AI can detect errors, anomalies, and trends that reveal their presence. This process can also filter out time-consuming and budget-busting false positives to free up your compliance officers to be proactive in catching actual violations early and avoid costly penalties. Keep your files clean by scanning incoming documents for compliance before introducing them to your system.

Regulatory compliance management

Compliance processes often require companies to produce detailed information based on complex legalese and technical rules. AI can be trained to follow the complex rules to sift through an organization's data and metadata to pinpoint information, roles and relationships to meet the regulatory requirements quickly and within mandated timeframes.

Claims processing

In the traditional process, insurance claims pass through multiple hands, introducing delay and errors. AI can process claims much faster than a human can and flag anomalies for manual review. Touchless claims use automated reporting, capturing, auditing, and communication to eliminate the need for human intervention other than dealing with exceptions.

Inventory management

The days of a fully stocked inventory are quickly diminishing as retailers realize that optimized stock equals more profit. Predictive analytics give retailers a better understanding of customer behavior to highlight areas of high demand, quickly identify sales trends, and optimize delivery so the right inventory goes to the right location. You can use AI to establish baseline requirements and then process real-time data to tease out patterns and relationships to determine demand behavior, which drives optimized inventory levels and replenishment plans.

Resume processing and candidate evaluation

The average job opening attracts 250 resumes, so the most immediate HR gains in efficiency are available in recruiting and hiring. Scanning resumes into an applicant tracking system can reduce the time to screen candidates from 15 minutes per resume to 1 minute. Natural-language processing and intent analysis take a step beyond keyword searches to find qualified candidates whose wording doesn't exactly match the job posting.

Virtual assistants interact with candidates to schedule meetings, an otherwise time-consuming and tedious task. By automating these time-consuming tasks, HR personnel have more time to focus on strategic tasks that require an interpersonal approach.

Chapter **17**

Media and Entertainment: Beating the Gold Rush

The twenty-first century delivered a seismic shift in the media and entertainment industry with technology playing the role of disruptor. Streaming media and subscription services spawned the cord-cutting movement, and 5G wireless liberated consumers from fixed appliances to consume media anytime and anywhere.

Artificial intelligence provides the infrastructure for key elements of this transformation. Intelligent recommendations form the foundation of most streaming media platforms, starting with music (Yahoo! Launch, Pandora, Spotify, and so on) and extending to video (Netflix, Amazon Prime Video, YouTube, and so on.) and podcasts (Spotify). (For more information, see Chapter 20, "Intelligent Recommendations.")

The influence of AI on media and entertainment continues to grow as it moves beyond personalization and the consumer experience into workflow optimization, search optimization, content localization, content compliance, marketing, and advertising.

Mining for Content

While the proliferation of digital media has certainly delivered significant benefits for consumers and producers, it has brought with it a new set of challenges.

Asset management

Content creators are digital hoarders. Some people never throw away anything, and they keep creating more, squirreling it all away in an increasingly larger cloud, available for possible reuse in the future — but only if they can find it.

Think about that recent popular clip, the one of the toddler holding an empty cone and crying while a puppy licks the fallen scoop of ice cream from the sidewalk. You knew that would come in handy one day, and today's the day. But where did you put it?

When your digital assets start numbering in the thousands or millions, finding the clip of the crying toddler can turn into a quest on the order of finding the seven cities of Cibola.

For example, look at News UK, publisher of some of the biggest and most popular British newspapers such as *The Times*, Britain's oldest daily national, and *The Sunday Times. The Sun* alone has more than 4 million readers each day. In addition to print, News UK operates several digital channels, including Sun Bingo, Sunday Times Wine Club, and Riviera Travel.

News UK receives and generates more than 100,000 new digital assets per day and manages more than 25 million assets in total. The assets include text, images, pages, video, graphics, and audio, which must be captured, indexed, and quickly made available to users across the business.

Granted, not everybody runs an operation the size of News UK, but trying to find one video clip in a library of several thousand can knock a big chunk out of your day.

Metadata

Even if you gather up your digital assets from the various servers, cloud storage, external drives, and USB sticks where they have been hiding and get them all in a pile (A.K.A. digital asset management platform), how will you track down that ice cream tragedy clip?

In a digital editing and distribution world where schedules are tight and deadlines perpetually loom, you have to find the right clips as quickly as possible. At any given time, there's no telling what you will need — a certain type of person, a distinctive setting, type of weather, time period, cinematographic style, a specific catchphrase buried in dialog, or even some combination of these elements in one clip. You have multiple ways to get hints about where to find the clip. Video editors search cinematographer's notes, camera-captured details, script queues — but the most effective method is to search the metadata.

Metadata is all the information about the asset that is attached to the image or video — location, people, objects, and such. News and entertainment producers and distributors rely on metadata *tags* to identify clips based on who, what, when, and where so they can turn B-roll into immediately relevant news footage.

Metadata is present because somebody typed it in when they added the asset to the system. And that means it is often incomplete, ambiguous, or nonexistent. Metadata tagging is the flossing of the content production world. If you are like me, you know you should do it, but you never quite get around to it.

Distribution

Until the 1970s, if you wanted to watch a movie you had two choices — a movie theater or television — and you watched it when they decided to show it. The VCR, and later the DVR, liberated people from arranging their lives around a broadcaster's schedule, but it would take another 30 years before technology truly liberated them.

In the twenty-first century, you can't swing a bag of buttered popcorn without hitting something with a screen, and the dominance of video isn't likely to diminish anytime soon. The Cisco Visual Networking Index predicts that by 2022, video will account for more than 80 percent of all network traffic.

This trend highlights the challenges of delivering digital content. You could be sending the content to something as small as a smartwatch or as large as a screen that takes up half the wall or anything in between. Your delivery infrastructure must support a seemingly endless variety of encoding formats, levels of video quality and bit rates, which complicates delivery workflow and increases fulfill-ment costs.

The industry is looking for a reliable yet flexible and intuitive distribution mecha-nism for content producers and content consumers that can deliver highly per-sonalized content over any network to any device.

Silos

Any enterprise needs an IT department to support the mission by maintaining the financial systems, customer relationship management (CRM), enterprise resource planning (ERP), email, web servers, and the like. In most companies, everything adjacent to technology is managed by the IT department.

However, media companies have highly specialized, resource-intensive technol-ogy needs focused on creating content such as books, magazines, websites, video, and advertising, plus all the marketing material associated with those properties.

These two IT shops use very different technology to achieve their goals and typi-cally are not vertically integrated. In fact, sometimes they rarely communicate with each other at all. The reality is that, although they have different missions and metrics for success, maintaining these functional silos prevents the gains in efficiency, productivity, and economy that comes from integration.

Content compliance

In 2019, China edged ahead of the U.S. in box office revenue to take the number one slot, with India coming in a distant third. When the film industry searches for wider distribution, cultural differences and regulations create pressure to adapt the content. Consider these films:

>> **Inside Out:** In the American release, Riley refuses to eat broccoli. In the Japanese release, Riley refused to eat green bell peppers. The studio also made 27 other changes in the film.

>> **Captain America: The Winter Soldier:** To create relevance with international markets, Marvel Studios created ten different versions of Steve Roger's to-do list that appeared at the beginning of the movie.

>> **Toy Story 2:** Behind Buzz Lightyear's soul-stirring speech before the cross-town trek, an American flag waves as "The Star-Spangled Banner" plays. For the international release, Pixar replaced the flag with a spinning globe and the national anthem with Randy Newman's "One World Anthem."

- **Red Dawn:** The 2012 remake was set to release in 2011, but the studio delayed the premiere and spent $1 million to digitally change Chinese flags to North Korean flags, edited a few scenes, and reworked the opening.

- **Demolition Man:** For the European release, the studio changed the lone survivor of the franchise wars from Taco Bell to Pizza Hut because unlike Taco Bell, Pizza Hut had an international presence.

- **Planes:** For the international release, depending on the country, Disney changed the color and the name of the character Rochelle, creating 11 different versions of the plane.

Editing a film to accommodate foreign markets starts with reviewing the film and tagging scenes or dialog where changes must be made, a time-consuming, labor-intensive task.

Striking It Rich

Many of the challenges facing the entertainment industry are particularly suited for an AI solution.

Metadata

The industry's track record of consistently tagging content is notoriously poor. The value of metadata is increasing exponentially as everyone contributes to the flood of content, but the industry lacks universally recognized standards, and as a result, one of the biggest barriers to asset discoverability is incomplete metadata.

Most marketers struggle to find that perfect moment in a video that captures the essence of their product, service, or membership. Instead of watching endless hours of video to find a scene where a specific person is speaking about the desired topic or an advertisement with a particular segment to reuse, marketers can use the discovery tools of an AI-powered digital asset management (DAM) system to isolate clips with the desired actors, objects, settings, and even dialog.

Digital distribution

Due to the explosion of end-user devices, screen types, and sizes, digital distribution is the fastest growing segment of media and entertainment, simultaneously creating new challenges and new opportunities for content owners and distributors.

Digital distribution uses compression and the existing communications infrastructure to replace the expensive legacy switching distribution network. Multicast brings even more economies of scale to the solution. AI-assisted digital distribution platforms intelligently push the right content in the best format for any device to deliver highly personalized content over any network. For those looking to personalize the customer experience, AI-assisted distribution enables you to track preferences, design unique content, and target it to the right people.

Digital asset management

A robust DAM system integrated with tiered storage, which locates data on higher- or lower-cost media based on business value, is more cost-effective than legacy systems and can locate and retrieve content regardless of the storage medium.

TIP

An AI-assisted DAM ensures compliance with usage rights, supports automated metadata tagging, allows you to perform complex searches to find the exact content you need for a project, and provides comprehensive tracking, auditing, and reporting. Imagine being able to quickly match relevant brand advertisers with content that is already in the film to maximize product-placement revenue.

Assaying the Algorithms

AI offers these capabilities in the media and entertainment industries:

>> **Machine learning** to automatically tag your image or text archive and deliver faster, more accurate searches.

>> **Intelligent recommendation algorithms** to identify relevant content to readers, listeners, and watchers.

>> **Recurrent neural networks and sequence-to-sequence learning** to translate subtitles.

>> **Supervised and unsupervised learning** to deliver the most relevant content to consumers to keep them engaged, from programming to advertisements.

>> **Advanced machine learning** during digital content distribution to enforce localization and contextual compliance, such as scanning for gore or nudity when delivering content to hotels or airlines.

>> **Image recognition and speech-to-text transcription** to automatically tag DAM content with metadata.

>> **Text mining and regression** to predict possible disruptions in the content supply chain, such as a content supplier failing to meet a deadline.

Examining the Use Cases

Now that you have taken a peek under the hood to get a glimpse of several AI techniques that are useful in media and entertainment, it's time to dig deeper into practical ways to use AI to turn your organization into a lean machine.

Search optimization

Media content producers are using AI to improve the speed and efficiency of the media production process and the ability to organize visual assets.

The first step is to process the media itself to harvest intelligence from the content to create extensive metadata synced with the video timestamps:

>> **On-screen optical character recognition** creates searchable metadata text from visual text on the screen, such as street signs, notes, pages from books, or the information on a clapperboard.

>> **Language detection and speech-to-text** creates subtitles, not just for viewing, but as metadata to allow everything to be searched, even dialog.

>> **Face detection** reports the number of people in a scene as well as their age, gender, and color.

>> **Facial recognition,** combined with celebrity databases, identifies known individuals by name and tags the content.

>> **Speaker tagging** indicates which people in the clip are speaking which lines.

The second step is to use powerful search capabilities on text, keywords, and other elements to locate very specific content instantly, such as when a certain character says a specific bit of dialog or all the scenes where an object or place is mentioned.

Workflow optimization

TIP

You can use AI to automate pre-production and post-production processes, such as scheduling and budgeting, breaking down a script, generating storyboards and shot lists, syncing and grouping clips, and analyzing dailies and cuts.

Globalization

Subtitling and translation are key areas that are witnessing large-scale adoption of AI. While leveraging AI for speech-to-text transcription is already popular, recent improvements in accuracy and time-coding capabilities of AI engines will help make the entire process of subtitling more efficient. Such tools are also catering to a growing number of regional languages, and their usage for subtitle translation will steadily increase.

With digital platforms enabling content suppliers to go global, compliance editing takes up more time and effort than ever before. Producers need to meet compliance requirements for multiple territories, which typically involves multiple rounds of viewing and editing.

TIP

AI can help swiftly identify objectionable content such as nudity, violence, smoking, drug abuse, and profanity. Leveraging AI to automatically identify content segments with compliance issues can reduce manual effort and operational costs significantly while providing scalability to handle peaks in volume.

3

Exploring Horizontal Market Applications

Chapter **18**

Voice of the Customer/ Citizen: Finding Coherence in the Cacophony

Voice of the customer (VoC) platforms support customer experience efforts focused on improving satisfaction, loyalty, and brand advocacy. VoC initiatives aren't new. In some ways, using VoC for market research goes all the way back to the start of branded retailing. Companies have been tuning into customer feedback for decades, using everything from polls to fan mail to gauge their target market's sentiment toward products and services.

Non-intelligent digital technologies of the 1990s and early 2000s, such as web crawlers, spreadsheets, and search engines, supported simple analysis of customer activity. AI has changed the game. It turbocharges VoC programs to give you the power to collect vast amounts of data for more precise and effective business decisions.

Today, AI-powered VoC solutions track what your customers are saying about your business, products, and services at key points throughout their buying journey. They identify the collective sentiment and intentions of customers and plug these findings into your enterprise applications to deliver insights directly to your teams. By studying your customers and prospects across a wide array of communication platforms, AI-enhanced VoC solutions unlock insights into opinions and experiences you can't access otherwise.

Hearing the Message in the Media

From traditional shopping-cart retail to online shopping and in-store pickup, your customers are exposed to a multifaceted experience that was inconceivable in the past. With this digital evolution comes new data for you to track. And, with so many different touchpoints shaping the customer journey and experience, you have more opportunities to understand your customer's preference, behavior, and satisfaction. However, while these complex customer interactions hold a wealth of information, many retailers have difficulty accessing this information to turn it into actionable plans. Creating a single version of truth at scale and extracting meaningful insights in a timely manner has become a tremendous challenge.

Consider one example of just how difficult it has become for larger companies to hear their customers' voices. Suppose a loyal customer of a national sporting goods store walks into his nearest location to purchase a new pair of running shoes. All goes well until the cashier is unable to access the customer's rewards account, which prevents him from accumulating more loyalty points. The cashier refers him to a help number, but the experience has left him unsatisfied and he abandons the transaction altogether.

Then he takes to social media to vent his frustrations and find he isn't alone in the issue. This location has been experiencing problems with loyalty cards for some time now. A whole network of once-faithful customers is now likely to take their business elsewhere, if they haven't done so already. But with such a large company, no one is keeping their pulse on this one regional segment of customers. Their feedback goes unanswered — in fact, completely unheard.

Experiences like these happen every day. For example, Gartner found that 96 percent of customers who had high-friction experiences reported being disloyal, compared to only 9 percent of customers with low-friction experiences. Nearly half of consumers have used social media to "call out" a brand or business for an issue such as customer service problems.

TIP

Customer sentiment is greater and more complex than ever before. It's simpler now for your customers to publish and share comments on social media, where a vast audience can access these opinions and experiences, versus emailing the company or contacting customer support. International trade has also introduced a broader range of products, and consumers have increasingly diverse tastes. The crisis of rising consumer expectations puts tremendous pressure on you to provide a superior customer experience and predict industry trends.

Providing a better, more personalized customer experience depends on your ability to tap into these customer insights.

Consider the vast, complex channels through which customer experiences take place today. The customer journey no longer consists of simply walking into a store, making a purchase, and leaving. Now, consumers spend significant time researching a product before they purchase, exploring everything from customer reviews to price comparisons. Beauty shoppers, for example, spend 80 percent of their purchase journey in the pre-search phase, analyzing multiple platforms for content that might influence their purchase.

REMEMBER

Knowing what your customers are saying about your products or services online is an important part of your strategy for attracting and retaining customers. Listening in on their feedback can shape decisions for future launches of new product lines.

Each of these channels has its own nuances, but the information is largely unstructured. How can you quantify and measure these ongoing conversations in real time to discover what they are saying about your brand and about your competitors? Clearly, the solution entails more than just having an intern monitor your Facebook business page.

Delivering What They Really Want

Using AI, VoC systems collect and analyze direct and inferred feedback across a wide array of sources, ranging from operational data to customer service calls, social and web content, and email. In doing so, they capture the entire customer journey in a single view. Here are some of the ways AI can help you deliver what customers really want:

>> AI allows you to aggregate customer feedback from all channels to analyze the broadest range of comments and opinions. This data can then be used to shape valuable insights for improving products and enhancing the customer experience, such as levels of brand awareness. For instance, you might use

AI to determine how many times your brand's name comes up in public conversations, an important indicator of brand value.

>> You can also use AI to gain insight into brand relevance. Text analytics allow you to uncover customer sentiment and understand the extent to which customers believe your brand has delivered on the value it promises. These insights can help create a deeper understanding of the customer's emotional connection to a brand, which ultimately drives loyalty.

>> AI also supports forecasting to help you anticipate upcoming trends. For example, a running shoe company might discover via online reviews that while long-time customers like the overall structural enhancements of their latest edition of sneakers, the new laces don't stay tied and make for an overall poorer running experience. A supplement company might gather from Instagram comments that consumers feel they're using too much packaging on their new line of multivitamins. These insights can be useful for designing and marketing future products and to let customers know, "We heard you."

A McKinsey study showed that companies that offer consistently best-in-class customer experiences tend to grow faster and are 80 percent more likely to retain customers than firms that don't.

TIP

Tracking customer sentiment allows you to meet these goals:

>> **Increase sales:** What is the most popular item in your new product line? You can use a VoC solution to answer this question, while also identifying the least popular products or services to inform your product, marketing, and sales strategies for the future. According to McKinsey, across private industries, successful projects for optimizing the customer experience typically achieve revenue growth of 5 to 10 percent.

>> **Uncover new cross-sell and up-sell opportunities:** You can use AI to detect purchasing trigger points and drivers throughout different phases of the customer journey, including in-store at the point of sale. With a deeper understanding of these decision points, you can recommend tailored offers aligned to customer preferences, which is important considering 75 percent of consumers are more likely to purchase from retailers that recommend options based on their purchase history.

>> **Reduce risk:** You can use machine-learning algorithms to analyze and monitor business outcomes, detect warning signals earlier, anticipate trends, and respond before your competitors do.

>> **Decrease customer churn:** To act on complaints, you must be able to access those complaints. VoC solutions enable social listening to unlock the criticisms

you can use to improve customer support, communication methods, and product features.

>> **Spot evolving trends:** You can use social listening to understand customer likes and dislikes regarding your products and services and use that information to refine product development decisions.

Answering the Right Questions

Unstructured sources such as social media, email, SMS, RSS feeds, and blogs can contain actionable information. VoC solutions access and collect data from documents of any format and use text mining to process raw text and extract mentions of specific attributes, including people, places, events, concepts, categories, and organizations. Sentiment analysis detects the subjectivity and tone — positive, negative, or neutral — by evaluating individual word choices.

Concept extraction identifies keywords and phrases using pattern-based algorithms. AI-powered systems use natural-language processing to distinguish abbreviations, speech patterns, and parts of grammar.

VoC solutions detect the language of the content and summarize documents by highlighting the most important phrases or sentences.

VoC solutions apply advanced analytics and machine learning to determine which specific consumer products in an entire line receive the highest star ratings online. Factors like price, size, color, and other attributes can be incorporated into reports and interactive dashboards along with ratings to identify correlations. For instance, customers might repeatedly categorize a more expensive desk as "sturdy" and "well-made," but give lower-priced models poorer reviews and ratings. VoC solutions can use these data patterns to create predictive machine-learning models that help to answer questions such as, "Which price points have the best customer ratings?" and "What are the most common complaints from customers among our poorly-rated pieces?"

Machine learning improves and becomes more intelligent as you test and refine the model, creating reusable analytic assets. These assets might include data visualizations such as word clouds, which cluster frequently used phrases and terms so that those repeated most often are prominent, or more standard-style frequency lists which rank mentions from highest to lowest.

TIP

You can share insights with operational users on demand via interactive visualizations as events unfold, which your teams can use to make data-driven decisions across product development, marketing, sales, customer support, and other key functions in a timely manner. Figure 18-1 provides an example of what a voice of the customer dashboard could look like, which would be modified to meet the specific need an organization is aiming to achieve.

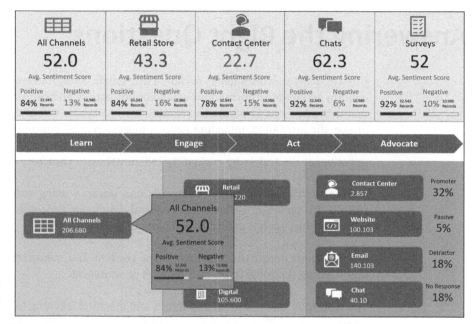

FIGURE 18-1: A sample voice of the customer dashboard.

Examining Key Industries

It isn't enough to determine what customers are saying about you. Your solution should answer these types of questions:

» What is the customer's level of satisfaction?

» What is the likelihood they'll purchase our products or services again?

» What is the likelihood they'll recommend our company?

With sentiment analysis, you can drill down to understand the "why" behind these interactions. Why is the customer pleased or upset?

TIP

VoC solutions also help you identify the root cause behind issues affecting your business, such as low satisfaction scores, diminishing sales, or increasing customer churn. You can use this data to make decisions in real time, prioritizing the customer experience by building positive, personalized, and consistent interactions and driving key customer outcomes such as spending, engagement, and retention.

Consumer packaged goods

If you are producing consumer packaged goods (CPG), you have one or more layers between you and your customer. If an issue arises, the consumer may not complain to you, may not even complain to the retailer, but there's a good chance they will complain on social media.

That's where AI and VoC come to your aid. You can bypass all the layers to hear from the customer and, most importantly, discover the specific point in the buying journey that is causing friction. You may need to adjust product design, production, or distribution. Maybe the problem doesn't lie with the product itself, but with shipping or a specific retail outlet.

For one global CPG company, customer engagement processes were spread across several teams that sorted, read, and responded to customer emails, each team using its own tools. Customers often gave up before their issue reached the right department. The VoC team was hampered with tedious, time-consuming tasks, such as pulling and consolidating data from the various customer support applications. Cross-functional collaboration was impossible.

The switch to a single AI-powered VoC solution unified all sources of feedback, gave the teams on-demand access, and enabled them to engage with customers in a more meaningful way, perform more accurate targeting, and make better decisions for the brand. As a result, their Net Promoter Score and customer satisfaction rates improved.

Public and nonprofit organizations

The value of VoC isn't limited to the private sector. For example, some cities have deployed VoC solutions to track the opinions of residents and tourists on key topics such as satisfaction with the blend of things to do around the city, transportation challenges, and access to services, to name a few.

These systems can surface common issues using features such as a word cloud generator that visually highlights frequently used terms across Facebook, Twitter, and other social media channels. If "parking" or "public transportation" bubbles to the top, they can launch a city-wide transportation app to highlight open parking spaces and map out bus routes with schedules.

IN THIS CHAPTER

» **Understanding how routine maintenance and preventative maintenance leave you exposed to risk and higher costs**

» **Discovering how you can use AI to power predictive maintenance and increase the output of your high-value assets and machinery**

» **Identifying the AI techniques that make predictive maintenance possible**

» **Exploring asset performance optimization use cases for AI**

Chapter **19**

Asset Performance Optimization: Increasing Value by Extending Lifespans

They say if it ain't broke, don't fix it, but anyone with high-value assets, whether a fleet of bucket trucks or drilling rigs, knows preventive maintenance is much more effective than performing repairs reactively. Servicing equipment before it fails reduces costly downtime and extends its lifespan, thus stretching your resources as far as possible.

This concept certainly isn't new. Routine equipment checks and preventive maintenance in general have been the responsibility of every maintenance department for decades. But here's the good part.

TIP

You can use AI and Internet of Things (IoT) sensors to go beyond preventive maintenance to implement predictive maintenance.

Preventive maintenance prevents failures with inspections and services performed at predetermined intervals. Predictive maintenance uses large volumes of data and advanced analytics to anticipate the likelihood of failure based on the history and current status of a specific piece of equipment and recommends service before it happens.

How do you like the sound of that? It's the sound of asset performance optimization. Figure 19-1 traces the evolution of this concept.

FIGURE 19-1:
The evolution from maintenance to asset performance optimization following the advent of data analytics, sensor technology, and AI.

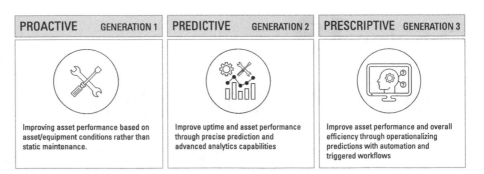

Spying on Your Machines

Asset performance optimization (APO) collects the digital output from IoT-enabled equipment and associated processes, analyzes the data, tracks performance, and makes recommendations regarding maintenance. APO allows you to forecast future needs and perform predictive maintenance before immediate actions are needed.

Although some machines run continuously with little need for maintenance, others require much more care and attention to operate at their best level. Determining which equipment needs more frequent servicing can be time-consuming and tedious. Often maintenance guidelines rely heavily on guesswork. Time frames for tune-ups tend to be little more than suggestions, based on information such as shop manuals and a recommendation from the lead mechanics rather than hard data, such as metrics from the performance history of each piece of equipment, including downtime and previous failures.

APO, on the other hand, analyzes both structured and unstructured data, such as field notes, to add context for equipment readings and deliver more precise recommendations. Using IoT devices, APO systems gather data from sensors, EIM systems, and external sources. It then uses AI to acquire, merge, manage, and analyze this information, presenting the results using real-time dashboards that can be shared and reviewed quickly for at-a-glance updates. Throughout the lifespan of the equipment, through regular use and maintenance, the system continues to learn and improve its insights over time (see Figure 19-2).

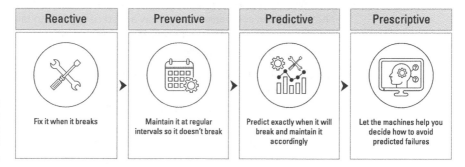

FIGURE 19-2: APO helps you decide how to avoid predicted failures.

Reactive	Preventive	Predictive	Prescriptive
Fix it when it breaks	Maintain it at regular intervals so it doesn't break	Predict exactly when it will break and maintain it accordingly	Let the machines help you decide how to avoid predicted failures

Fixing It Before It Breaks

APO allows you to take a strategic approach to predictive maintenance by focusing on what will make the greatest difference to your operation. Unforeseen equipment malfunctions and downtime cause disruptions, which can ultimately jeopardize project timelines, customer satisfaction, and business revenue.

REMEMBER

These are benefits of APO:

>> **Smoother, more predictable operations:** Equipment issues are addressed preemptively instead of after a disruption occurs, leading to greater overall operational efficiency. Implementing APO can help companies achieve a 70-percent elimination of unanticipated equipment failure.

>> **Reduced downtime:** Preventive maintenance typically reduces machine downtime by 30 to 50 percent.

>> **Boosted productivity:** In addition to reducing downtime, predictive maintenance allows you to become more strategic in scheduling maintenance. This also can uncover any routine maintenance tasks that can be performed at less frequent intervals.

>> **Lowered costs:** APO can reduce the time required to plan maintenance by 20 to 50 percent, increase equipment uptime and availability by 10 to 20 percent, and reduce overall maintenance costs by 5 to 10 percent, according to a Deloitte study.

>> **Increased customer satisfaction:** Assets nearing failures can sacrifice production quality, cause service outages, and create other circumstances that ultimately affect the customer. By preventing these issues from happening, APO helps companies achieve and maintain better customer satisfaction.

>> **Improved safety outcomes:** Equipment malfunctions can result in serious injury, but often companies don't know a system is about to fail until it's too late. PwC reports that APO and predictive maintenance can improve maintenance safety by up to 14 percent.

>> **Reduced risk of litigation and penalties:** With fewer breakdowns and disruptions to service, organizations can minimize their risk of costly fines, lawsuits, and subsequent reputational damage.

Ultimately, in any industry with high-value equipment, or even large numbers of low-cost assets, APO pays off. It directs technicians' efforts to the machines that need attention the most, instead of performing inspections or maintenance on the equipment that doesn't need it. This leads to predictable and seamless operations, improved uptime, increased revenue opportunities, and greater customer satisfaction.

Learning from the Future

APO solutions allow you to enhance your operations by making your machines smarter and sharing that intelligence with your workforce, thereby maximizing the value of both your human teams and your mechanical equipment. As the age of AI advances, the companies that thrive will be those that find the best ways to harness data for improved operational performance.

Data collection

APO continuously collects data on mechanical performance from IoT sensors in virtually any type of device or machine, ranging from hydraulic brake system sensors on a train to temperature monitors inside industrial and medical refrigerators holding sensitive products. The system collects numerous data points from the sensors, blending them with other sources, and analyzes the results.

For example, in the case of a hydraulic brake system, APO compares current data to historical performance records, including failure reports, to deliver predictive maintenance insights. When further data inputs are blended with this specific brake data, even richer and more accurate recommendations can be delivered.

Additional input samples from internal and third-party sources can be blended to provide context and greater insight; these types of input can be invaluable:

>> Weather data

>> Maintenance recommendations from manuals

>> Supplier quality data

>> Historical brake maintenance schedules and failure rates

>> Passenger travel analysis

>> Heavy or unusual usage data

TIP

Using this comprehensive blend of data, you can implement an APO solution to recognize patterns and perform an in-depth analysis in multiple applications, from manufacturing plants to utilities and even healthcare. The data can include metrics such as temperature, movement, light exposure, and more collected from IoT sensors on fleets, plants, pipelines, medical imaging equipment, jets, grids, and any other Internet-enabled device.

Analysis

AI uses big-data analytics and natural-language processing to derive key data points from structured data as well as unstructured content such as field notes and equipment manuals.

TIP

You can use AI to analyze this information and relevant historical data to identify patterns and generate questions that help engineers, maintenance supervisors, production managers, and other key personnel make informed and timely decisions. APO solutions use these patterns to make predictive conclusions that help you answer questions in various areas, such as these:

>> **Timing:** Am I performing inspections at appropriate intervals? Would shortening the intervals improve overall uptime? Or could I afford to lengthen the intervals to reduce resource expenditure?

>> **Quality:** Could defective components be slipping through my inspections and leading to downtime? If so, how can I improve the inspection process to prevent this issue moving forward?

>> **Design:** Can my design be modified to reduce future failures?

For example, a predictive conclusion formed by the patterns observed in the case of the train brake system might indicate the need for shorter inspection intervals. This is where humans come in and leverage all of these valuable findings to improve their business.

Putting insights to use

After patterns are identified and their related questions are answered, the predictive conclusions provided by APO solutions can then be implemented. For example, train maintenance workers can schedule inspections more frequently to check for a key component in the hydraulic brake system that has shown a tendency to fail. Or perhaps the APO solution discovers that a defective component in the train needs attention. Field engineers can use a digital model of the train to determine a repair strategy. If the part cannot be repaired, the APO solution can trigger a replacement part order through the supply chain network, using automation to streamline the process of getting the train back up and running.

Examining the Use Cases

The best uses for APO vary not only by industry, but also from one organization to the next. As with all AI-powered solutions, the beauty of APO lies in the fact that it can be customized according to the needs of any equipment, process, and company.

TIP

To use APO most effectively, start by looking at the biggest challenges your business faces. Here are some questions you might ask to help pinpoint the best starting points:

>> Which pieces of equipment are experiencing the highest failure rates?

>> Which machines are experiencing the most downtime?

>> Where am I spending the most time on repairs?

>> Which assets are costing me the most to repair?

>> How often do I perform preventive maintenance? Which assets currently receive the most maintenance?

>> Which machines pose the greatest safety risks if they were to malfunction?

>> Which equipment would have the biggest impact on our business if it were to fail?

>> Does the equipment I want to analyze already have IoT devices in place, or do I need to equip them with new sensors?

>> Beyond IoT sensors, are there other data sources I can pull from to make maintenance predictions even more accurate, such as weather data, customer usage data, and so forth?

After you've decided where to focus your efforts, you can implement an APO solution that meets the needs of your organization. As with any AI-powered platform, the system will become more intelligent the longer you use it. It will learn from historical data and refine its predictions over time, delivering insights through a range of data visualization options, such as graphs, reports, and dashboards. The ability to be shared and viewed on any device is important for most applications, because teams working in the field, on the factory floor, and in the office are all likely to need access to these data visualizations.

Production automation and quality control

To stay competitive in the declining manufacturing and service sectors, organizations such as steel mills are looking toward technology as a solution for reducing costs and accelerating business. Here's how one steel producer uses APO to drive productivity.

Within the plant, sheets of steel are pushed through rollers, where they're flattened. When sheets move through too quickly, however, they move off center and crumple. Operators must manually feed new sheets of steel through the rollers, which results in unplanned downtime.

The plant installed a break-out predictor, which senses sheet movement and adjusts production line speed as needed to prevent problems. With an APO solution, the plant can gather data from the break-out predictor. It analyzes the data to detect patterns that could indicate a problem. With better insight as to when, where, and why these issues occur, the steel mill went from dealing with unplanned problems to proactively addressing production issues for better operational efficiency. Figure 19-3 shows how predictive maintenance can drive optimum value.

Preventive maintenance

Maintaining big trucks is resource-intensive, requiring an entire department dedicated to inspecting, servicing, and repairing fleets in trucking companies. AI-powered solutions help fleet managers identify issues before they arise, resulting in more on-time deliveries, reduced downtime, and greater overall customer satisfaction.

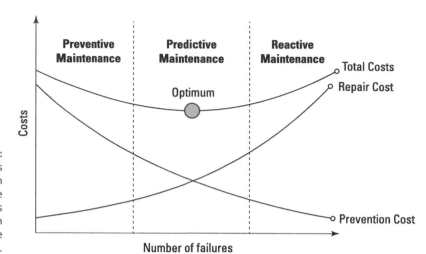

FIGURE 19-3:
Cost levers driving optimum economic value in operations through predictive maintenance.

TIP

With AI-powered analytics and IoT sensors that track key truck data, you can use an APO solution to compare current and historical data to determine whether the part should be replaced early to prevent unplanned downtime. IoT sensors pull a wealth of information from equipment in operations, including data points such as tire pressure, speed, and acceleration and deceleration patterns. Additional data, such as warranty information, can be analyzed to determine whether it will be worthwhile to replace the part before the warranty expires.

For example, in the case of exhaust gas recirculation (EGR) valves, replacement may be needed long before the component breaks completely, even if it means foregoing the warranty. These valves can get stuck open or closed due to a buildup of soot and therefore fail to recirculate exhaust into the combustion chamber to decrease the combustion temperature. If they do fail, they can cause serious malfunctions throughout the rest of the emissions system, which can be expensive to repair. APO systems track breakdowns and watch for triggers that could indicate future failures in parts like EGR valves, using historical data to predict when it's financially appropriate to replace them instead of waiting for a complete failure that would be covered under warranty. Figure 19-4 shows how conducting maintenance with AI and IoT sensors reduces number of maintenance events over time.

TIP

Beyond preventing downtime, you can use an APO solution to maximize the uptime of high-value equipment. For instance, pulling data from weather and traffic reports helps logistics managers and drivers plan the best routes, avoiding hazards like bridges on especially windy days or delays caused by construction or motor vehicle accidents. With these insights, they more accurately project pick-up and drop-off times and make the most of their time by strategically using time spent on the road to cover the greatest distances.

Preventive Maintenance (Scheduled)

FIGURE 19-4:
Conducting
maintenance with
AI and IoT
sensors reduces
the number of
maintenance
events needed
over time.

Predictive Maintenance (at the Optimal Moment)

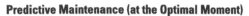

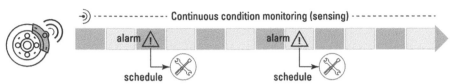

Process optimization

Pumps are essential components within an oil drilling rig. Many models exist, each with a unique method of functioning. Centrifugal pumps, for example, use centrifugal force to draw liquid into the pump intake. This pump type is the most popular in the industry and is commonly used for transferring low-viscosity fluids with high flow rates.

When they're running at optimal levels, centrifugal pumps can pump several hundred gallons of liquid in a single minute. Yet several factors can influence rates, including the pump's discharge flow control valve and the quality of the liquid. To help oil and gas companies maximize their operations, AI-enhanced analytics determine the value of the variables that yield the greatest quantity of liquid in the shortest amount of time.

Chapter **20**

Intelligent Recommendations: Getting Personal

Which movie recommendation would you trust more — a Rotten Tomatoes score, or a tip from your best friend? It comes down to who knows you best.

Hopefully, your best friend knows you better than a website does, but there's always that one friend who tries to convince you to go see the movie they're excited about, even though it's exactly the kind of movie you avoid at all costs. Time and experience reveal whom to trust and whom to ignore.

Does your recommendation system know your customer, or does it cycle through a one-size-fits-all, static list of high-margin or overstocked items?

You can use intelligent recommendations to convert casual customers into devoted fans and increase revenue through cross-selling and up-selling.

Making Friends by the Millions

"A lot of times, people don't know what they want until you show it to them."
— STEVE JOBS

Most likely, you have experienced intelligent recommendation systems in action. Every visitor to Amazon encounters additional product choices that are "Inspired by your browsing history" or "New for You." Similarly, Netflix, Amazon Prime Video, and other streaming content sites constantly reevaluate customer orders and social media activities to better inform their recommendations. Suggestions from online retailers are produced by intelligent recommendation systems.

An intelligent recommendation system is an AI-powered platform that studies your customers and prospects, enabling it to present the most appropriate offers for each individual. Intelligent recommendation systems identify a customer's buying propensity by evaluating their behavior based on a broad spectrum of digital sources.

Although that sounds simple, when you consider the many types of customer data available today and the level of effort required to acquire and evaluate the implications for your needs, turning all this data into a good recommendation is a nontrivial exercise. Certainly, structured data such as product ID numbers, pricing information, or even opinion survey data is easy for software to import and analyze. The problem is that all the interesting information, the stuff of insight into behavior and preference, lies in unstructured data.

Customers contact your company through email and instant messaging and by phone, where they tell you exactly what they think. In the larger world, they leave reviews on Yelp and other platforms and talk about you to their friends and family on Twitter, Facebook, and Instagram. Imagine the potential of harnessing that information.

Each of these sources presents its own challenges for harvesting customer sentiment and intent, not the least of which is that much of the information is unstructured, written in natural language.

How do you quantify and measure a conversation across millions of customers in real time? You do that with artificial intelligence and machine learning.

Listening to social media

Customers have always talked about brands. Word-of-mouth drives up to one-fifth of buying decisions. In the twenty-first century, you can find out what they are saying in real time and recommend products to them that reflect their taste and preferences. Social listening refers to the process of scanning the intentionally generated, unstructured content that your customers share with the world, such as social media posts, emails, and texts.

Mining data exhaust

As you navigate through your life online, you unavoidably leave a trail of digital ephemera in the form of cookies, temporary files, stored preferences, and the like. This information can be as narrow as items previously purchased or as broad as which newspapers or magazines people read, who they chat with on Facebook, or what time they drove across the Golden Gate Bridge, as tracked by an RFID automated toll tag. Data mining harvests this information to build a profile that a recommendation system can use to target the most suitable products to the customer.

Reading Minds

When your friends recommend something that you come to enjoy, not only do you trust them more, you appreciate their taking the time to learn your tastes and preferences. When your business provides targeted offers, those insights into individual customer preferences not only enhance sales and increase profits, they also improve customer satisfaction and reduce churn. The resulting impact on future product development can reduce the stress on product management and customer services budgets.

TIP

Companies implement intelligent recommendation systems to accomplish these goals:

>> **Improve retention:** Continuously catering to users' preferences makes them more likely to remain loyal subscribers of the service.

>> **Increase sales:** Companies can boost up-selling revenue by 10 percent to 50 percent using "You Might Also Like" product recommendations.

Knowing Which Buttons to Push

An intelligent recommendation system analyzes the available information to produce a detailed, individualized picture of each customer and make predictions about their preferences and behavior, specifically their buying propensity.

Many offers are irrelevant to consumers or may even strike the wrong note. For example, you aren't putting your best foot forward by recommending a romantic getaway to someone in the middle of a messy divorce, or by listing the benefits of retirement community units to someone under 30. For some customers, the sheer number of offers could annoy them to the point of deleting them all, unread.

Popular product recommendation

The simplest method is to recommend popular products. Recommending what's popular requires very little analysis. For example, a server in a restaurant uses this method when you ask what they recommend, and they say, "Our Spam tartare is very popular." Popularity-based recommendations do not consult or track the tastes or behavior of the individual customer. If it's trending, it's recommended. This approach will likely perform better than recommending a random product from the catalog, but that isn't an intelligent recommendation.

Market-basket analysis

A slightly more sophisticated approach, market-basket analysis, takes into consideration what other customers have bought. A common example is Amazon's recommendation: "Customers who bought [what you're interested in] also bought [this other product]."

For example, a basket that contains disposable diapers might also contain baby food, logically enough. Fed by millions of data points in buyer behavior, this approach can provide strong statistical support for intuitive associations, like shelving tissues with the cold and cough medicines. However, this approach can also be thrown off by short-term events (maybe the diapers and baby food were for a visiting relative) or coincidences that don't actually reveal significant trends. For example, the Harry Potter books are so massively popular on Amazon that they provide hardly any clues about what other titles not about a boy wizard would appeal to that purchaser.

Propensity modeling

In this use case, AI creates value by leveraging propensity modeling to help you avoid those pitfalls and instead target the right offer to the right customer. Jerry Strickland, a Senior Data Specialist with USAA, distilled the various types of propensity modeling into six examples:

>> **Predicted Customer Lifetime Value (CLV):** Instead of looking at the size of individual purchases for big spenders, this metric estimates the total net profit

that a given customer will bring to the business for the length of their relationship. It is a prediction of future sales, not a summary of past sales. Predictive modeling evaluates everything you know about the customer, including past sales, demographics, social listening, and other channels, to draw inferences from similarities with the behavior of other customers.

>> **Predicted Share of Wallet (SOW):** Instead of attempting to grow the percentage of sales in a category (market share) by attracting new customers, growing wallet share focuses on increasing the amount an existing customer spends on your brand at the expense of the competition. Predictive modeling looks for growth customers instead of growth markets; that is, it identifies current customers who are spending more with a competitor than with you, introducing opportunities for marginal increases of existing business.

>> **Propensity to engage:** Instead of blasting out emails or social media posts to every customer, match the channel to the customer. AI uses social listening and other techniques to identify the customers most likely to click, reply, or comment so you can maximize your digital marketing efforts.

>> **Propensity to unsubscribe:** Conversely, AI can also identify customers who are less responsive to digital marketing push strategies so you can use other strategies for customers with high CLV and a high propensity to unsubscribe.

>> **Propensity to buy:** You use a different engagement strategy for a customer who is comparison shopping or just looking than for the customer who is ready to buy right now. Propensity modeling uses data from various sources to help you tell the window shoppers from the serious shoppers so you can apply the strategy that encourages a sale without unnecessarily cutting into margins. For example, you might tempt comparison shoppers with a discount, but a customer with a high propensity to buy might be more interested in features and upgrades than discounts.

>> **Propensity to churn:** Some businesses — Internet and TV service providers come to mind — seem prone to maximizing their margins until a customer threatens to cancel, and only then attempt to keep them from jumping ship. Propensity modeling alerts you to customers who are at risk so that you can proactively reach out to them, especially for customers identified as high-value by your system.

These predictive marketing approaches date back at least to the mid-twentieth century and the rise of catalog and direct-mail outreach, when punch cards and simple spreadsheets were among the few tools that could crunch the numbers and add statistical support to a merchandising manager's intuition. The ability to effectively predict and act on buyer behavior came with the arrival of technology that can collect and analyze literally billions of records and transactions, combined with the Internet to facilitate instantaneous communications.

Of course, the information used to predict customer behavior resides in enormous volumes and is encoded in a dizzying variety of data types, from structured data in databases to freeform text in documents, emails, scanned images, and social media feeds. It quickly becomes apparent that machines provide the only efficient method of parsing, understanding, and gaining value from the information. Only machines — which is to say, artificial intelligence — can read at the pace required to acquire and process thousands of documents and articles every second, and then merge, aggregate, and persist the information while analyzing it for content and tone.

The main tools that AI uses to tackle these huge volumes of structured and unstructured data are data mining and text mining. Of course, these techniques can address a wide range of AI business cases besides intelligent recommendations (which are addressed in other chapters). But first, let me provide a brief overview of these important terms in enterprise AI.

Data and text mining

As discussed in Chapter 1, machine learning uses information acquired through data mining and text mining to make associations and draw inferences.

Data mining processes structured data such as is found in corporate enterprise resource planning (ERP) systems or customer databases or in an online shopping cart, and it applies modeling functions to produce actionable information.

Text mining uses natural-language processing to extract data elements to populate the structured metadata fields such as author, date, and content summary that enable analysis.

Depending on the characteristics of the domain, the quality of available data and the business goals, recommendation engines apply various data-mining techniques such as these:

>> Collaborative filtering (CF)

>> Content-based filtering (CBF)

>> Knowledge-based methods

>> Case-based methods

The filtering techniques are the most commonly used techniques for intelligent recommendations.

Collaborative filtering (CF)

Because it relies solely on readily available and easily analyzed transaction-level data to find correlations in consumption patterns, collaborative filtering, shown in Figure 20-1, is one of the more popular recommendation techniques. Several types of collaborative filtering algorithms are available:

>> **User-based CF** measures the similarity between target users and other customers by computing a similarity score for every customer pair, and then offers products that similar customers have chosen in the past. It answers the question "What did customers with similar tastes find interesting?"

>> **Item-based CF** measures the similarity between the items that target customers interact with and other items by computing a similarity score between every product pair. It answers the question "What items are similar to the item this customer finds interesting?"

>> **Context-aware CF** adds another dimension to the user-based and item-based CF in the form of contextual information such as time, location, and social information. It answers the question "What else do I know about this customer that might affect the level of interest in an item?"

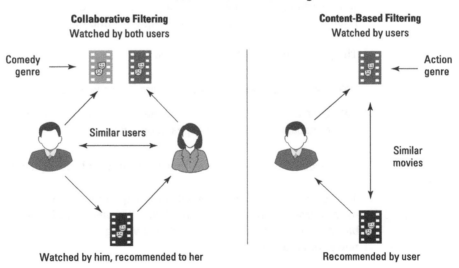

FIGURE 20-1: Differences between popular recommendation methodologies.

Because it is based on comparing shopper behavior, user-based CF is very effective. However, because it must compute a similarity score for every customer pair, it is time- and resource-intensive. A database of N customers generates $(N * (N - 1)) / 2$ unique customer pairs. For example, 100 customers produce 4,950 unique pairs. If you have 5,000 customers, you would have 12,497,500 unique customer pairs. As you can see, for large user bases, this algorithm is hard to implement without a very strong, parallelizable system.

Item-based CF does not need to compute similarity scores between customers, only between products, and the number of products is likely to be much smaller than the number of customers. As a result, it is less resource-intensive and takes much less time. In addition, if you have a fixed set of products, you can perform the computation once and you're done.

Context-aware CF enhances a recommendation engine with context, expanding the ability to establish relevance.

Content-based filtering (CBF)

This personalization technique builds a profile of the customer's interests based on the item metadata in the customer's buying history and looks for matches with the item metadata for other products. For example, if a customer buys a book on woodworking, the metadata of that purchase could be matched with metadata for related products, such as woodworking tools and protective equipment.

The process involves two main tasks:

>> Identify metadata attributes to be associated with each item.

>> Build user profiles of items a user has interacted with, giving more weight to metadata attributes that appear more often.

User feedback is critical to fine-tune the profile and subsequent recommendations.

TIP

The accuracy of CBF relies heavily on the quality of metadata, and the results are usually less accurate than CF methods. Simpler techniques such as popularity-based methods or market-basket analysis generally also lack high predictive power or accuracy.

Cross-validation

Intelligent recommendation systems are typically deployed with the goals of identifying and raising the effectiveness of cross-channel/cross-product sales campaigns, identifying a customer's affinity for specific products, reducing customer churn and boosting revenue. So how do you assess how well your recommendations perform?

Cross-validation is one technique used to test the accuracy of the recommendations by calculating the receiver operating characteristic (ROC) curve to produce a metric called "area under the curve" (AUC). This exercise compares predictions (recommendations) to actual outcomes (purchases) to quantify the likelihood that items with the highest ranked recommendation will be purchased.

Historical Fact: The seemingly strange-named Receiver Operating Characteristic curve dates to WWII and was used to measure the effectiveness of a sonar signal to differentiate between a whale and a submarine.

You can customize your intelligent recommendation system to track key performance indicators to optimize performance using these values:

>> **Click-through rate (CTR):** How often does the customer explore the recommended offerings?

>> **Conversion rate (CR):** How often does the customer purchase an item based on the recommended offerings?

>> **Conversion time:** How long does it take to convert a casual shopper into a loyal customer?

>> **Average order value (AOV):** Does the average order value go up?

Other business metrics to consider include ROI and customer lifetime value. However, these metrics depend on several unknowns and thus can be difficult to measure at times.

Data visualization

Data visualization is one of the most important elements of any analytics solutions. This is especially true for predictive analytics software where the results provide actionable insight to improve decision-making. Enterprises can't afford to leave the interpretation of the results to data scientists; they must be easily digestible by the people who will actually work with them: end-users and business managers.

Data visualization can produce a single view of multi-dimensional datasets to help you with these tasks:

>> Assimilating a large amount of information in a glance and focusing on what matters most

>> Recognizing the correlation between consumer behavior and metrics such as customer life value and share of wallet

>> Identifying trends and connections and preparing strategies in advance

>> Improving collaboration between teams

TIP

Most predictive analytics solutions provide a range of data visualization capabilities including charts, graphs, reports, and dashboards. The best predictive analytics software will give you easy-to-use, self-service features where users can define their own visualization capabilities to display the results in the way they want.

Examining Key Industries

With all that terminology and algorithmy under your belt, you're ready to dive into the use cases.

Finance

The challenge of understanding buying propensity is particularly acute for banks, investment firms, and similar financial organizations. An ever-growing proportion of the population has savings and investments, such as a retirement account, and could benefit from guidance on how to manage their money. But not everyone can afford a private financial advisor. Many look to their current partners to guide them.

However, banks have inserted themselves into many lines of business, from home mortgages and credit card protection to auto-paying utility bills and even retail shopping. They have millions of potential combinations of offers, customers, times, and channels to market — desktop, mobile, kiosk, partner site, and more.

This is exactly the type of problem that a truly effective AI-augmented intelligent recommendation system is designed to solve. By focusing a solution on the issues unique to their challenges, financial companies can mine not just structured data, such as a consumer's past online activity, credit score, and demographic profile, but also behavior patterns of similar customers, retail partners' purchase histories — even the unstructured data of a customer's social media posts or comments they've made in customer support chats.

It can keep score of the myriad permutations of offers — headline, offer wording, size of the discount, the particular products displayed — like the world's biggest A/B test. Even abandoned orders can be a rich source of insight. They show that something attracted the customer initially, but then something else put them off, which the AI can tease out. With every interaction the software observes, it gets smarter.

Credit card offers

The customer churn rate within financial services is extremely high. In 2017, one in five U.S. customers left their provider, making financial services the third-worst industry for customer attrition.

Meanwhile, in Asia, customers are beginning to cut down the number of cards they have. Their choice is based on the level of service they receive in terms of the benefits and rewards on offer. Anthony Chiam, service industry practice leader at J.D. Power, said, "With nearly 25 percent of cardholders considering switching from their primary card issuer — either for a better rewards program or better benefits — it is important that issuers consider their long-term engagement strategies to minimize customer attrition."

Of course, not all customers are good customers. A credit card provider needs to be able to distinguish between good and bad customers — in other words, profitable versus unprofitable/delinquent. For example, companies often think that the more times a customer contacts the call center, the more likely they are to be a bad customer. This may not be the case. Instead, the content of the last contact is likely to be more revealing.

TIP

AI allows you to automatically convert call center logs to text to enable sentiment analysis, which can build a picture not just of the customer's interactions with the company but also their perceptions and opinions on the company and its products and services.

With a robust enterprise AI approach, you can work with all the structured and unstructured information you have on a customer, including enterprise applications, social channels, transactional information, and call center interactions. Then you can use the analysis to identify the attributes that make someone a good customer for you, create accurate profiles of the customers at risk you want to retain, segment those customers based on buying behaviors and preferences, and tailor their promotions and rewards accordingly.

Retail

As Amazon has demonstrated, retail shopping is a prime candidate for intelligent recommendations, and for good reasons. Two psychologists from Columbia and Stanford University published a study in 2000 about how choice affects buying behavior. They set up a booth at a food market with various flavors of jam: 24 varieties on some days and 6 on others. While the larger selection generated more interest, the smaller selection generated more sales. Further studies indicated a direct relationship between sales and the ease of making a decision.

TIP

You can boost sales by reducing the range of choices. And if those choices are targeted to the customer's preferences, you can boost them even more. Accenture found that 75 percent of consumers are more likely to buy from a retailer that recognizes them by name and can recommend options based on past purchases.

Mass customization and personalization takes the recommendation further to tailor the product to the customer. Through data mining and text mining, you can personalize the product to a specific customer, and you can discern trends across segments and use the information to inform product development. Figure 20-2 provides an conceptual overview of how such a system can function.

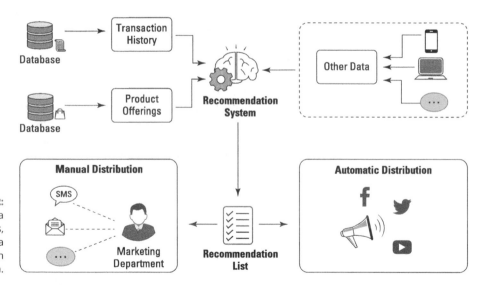

FIGURE 20-2: The flow of data inputs, outputs, and activities in a recommendation system.

The Direct Marketing Association found that of the various customer engagement tactics, such as blanket emails, activity-based triggers, and lifestyle-based triggers, 58 percent of all revenue came from targeted emails.

Harvard Business Review describes four approaches to product customization:

>> **Collaborative:** Offer a unique product based on conversations about needs and preferences.

>> **Adaptive:** Offer a user-customizable standard product.

>> **Cosmetic:** Offer a base product that can be easily personalized for the customer.

>> **Transparent:** Offer unique products to each customer without disclosing the customization.

Collaborative customization involves a dialog with the customer, while adaptive customization provides flexibility for the customer to customize for themselves. Both are hands-on approaches to targeting the needs of the customer. Cosmetic and transparent customization personalizes the product based on determining customer preferences. Gartner predicts that smart personalization engines soon will be able to recognize customer intent. Enabled by AI, mass customization delivers better customer service, enhances brand experience, and increases brand loyalty by moving the conversation from price to benefits.

REMEMBER

It's easy to see the benefits of AI for retail customer experience. If your computers do more than process data — they learn and interpret it — you have a system that can truly produce the real-time, actionable insight needed to improve decision-making.

Incorporating AI allows retailers to gain a laser focus on the customer by having access to data from all sources to create a single view of the customer. You can understand your customer at a transactional and an emotional level. Importantly, AI-enhanced analytics can help break down the barriers between data silos and analyze the information that previously was trapped in unstructured data and other forms of content.

When you combine AI, machine learning, and analytics, you multiply the power of your efforts in several ways:

>> Machine-learning algorithms offer an additional factor in analyzing and monitoring business outcomes.

>> AI and machine learning can sharpen analytic algorithms, detect more early warning signals, anticipate trends, and enable you to have accurate answers faster than your competitors.

>> Real-time analytics bring different business areas together, facilitate collaboration, and improve productivity.

Chapter **21**

Content Management: Finding What You Want, When You Want It

I f you're like most people, you're on the verge of drowning in content. Or maybe you're already going down for the third time, disappearing under a wave of spreadsheets, documents, web pages, industry studies, and technology updates. And don't forget the texts, emails, voice mails. Statistics show that the deluge continues to grow, with 2.5 quintillion bytes of new data being produced every day. That's right now. I'd rather not imagine the numbers for the next year or the next decade.

The problem is that most of that content is not labeled and filed in neat little rows and columns and databases, optimized for accessibility, searchability, and summarization, dripping with instant insights and actionable bullet points. Instead, it's locked up in unstructured data, and mining unstructured data for actionable insights can seem as tedious as blasting through bedrock to extract precious metals. In fact, most business professionals believe that more than 70 percent of their enterprise content is unstructured.

Traditional data storage technologies lack the nuance required to extract and store the value found in disorganized, unstructured data. That's where AI comes in.

Introducing the Square Peg to the Round Hole

I'll let you in on a little secret. When it comes to data management, AI is in its element. Especially when it comes to unstructured data, and more specifically, when it comes to processing natural-language content.

Natural language is English "as she is spoke" out in the wild. Sometimes it follows the rules, sometimes it don't. Think of text messages, tweets, social media posts, emails. Think of questionnaires and applications and intake forms. All these things can be rich with information, but the information is not as easy to extract and summarize as information in a spreadsheet or a database.

Often, just making sure a document gets to the right place is a tedious and time-consuming job. For many organizations, assessing the value, possible risk, and potential gain associated with the information with any degree of timeliness and accuracy is more of an aspiration than an actuality.

In fact, until recently, most of that information lay dormant in filing cabinets or legacy document management systems. To find the value, you had to find the relevant documents, sit down, and read them. Who has time for that? Nobody. Especially not you.

Categorizing and organizing content

Yet the fact remains that effectively categorizing and organizing content is essential to most critical business processes. More importantly, you don't just need to capture that information; you must understand the implications, regardless of the type or format of the data, at the earliest possible point in your business processes.

You likely already have a content management system. You may even have several. In recent years, the number of content systems that companies use to make sense of their data has grown by nearly 30 percent, and their operational complexity has increased right along with it.

The discouraging fact is that despite the growth in the number of content systems, for most companies more than 50 percent of their critical business content remains outside of those systems.

Automating with AI

This is where AI comes to the rescue. AI-enhanced content management provides a single, seamless system for automating the classification and management of enterprise content. It pinpoints high-priority content to minimize risk and improve decision-making across the organization. Using AI capabilities such as natural-language processing and text mining, an AI-enhanced content management system derives meaning from unstructured content and categorizes it appropriately. As a result, you gain deeper insights from your content, streamline processes, and improve decision-making.

But you don't have to stop at streamlining processes and increasing your competitive position. The same system can help you navigate the shifting regulatory landscape of legislation such as the European Union's General Data Protection Regulation (GDPR) and the California Consumer Privacy Act (CCPA).

Sure, tapping into unstructured content lets you increase business intelligence to minimize cost and maximize revenue. That's enough right there, but missing potential regulatory landmines in your textual data could wind up offsetting those gains, such as missteps in collecting and managing personally identifiable information (PII).

TIP

Chances are good that you already have a wealth of PII lurking within your databases. From customer PIN codes in financial services to home addresses stored by service providers, there's no shortage of private information circulating across virtually every industry. Getting a better grip on what information you have and where it lies within your organization can help you sidestep costly fines and reputational casualties.

Finding Content at the Speed of AI

AI can help you make sense of all the data you have at your disposal. Here are some ways in which AI can corral that data and harness its power:

>> **Increase the value of content:** An AIIM study estimates that 70 percent or more of today's enterprise data is unstructured, textual data. Yet, 71 percent of enterprises struggle to manage, protect, and harness the value of this content.

According to a recent Panopto study, the associated inefficiencies in knowledge-sharing can result in a financial loss of up to $47 million per year. AI-enhanced content management helps you maximize the value of your structured and unstructured data to support better overall performance.

>> **Connect the enterprise:** If you don't currently have a single, unified system to promote collaboration across different functions, you might have noticed that information gets siloed in various departments across your organization. AI-powered solutions give your employees the ability to share insights in ways that are digestible and easily accessible, creating cross-functional collaboration on initiatives that truly align with and support your overall strategy.

>> **Eliminate redundant data:** Think about every time you've lost track of a document on your computer and after 10 or 15 minutes of digging around in different folders and drives, you gave up and tracked down the source and downloaded it again. Now, picture that exercise in frustration across an entire enterprise. That little scenario illustrates how your company becomes infested with redundant, outdated, trivial data (ROT).

This type of data typically comprises 30 to 50 percent of the data you currently have in your system, or that you plan to retain during a migration. Keeping data that has no value to your organization drives up storage costs. Eliminating ROT can save expenses, both now and in the future.

>> **Reduce process completion time:** Manually searching through risk-prone content across repositories, or giving up and re-creating documents, wastes time. AI-enhanced content management solutions assess, classify, and automate content to process information and trigger the next action based on contextual classifications, reducing process completion time by up to 75 percent.

>> **Cut compliance costs:** Compliance means something different for every industry and location. For companies in California, for example, CCPA gives consumers the right to know which types of PII companies collect from them and what they do with it. Each violation can cost up to $7,500, possibly posing a significant financial burden for your company. And that is only one aspect of one law. Utilities, healthcare, financial services, and other highly regulated industries all have their own regulations in place. Ignoring regulations increases financial risks. Maintaining compliance requires a significant investment of time and manpower when you use manual processes to manage your content. An AI-powered content management solution can cut compliance costs by 50 percent.

>> **Improve business outcomes:** Information fuels your decision-making. With the ability to make sense of your data, you can clear away the chaos of increasing volumes of unstructured content to get better clarity, which you can apply to multiple business initiatives, ranging from anticipating the wants and needs of your customers to improving the buying journey and overall customer experience.

Expanding Your Toolbox

AI-enhanced content management involves tools to access content, extract concepts and entities, categorize and classify content, automate processes, and recommend next steps.

Access the content

To successfully deploy an AI-enhanced content management system, you must first determine what unstructured, textual data is relevant to the business challenge you're facing. For example, if you have a bank with customers in California, the CCPA applies to you, so you must identify which PII you collect from your customers and how you store it. It might affect content repositories spanning multiple databases, including email and the system you use to process and store customer applications. Whatever your specific use for a content management solution, the first step is always accessing the textual data.

TIP

AI-powered content management solutions can give you a clear picture of how your information is distributed across systems. For example, it can break down documents by file type, size, and creation over time, which helps you understand where your textual data lives.

Extract concepts and entities

AI-enhanced content systems use machine learning, text mining, and natural-language processing to process your content, identify key elements, extract them, and store them as structured metadata data to accelerate retrieval and increase the value you can derive from the information.

The concepts and entities that the system extracts can include names of people and places, dates, GPS coordinates, and customized information to suit your business needs. For example, you might want to pinpoint documents with a specific product or part number.

AI uses natural-language processing to go beyond simple extraction to accomplish these tasks:

>> Summarize important information within the data

>> Detect tone and sentiment, differentiating factual information from opinions and determining whether statements are positive, negative, or neutral

>> Uncover the emotion and intent behind specific sentences

The system can also clean up data to enforce integrity and consistency policies and determine which content you must keep for compliance purposes and which content can be destroyed. This is particularly useful for content migration, as the use cases discussed later in this chapter show.

Categorize and classify content

With the ability to crawl thousands of documents and use what it learns, an AI-enhanced content management system can automatically classify your content based on type and entities, solving a significant business problem by applying metadata. It can also provide visualizations, including a comprehensive risk score. Visualizations may also include dashboards, tag clouds to illustrate the most frequently used terms in a document, and other display options to help you sort and quickly identify important ideas.

Using predictive analysis, AI-enhanced content management systems can classify content to guide and prioritize actions and synthesize inputs on content requirements, regulatory requirements for PII, and so on. AI can give you the power to realize the insight buried in millions of documents spanning decades, a task that would be cost-prohibitive on a human scale. For example, you can use AI to analyze those documents to answer business questions such as, "Where are my risks, and where do I need to take action?"

TIP

You can use a privacy dashboard to quickly identify any PII lurking in your data and set up other flags for different risk areas. With these insights, you can prioritize actions and work on areas that are most important first.

Automate or recommend next best actions

To ensure that you're maximizing the benefits of cost savings and efficiencies, you can use content management tools to trigger actions. Although humans can address outlier cases, the ability to scale and address challenges without employing an army of knowledge workers lies in the ability to automate routine tasks. A high-risk score, for example, might trigger an investigation from an employee, while a low-risk score might simply kick-start a workflow in which the content is routed to the appropriate repository.

Examining the Use Cases

Now that you have a grounding in the fundamentals of AI-enhanced content management, it's time to look at some applications in a representative sampling of industries and applications.

Legal discovery process

Law firms must gather, sort through, and analyze thousands of documents during the discovery process. While many firms and corporate legal departments still complete these processes manually, this causes the cost and timeline of legal cases to soar. Extracting key information is critical to building a strong case, but having highly paid attorneys manually sort through massive amounts of content is neither practical nor financially feasible.

TIP

AI-enhanced content management solutions help legal teams classify and manage their documents to automate the repetitive, time-consuming aspects of the discovery process. With the ability to analyze billions of records quickly and classify it accordingly, AI speeds up legal review and allows legal professionals to make faster, better decisions. It can also automatically pinpoint sensitive information within documents, such as Social Security numbers and phone numbers, to protect clients' privacy.

Content migration

From switching data warehouses to managing acquisitions, data migrations have become a routine activity in the Digital Age. Yet, the process can still be clumsy and complicated. Many organizations lack visibility into their data and are unsure of where their priority data is located. These projects often take far longer than expected and fail to yield desired results, such as reducing and effectively controlling overall enterprise data.

TIP

AI-driven content management solutions analyze the metadata of your content to help you determine what needs to be migrated and what doesn't. It also enriches documents with details about its contents, making it easier for teams to take the next best action. It can also deliver migration insights so you can keep track of your data. In all, AI-enhanced content management solutions can help you speed up data migrations by up to 20 percent.

PII detection

Global enterprises could face up to $20 million in noncompliance costs; to avoid legal risks and fines, many companies spend millions of dollars on compliance. Data with PII is a growing concern for large organizations, especially in the wake of regulatory changes such as GDPR and CCPA. These laws require companies to disclose the type of personal information collected and from whom, who it's shared with, and how it's stored. To satisfy these requirements, compliance officers must first know the sources and types of PII their companies have. This could include full names, PIN codes, ethnic origins, religious beliefs, and many more pieces of sensitive data.

TIP

AI-enhanced content management optimizes compliance by organizing, centralizing, and contributing to PII management. It can crawl thousands of documents and use what it learns to automatically classify which documents have PII and what type of information is contained within them. It therefore makes categorization swift and simple when timeliness is critical. It can also provide interactive visualizations with risk insights that allow you to drill down to locate PII. In addition, it allows for automated routing or recommendations for the next best action to safeguard privacy and mitigate risk.

Chapter **22**

AI-Enhanced Content Capture: Gathering All Your Eggs into the Same Basket

C hances are good that you've sent an email to a customer service department at one point or another. Perhaps your order was late, items were damaged in shipping, or you needed to know how to initiate the return process. You may have found that while some companies are prompt in sending a reply and resolving your issue, you may not hear back from others for days. Although the timeliness of their response may have something to do with the nature of your issue, it's also likely to be influenced by whether the company is still using manual processes to sort through incoming emails.

Retailers that offer a prompt resolution are likely using advanced capture technology. These solutions offer the ability to quickly process incoming data, but they don't stop at email. Advanced capture technology can process handwritten notes, snail mail, and even social media.

Counting All the Chickens, Hatched and Otherwise

Since the rise of the digital age, the speed at which files can be sent, received, and processed has increased tremendously. In the past, the journey of a document from the time it was filled out until it was received and processed might have taken days. Now, it happens in minutes or seconds.

Streamlining content capture took its first step with the introduction of electronic forms, but a fair amount of tedious, repetitive work remained, such as spanning the air gap between systems. You might remember having to key in data from one form or system to another. You might even still be doing it.

The flow of paper and electronic documents continues to bog down employees, with manual tasks consisting of everything from inputting invoices and orders to processing files for new hires. This administrative burden takes its toll on workplace productivity, which increases costs. Although the estimated cost of 63 cents per document may not seem like much, consider the fact that the U.S. manufacturing industry spends more than $1 billion on data entry.

Of course, manufacturing isn't the only industry challenged by document-routing obstacles. Healthcare, financial services, and government are some of the most paperwork-intensive industries, with Health Insurance Portability and Accountability (HIPAA) forms, mortgages, and police statements still largely processed via physical paper. Yet, some forms are also collected and stored in digital databases, making the volume and complexity of content especially challenging to manage.

Tracing the history of capture technology

To process paperwork more rapidly, many organizations have embraced basic content capture technology. Originating in the 1990s, these systems scan and capture information from machine-typed documents into digital form using optical character recognition (OCR).

As you might imagine, the earliest OCR systems had their fair share of errors. Before it was refined, it could do more harm than good with the potential to misinterpret characters and introduce errors into databases.

Fortunately, intelligent character recognition (ICR), an enhancement of OCR, brings machine learning to capture. In doing so, it expands the material it can read, from high-quality, machine-typed characters to handwriting, poor quality scans, and multi-language documents. Intelligent capture improves on the accuracy of OCR, typically with the help of multiple data extraction engines. These systems can route documents based on content or keywords. They can also extract and analyze document data and validate information quicker than a human, thereby streamlining business processes for time and money savings.

Yet, despite their robust nature, intelligent capture solutions have some limitations. While many documents are simple for machines to capture and route based on easily defined keywords or other classification criteria, others are more ambiguous. In such cases, determining where a document should go next and who should do what with it once it gets there requires human intervention. That is true unless your organization is equipped with AI-enhanced content capture.

Moving capture technology forward

AI takes capture technology a step further with smart features such as the ability to read and interpret a much broader range of documents with a high degree of accuracy. From smudged carbon copies to wrinkled paperwork, the precise character rendering of AI-enhanced content capture can infer characters from a complex array of hard-to-read sources by using context to catch OCR mistakes. The technology pinpoints key information in a document, such as policy numbers and customer names, with automatic highlighting.

REMEMBER

AI-enhanced content capture is an end-to-end solution that automates paperwork and electronic document processing from the moment it crosses the transom to when it reaches its final destination. It uses natural-language processing, context processing, and analytics.

Monetizing All the Piggies, Little and Otherwise

Although intelligent capture solutions are effective for transforming massive volumes of documents into data that you can use across your organization, AI-enhanced content capture adds tremendous value to this process. Not only does it digitize and extract all textual data from content sources such as notes, social media posts, spreadsheets, and emails, among others, but it also applies AI to differentiate among this information contextually. From there, it routes documents to the appropriate workflow, saving a significant amount of time and effort across the organization.

AI also improves capture by intelligently prioritizing captured content. It uses predictive analysis to determine risk, which may not be readily apparent to individuals involved in a process. For example, it can extract key terms from customer emails to determine whether an immediate response from a customer service representative is warranted. It can also uncover issues within a workflow, such as when a specific employee is delayed in signing off on a critical report, creating a bottleneck in the process of elevating the issue to a manager. The system can even re-route documents or reprioritize steps.

REMEMBER

AI-enhanced capture doesn't just alleviate the burden of collecting and managing a vast pool of complex data. It also enables enterprises to turn their unstructured content into actionable data for improved business outcomes. These solutions don't simply turbocharge the capture process; they also act as data quality engines to extract valuable information from content.

Streamline back-office operations

Not only has the digital age hastened the speed of document exchange, it has also significantly increased the volume of data you share. Forbes reports that within large organizations, roughly 2.5 quintillion bytes of data are produced and received daily. The processes of capturing and routing that information to the right recipient or repository are resource-intensive, with entire departments of people overseeing these tasks. AI-enhanced content capture automates these processes to increase efficiency and save the enterprise significant time and money. Beyond this obvious benefit, there are many additional ways the solution can help an organization.

Improve compliance

As regulatory requirements evolve, it's becoming more important than ever for organizations to protect personally identifiable information (PII). Not only do these solutions typically have built-in security components to limit access to sensitive data, but they also simplify and streamline the process of indexing and searching documents needed for legal requirements. With a traceable log of activity and approvals, the systems help organizations make a defensible legal case for regulatory compliance if need be.

Reduce risk of human error

AI reduces the risk of human error, which is widely believed to be 1 percent. The 1-10-100 rule of data quality says that it costs $1 to verify data accuracy, $10 to correct data errors in batch form, and $100 or more for each record with errors on which no action is taken. Thus, even a low error rate can cost you a significant amount.

According to a 2009 experiment, university students who manually entered 30 data sheets had an average error rate of 10.23 errors. That may seem small for 30 sheets worth of information, but contrast that with the average mistake rate of 0.38 errors made when using capture software. And remember, the experiment was carried out more than a decade ago. The technology has improved significantly since then.

Support business transformation

Businesses across every industry are recognizing the need for quicker, more convenient services, and AI-enhanced capture is helping them achieve that goal. The lengthy process of settling an insurance claim serves as a noteworthy example. While it can take 7 to 14 business days in many cases, the introduction of mobile applications and capture technology powered by algorithms and other AI tools has significantly accelerated the process.

Some car insurers offer policyholders the option to take a picture of their damaged vehicle and upload it for review. The ability to process photos, forms, and other file types allows claims officers to rapidly resolve claims in moments instead of days. Similar transformations can be realized across other sectors to streamline business processes, provide better service, and support competitiveness.

Improve operational knowledge

AI-enhanced capture empowers the workforce by delivering information directly to the employees who need it, bypassing the paperwork shuffle. When data is processed in less time, information becomes accessible sooner.

Capture technology makes it easier to perform data analysis and trend spotting, which can help you uncover patterns that may need attention. It can also reveal inefficiencies in the workflow, automatically highlight key information, and flag any edge cases so they can be addressed promptly.

For example, a web-based clothing store might have a contact form on its website that serves as a catchall for customer inquiries. Some matters, such as inquiries on shipping status, may not require as prompt a response as others, such as questions about a coupon code issue from a shopper who already has an item in their cart. With the help of AI capture technology, you can prioritize these items strategically and trigger a workflow for the most urgent inquiries.

Getting All Your Ducks in a Row

Several technologies come together to make enhanced content capture possible.

Capture

The workhorse of the capture technology is, of course, its ability to capture data from any source, including handwritten forms, emails, PDF files, Word documents, and more. Advanced OCR technology recognizes both machine- and hand-printed characters in any major language. AI-enhanced capture can also recognize specific forms and can manage complex capture workflows across different departments quickly. Most systems also capture mobile information, such as forms submitted via smartphone.

Digitize where needed

Based on predetermined configurations, capture technology can convert the information it captures into editable text or a searchable PDF file, depending on your needs. For example, some paperwork-heavy industries, such as medical offices, have begun scanning documents primarily for archival purposes, while others are transforming their entire business processes to become digitized.

Process, classify, and extract

AI uses machine learning, including natural-language processing and sentiment analysis, to gain a contextual understanding of the data. After it reads and understands content, it applies advanced recognition and auto-classifies it based on these findings.

REMEMBER

AI-enhanced capture uses two types of technology to drive speed and accuracy:

>> **Zonal extraction:** This approach uses a template that identifies fields to capture and their locations. It's most effective for recurring documents, such as claims forms or vendor invoices.

> » **Freeform extraction:** Using keywords and text analysis, freeform extraction is a flexible solution for retrieving data from documents that come from different sources. For instance, vendors may send your company invoices in multiple formats. AI-enhanced capture uses this technology to apply freeform rules that enable the extraction of key data from the invoices.

Together, these technologies automate data extraction to save time and reduce the risk of human error.

AI delivers clear, actionable insights and even predictive analytics. It also prioritizes content based on any additional established or learned criteria to trigger a machine-initiated workflow. For example, in the contact form scenario mentioned above, AI can quickly determine whether emails from customers have a positive, neutral, or negative tone. This ability to read and analyze sentiment allows the system to prioritize appropriately, so customer support personnel can deliver answers in a timely manner to the customers who need them most. Similarly, it can detect important differences between internal documents. For example, it can appropriately process invoices sent to customers versus invoices received from vendors requiring payment. Figure 22-1 shows how AI can ensure optimized performance over time.

FIGURE 22-1: The process flow from capture through the application of AI, management, and monitoring to ensure optimized performance over time.

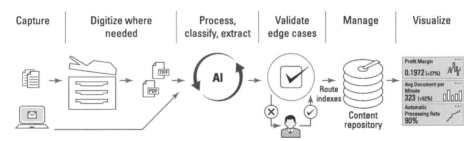

Validate edge cases

Another standout quality of AI-enhanced capture is its ability to help humans focus on challenging tasks. Not only does it reduce the tedious processing of data without the need for manual intervention, but it also brings edge cases to the attention of the right person for validation.

For example, an admissions department at a community college may be able to process most transcripts rapidly using capture technology. They extract the information and send the files to the appropriate repository. Yet, in some cases, the system might flag missing information or errors that exceed value thresholds. In these scenarios, these specific transcripts can be brought to the attention of the appropriate admissions officers so they can follow up with students or take other actions as needed.

REMEMBER

AI-enhanced content capture becomes more intelligent over time. It learns from historical data to determine which cases can be considered normal and which require human intervention. It can also make decisions based on pre-established thresholds to deliver value to your organization right away.

Manage

AI-enhanced content capture also simplifies document management. With its ability to read and make meaning of data, it routes and indexes information to the appropriate place within the content suite repository. Because it also can extract keywords, it makes your data and content easier to search.

TIP

You can use AI-enhanced capture to automatically assign metadata from keywords to each piece of content that enters the enterprise, effectively acting as comprehensive translators. Although functions like HR, finance, and sales all have their own unique document types and language, these systems are sufficiently intelligent to understand their specific nuances. They can therefore manage content across the entire organization and link various functions seamlessly through simplified sharing and connections to line-of-business applications.

Visualize

Finally, AI-enhanced capture offers key analytics via dashboards and reports. It can deliver key performance indicators to help you spot inefficiencies in your business processes.

Examining Key Industries

Remember those paper-heavy industries from the beginning of the chapter? Here are some ways AI can help with the clutter.

Financial services

Financial services organizations receive thousands of pieces of mail daily. Processing and scanning each document requires an entire team, not to mention determining the purpose of each piece of mail and routing it to the appropriate recipients.

You can use AI-enhanced capture to rapidly process huge volumes of paperwork, significantly reducing the manpower needed to handle incoming mail from the moment it enters the facility. AI-enhanced capture also ensures any documents that need to be seen are received by the individuals who can intervene when needed.

Processing physical mail isn't the only way financial services can benefit from AI-augmented capture.

You can use AI-augmented capture to streamline the process of applying for mortgages online, smoothing the on-boarding process to ensure that application documents are properly indexed, routed, and classified. It can even help to assess risk based on the information provided in the application. To ensure your teams have the information needed to finish the on-boarding process promptly, the system will also apply metadata, which facilitates the appropriate routing of the form.

AI-enhanced capture is particularly useful for insurance companies. These companies receive huge volumes of claims and supporting documents, some of which may be sent via email, fax, and even traditional mail. Appropriately routing these documents has traditionally been time-consuming, but AI can ensure incoming information is sent through the proper channels based on key identifying data, such as claim or policy numbers.

State government

While there are many areas of opportunity for AI-enhanced capture in the private sector, the public sector can also benefit from this technology. State governments receive millions of tax forms each spring. Processing these forms manually isn't just cumbersome and time-consuming; it also winds up costing taxpayers more in the long run. Many state governments have therefore turned to capture technology to help process document types related to tax returns.

The Minnesota Department of Revenue embraced this solution for its tax processing activities to determine whether a return is complete, and if so, route it to the right workflow, depending on its contents. As a part of a larger digital transformation, this system has helped them save more than a million dollars.

Healthcare

Healthcare documents tend to be extremely repetitive in nature. Oftentimes, patients are asked to fill out forms online and required to redundantly fill out physical paperwork at the time of their appointment. In some cases, they must fill out the same paperwork because information is siloed in different registration systems or locations, an obstacle that is exacerbated when HIPAA regulations restrict access. Yet, these forms require approval and must therefore still be processed.

Historically, healthcare systems haven't had the data intelligence to eliminate this redundant paperwork.

TIP

You can use AI to assign key identifiers such as patient name, birthdate, and physician so your clerks can verify that patients have already registered for an appointment or procedure, allowing them to bypass additional paperwork. This is just one example of how AI helps healthcare providers smooth tasks for both patients and staff to save time and enhance the quality of service.

Chapter **23**

Regulatory Compliance and Legal Risk Reduction: Hitting the Bullseye on a Moving Target

Two dozen federal regulatory agencies exist in the U.S. plus several dozen in the E.U., not to mention the state-level agencies. Regardless of your industry or nonprofit focus, some agency somewhere is scrutinizing every jot and tittle of the law to see if you're up to snuff. If you're lucky, you might be answerable to multiple regulators regarding different aspects of your market.

The rules are constantly in flux. In 2017, Thomson Reuters Regulatory Intelligence captured 56,321 regulatory alerts from more than 900 regulatory bodies worldwide, averaging 216 updates a day, up from 10 per day in 2004. If you worked around the clock, you could get through the stack if you interpreted and implemented one change every 7 minutes. And it's not so easy on the regulatory agency functionaries either.

You can see why financial institutions estimate that 10 to 15 percent of their total workforce is dedicated to governance, risk management, and compliance, and why in 2018, 66 percent of financial services firms worldwide expected the cost of senior compliance staff to increase.

You can also see why this problem is a prime target for an AI-powered solution. With pre-defined targets and all that big data lying around, organizations are turning to AI to help them make better decisions, increase customer confidence, and win more business by getting control of compliance and risk.

Dodging Bullets

It's the fines that dominate the headlines. They come from all directions: the Federal Trade Commission (FTC), the Securities and Exchange Commission (SEC), the Consumer Financial Protection Bureau (CFPB), the U.S. Department of Justice, the U.K. Information Commissioner's Office (ICO), attorneys general at state and federal levels, the Netherlands Public Prosecution Service, Denmark's Financial Services Authority, the European Banking Authority. If the General Data Protection Regulation (GDPR) is involved, fines can be up to 4 percent of the company's annual revenue.

Fines

In July 2019, the regulators had a busy month, with four mammoth rulings.

Marriott, $124 million: The ICO fined Marriott for a 2014 data breach of guest reservation data affecting 339 million guest records for Starwood hotels, which Marriott acquired in 2016. The personal data (name, mailing and email address, phone number, passport number, date of birth, gender, arrival and departure information, Starwood accounting information, reservation date, communication preferences, and encrypted payment card numbers) were exposed globally by this cyber incident. Marriott reported the breach in November 2018, six months after GDPR was in effect. The fine was almost 200 times over the maximum penalty of $627,000 under the previous act. Even so, the higher fine amounted to merely 0.5 percent of Marriott's 2018 revenue.

British Airways, $230 million: The ICO levied this record-breaking fine for the 2018 theft of data from BA's website affecting 500,000 customers. Customer details (login, payment card, and travel booking information) were diverted to a fake website over a period of four months. The fine amounted to 1.5 percent of British Airways' 2018 revenue.

Equifax, $700 million: Multiple U.S. agencies and states negotiated a settlement with Equifax for unfair and deceptive practices in connection with a 2017 data breach that affected 147 million consumers. The fine amounted to 2 percent of Equifax's 2018 revenue.

Facebook, $5 billion: The FTC issued this record-breaking fine for privacy violations, including misrepresenting the ability of a user to control the use of facial recognition, sharing user data with third-party app developers, and employing deceptive practices when collecting users' phone numbers for a security feature to be used for advertising. The fine amounted to 9 percent of Facebook's 2018 revenue.

Although the January 2019 Google GDPR settlement six months earlier was the largest fine issued up to that date, in retrospect the $57 million settlement for not properly disclosing how it collects data to present personalized advertisements seems little more than a slap on the wrist. The fine amounted to 0.0004 percent of Google's 2018 revenue.

But don't forget the banks:

>> In 2012, the Dutch bank ING paid a penalty of $619 million for facilitating billions of dollars' worth of payments through the U.S. banking system on behalf of Cuban and Iranian clients. Six years later, it paid $900 million to settle a case for failing to spot money laundering after multiple warnings.

>> In 2012, U.K. bank HSBC paid a fine of $1.92 billion for, among other things, allowing Mexican drug cartels to launder hundreds of billions of dollars of drug money.

>> In an ongoing investigation that started in 2017, Danish bank Danske Bank is possibly facing fines of $2 billion for a money laundering scheme spanning seven years and involving $220 billion.

Not even lawyers are exempt:

>> In 2017, 22 percent of law firms experienced a cyber attack or data breach, up from 14 percent the year before.

>> In 2015, hackers hit multiple law firms in New York City and downloaded files regarding planned mergers. The investigation linked the hacks to three Chinse traders who used the information for insider trading, gaining more than $4 million.

>> In 2016, Panama-based law firm Mossack Fonseca, global keeper of the financial secrets of the rich and famous of all stripes, paid no attention to Know Your Customer (KYC) rules put in place to prevent bad actors from doing bad things with their money. That became a problem when 2.6TB of data containing 11.5 million documents was copied from their servers and leaked to the public. By the end of the year, governments and companies in 79 countries had opened 150 inquiries, audits, or investigations into the law firm, its intermediaries, and its clients.

>> In 2016, seven hackers from the U.S., Russia, and Ukraine broke into the SEC's corporate filing database over a five-month period and downloaded information that they used to make $4.1 million through insider trading. The breach was discovered a year later.

Healthcare is not immune either. In 2018, the U.S. Department of Health and Human Services, Office for Civil Rights, fined Anthem, Inc. $16 million because of a 2015 breach that compromised the electronic protected health information of 79 million patients, including names, Social Security numbers, medical identification numbers, addresses, dates of birth, email addresses, and employment information.

Increasing regulation

According to a PwC survey of U.S., U.K., and Japanese technology executives conducting business in the E.U., 40 percent of respondents had budgeted more than $10 million for GDPR compliance.

Finance

Of the industries recently surveyed by Accenture, financial services were hit hardest by cybercrime at an average of $18.3 million per company surveyed. As an industry built on trust, for financial services the impact of a breach goes beyond the direct cost of containment and mitigation. It can affect brand loyalty and customer churn.

A 2018 RMA survey of bank officers found that more than 50 percent increased compliance spending over previous years, and 62 percent ranked keeping up with regulatory changes as the top challenge for bank directors. About one-third of the banks said that increased regulatory demands reduced product flexibility and responsiveness to customer requests.

For example, a 2017 Mitek report on compliance costs for U.K. banks revealed that 25 percent of new customer applications were abandoned because the KYC verifications introduced too much friction into the process. In addition, each KYC check cost the bank from £10 to £100.

Remember HSBC's $1.92 billion fine in 2019? Since then, the bank has ramped up from 1,750 employees working in risk and compliance to 7,000. That means that for every ten employees, one is watching the other nine for signs of risky business. In the wake of increased regulation, most other financial institutions are following suit. The RMA study showed that half of those surveyed were spending between 6 and 10 percent of their revenue on compliance.

TIP

Most corporate offices hold treasure troves of valuable information. It stands to reason that if cyber-thugs hit low-value targets such as home computers, an enterprise is at risk. However, for some industries the greatest weakness is from within, where 40 percent of breaches originate from internal sources. These types of breaches can go undetected for months or longer.

Legal

In a 2018 Kaplan legal operations survey, 69 percent of respondents reported that data privacy regulations have changed the roles and responsibilities in their organization regarding security and compliance, and 80 percent of respondents said that data privacy concerns affect how they handle discovery and investigations. This is particularly important given that 49 percent reported that the volume of government or regulatory investigations has grown since the survey.

Initial results from the 2019 Kaplan legal operations survey indicate that 94 percent of respondents have data security concerns about distributing electronically stored information to multiple discovery vendors and law firms — up from 91 percent in 2018, 89 percent in 2017, and 72 percent in 2015.

Healthcare

One consequence of the near constant change in regulations is the cost of upgrading related line-of-business of applications. For example, in 2017, U.S. healthcare providers spent $39 billion coping with 629 discrete regulations. In addition, an average-size hospital maintains 59 full-time employees just for compliance, and more than a fourth of those are doctors and nurses. Regulations change so quickly that it significantly impacts time spent in patient care and often results in inefficiency due to duplication of effort, as reported by the American Hospital Association. Case in point, in the first half of 2019, 38 U.S. states passed a total of 97 new laws regulating healthcare.

Data privacy

One of the most sensitive aspects of modern commerce is the collecting and sharing of data. One-third of consumers have fabricated personal details to avoid giving away personal data, but more than 75 percent of people are more willing to share various types of personal data with a brand they trust. And almost everyone (85 percent) wants more control over their personal data stored in corporate servers.

Consequently, it isn't surprising that most of the news stories about fines for violating regulations relate to personally identifiable information (PII). But the scope of regulation is much wider and growing, and every company is a target, no matter how large or small.

The first to fall prey to the General Data Protection Regulation (GDPR) was a sports betting cafe in Austria that was fined €5,280 in 2018 for failing to post a notice that their surveillance cameras covered the street and parking lot and failing to purge personal images from the archive within 72 hours.

However, it appears that the E.U. will give you an E for effort. In 2018, a social media company in Germany exposed the personal data of 330,000 users. Despite the size of the breach, regulators imposed a fine of only €20,000 because the company demonstrated it was making best efforts to comply.

When the GDPR launched in 2018, only 20 percent of companies in the E.U., U.K., and the U.S. were ready and another 50 percent were working on it. As of this writing, more than 20 countries and 12 U.S. states have introduced similar legislation.

Strategy

After this walk through the rogue's gallery, one thing becomes apparent: It all comes down to the data. All the regulations, all the processes, all the fines — it's all about data.

TIP

The first step in dealing with regulatory compliance and legal risk is to get a handle on your data. Here's how:

>> Research the regulations in your industry that specify what information is protected and how it must be handled. You will come back to this step often because regulations are constantly in flux.

>> Document where the information is currently stored — local drives, servers, cloud storage — and determine the risks associated with each system. How easy is it for unauthorized personnel to access?

>> Document the data management process, such as backup and/or mirroring processes, backup frequency, and restore options.

>> Determine when and how data moves through the system, from intake to routine use to backups. Data in transit is usually protected using an encrypted virtual private network.

>> Determine who should be restricted from access, who should have access, and at what level. You can be at risk for fines if access is not restricted to authorized users, especially in healthcare environments where electronic protected health information is involved.

If it sounds time-consuming, complicated, and costly, it can be. A 2018 LexisNexis report placed the annual cost of anti-money-laundering (AML) compliance in the U.S. at $25 billion.

Shooting Back

Given the potential severity of a compliance violation, it should come as no surprise that the word compliance often prompts a negative reaction. It conjures thoughts of punishing fines and costly remediation projects.

This reaction is a bit ironic, considering that, for the most part, the outcomes spelled out in regulations are exactly the thing you want to happen. Who doesn't want their data to be secure from hackers? Who doesn't want their money protected from fraud? Who doesn't want their privacy guarded against exposure?

Most of the regulations on the books require businesses to treat you the way you want to be treated. As such, the ability to demonstrate compliance is actually a competitive advantage. In fact, an AI-powered compliance program can drive revenue, expand performance capabilities, and increase organizational resilience.

Make better decisions

Regulation can be a catalyst for improved information governance, data analysis, and reporting. In fact, best practices for information management are often driven by compliance needs. Review these best practices:

>> Clean up obsolete content, including personal data that should have been disposed of when the purpose for collecting it was completed.

>> Standardize naming, tagging, and classification of unstructured content.

>> Ensure clarity regarding what things are, what they are called, and how they are described.

>> Harmonize systems, create unified repositories, and retire outdated legacy applications.

>> Establish good record-keeping and compliant records management practices.

One collateral benefit of data hygiene is the savings on storage and the ability to combine the resulting classification structures with other semantic metadata extracted from the content to build more robust AI solutions. Another benefit is that it mitigates the risk of litigation with respect to data retention policies.

Good data management means faster access to higher quality data. Time spent cleaning up your data means less time wasted on trying to find the relevant data and then wondering or trying to discover how accurate it really is. Having the right data right now means better decisions and accelerated time-to-action.

Increase customer confidence

When you are looking for suppliers, do you prefer to develop a relationship with a company that follows the rules? That might sound like a silly question, but when you turn it around, you can see the implications for your own organization: "If I develop a strong ethics and compliance culture, will that make my company more attractive to customers and business partners?"

For the most part, customers prefer to do business with vendors and suppliers who share their values and have a strong ethical culture. In fact, many customers actively seek such partners, making it part of their due diligence. As a result, environmental responsibility and social responsibility continue to play a greater role in the success of a company.

Surveying more than 53,000 consumers, the Natural Marketing Institute discovered that 58 percent of consumers consider a company's impact on the environment in considering where to purchase goods and services and are more likely to purchase from companies that practice sustainable habits.

It works the other way too. Trust and brand reputation can become casualties of failure to demonstrate strong compliance practices because consumers are less willing to engage with a business that compromised their data. In fact, a Gemalto survey found that 64 percent of consumers are unlikely to do business with a company where their financial or sensitive data was stolen.

Win more business

In some cases, regulatory compliance goes beyond a preference to a hard requirement, meaning the difference between winning and losing the business. For example, protecting sensitive data is important from a compliance perspective, but when a company evaluates a cloud services vendor or managed services provider, noncompliance with the relevant security and data privacy standards and regulations is likely a showstopper.

According to Forrester, "DPOs and CISOs are going to require that every vendor that comes in contact with any customer data — from device IDs to Social Security numbers — is compliant with GDPR and ePrivacy. The requirements will be written into every RFI and RFP."

Boost the bottom line

A well-considered compliance program extends beyond the organization to its third parties. From 2017 to 2018, supply chain attacks increased 78 percent. Regulators are also focusing more attention on the supply chain, challenging organizations to better manage their risk. For these reasons, third-party risk management continues to be one of the biggest challenges facing chief compliance officers.

TIP

Assessing the behavior of your third parties requires a deep dive into your supply chain and the patience to follow the trail to the source. If you do this well, you achieve not only greater visibility in your own supply chain, but in your suppliers' supply chains, and so on. This visibility and tracking promotes smarter working terms, improved efficiencies, and greater cost savings, all of which affect the bottom line.

According to Global Trade Review, adopting regulatory technology (regtech) solutions for anti-money-laundering and Know Your Customer compliance could save banks an estimated $3.4 billion per year.

According to Reuters, despite decades and billions of dollars of industry investment in flagging suspicious transactions, more than 95 percent of system-generated alerts are closed as false positives in the first phase of review. Artificial intelligence goes deeper to identify patterns and relationships to flag relevant activity and remove 80 to 90 percent of your manual processes.

Remember those 200 daily regulatory changes I talked about at the beginning of this chapter? What if you had a system that could monitor all those changes, condense the wordy and complicated language into skimmable abstracts, and notify you only when it found a change that applied to your business? Using AI to do that work for you might get you a piece of that $3.4 billion.

TIP

You can also turn the focus of your AI engine inward to monitor your own contracts, policies, and documents to assure that contracts and policies are updated and that your teams comply to regulations and proactively adjust when actual practice veers away from compliance.

You might even want to extend your focus to monitoring your social media exposure, because the SEC is already there. In 2018, the SEC fined boxer Floyd Mayweather Jr. $614,775 and music producer DJ Khaled $152,725 for promoting cryptocurrencies via social media without revealing that they had been paid to do so. If the SEC has a boxer and a producer on their radar, it's a good bet your organization is on it too.

The first wave of GDPR-readiness involved companies doing the bare minimum to become GDPR-compliant by the deadline, however manual or inefficient their processes. Smart organizations are moving to the second wave. This phase features the move from a checkbox, penalty-avoidance culture to developing a culture of digital ethics and true information governance. Organizations that internalize a privacy-first culture integrate and centralize privacy processes and optimize those processes through automation. They see data privacy as the right thing to do, a key principle that must be embedded into all facets of the business.

Building an Arsenal

The ability of AI to process large volumes of data with speed and accuracy can transform regulatory compliance. In the short term, you can use the technology to assist business leaders in understanding compliance requirements easily and take apposite action. Eventually, the continued use of AI in regulatory compliance can eliminate the need for humans to stay down in the weeds when it comes to compliance and risk.

AI uses unstructured data mining, robotic process automation, statistical data aggregation, and natural-language processing to read and interpret compliance documents, interpret metadata, pinpoint roles and relationships, and cognitive-process automation to deliver concise, actionable insights.

AI uses supervised and unsupervised learning, natural-language processing, and intelligent segmentation to capture, analyze, and filter possible compliance violations to filter out false positives that waste the time of compliance officers.

AI uses machine learning to automate the workflow of compliance departments.

AI uses structured and unstructured data mining and natural-language processing to monitor internal and external records, documents, and social media to detect errors, violations, and trends to allow your compliance department to be proactive and avoid costly penalties.

AI uses natural-language processing, statistical data aggregation, and machine learning to detect fraudulent activity.

AI uses robotic process automation, natural-language processing, and machine learning to identify potential violations of KYC and AML regulations.

Accenture reports that because of alarm saturation, most security teams only look at 5 percent of the alert flags they receive. AI uses unsupervised machine learning to rapidly assess security notifications to identify the high-risk attempts and point your team to the situations most in need of intervention.

Examining the Use Cases

Due to an abundance of data and well-defined parameters, artificial intelligence is well suited to take on managing regulatory compliance and legal risk.

Manage third-party risk

A well-managed supply chain can give you a competitive advantage. However, that advantage can turn into a liability if you don't monitor and manage risk. AI augments third-party risk management by reviewing relevant documents, such as transactions, status reports, and performance reviews, classifying high and low performers, identifying compliant and noncompliant partners, and flagging anomalies for human review. Using AI scales up your productivity while improving the quality of your decisions.

Manage operational risk

A Risk.net survey ranked the top five risks for 2019:

>> Data compromise

>> IT disruption

>> IT failure

>> Organizational change

>> Theft and fraud

It practically looks like a list of AI use cases.

A 2017 McKinsey study identified five building blocks for addressing operational risk:

>> Improve the quality of risk management data.

>> Embed advanced analytics.

>> Strengthen risk controls.

>> Foster a strong risk culture.

>> Bolster people and skills.

A follow-on white paper explored how AI, and specifically machine learning, can address those building blocks:

>> AI can perform labor-intensive, time-consuming tasks quickly and accurately, giving high-value employees more time to devote to the areas of operational risk that require a human touch.

>> AI can process freeform text descriptions to extract relevant information and insights that have lain dormant in your data for years.

>> AI can acquire information from a wide array of unstructured sources such as social media, email, voice mail, and others, and summarize the content and sentiment in that data to bring new intelligence and insight to support operational risk decisions.

>> In the course of developing AI projects to address operational risk and taking actions on the insights, your team gain skills that strengthen their effectiveness and the risk-aware culture.

>> AI introduces economies of scale that free your team to expand their understanding and skill to better engage the risk landscape.

Monitor compliance risk

Are you paying one employee in ten to keep an eye on the other nine, like HSBC? Would you like to change that to 1 out of 20 or better? Or you can look at the other side of the equation. Would you like to minimize your risk of a headline-making fine from the regulatory agency of your choice?

TIP

You can use AI to monitor internal and external records, documents, and social media to detect errors, violations, and trends that indicate potential violations of regulations, such as KYC and AML, to filter out time-consuming and budget-busting false positives to free up your compliance officers to be proactive in catching actual violations early and avoid costly penalties. Scan incoming documents for compliance before introducing them to your system. These are some potential uses:

>> **Life sciences:** Off-label promotion, misbranding, drug pricing, inflated or inappropriate spending on travel and expenses, payment anomalies, kickbacks, over-utilization of specific providers, non-policy payments to providers or speaker program attendees

>> **Healthcare:** Data privacy, drug pricing, contracts (physician and non-physician), patient access, pharmacy dispensing and security, joint ventures, third-party vendors, coding, and charge capture

>> **Finance:** Money laundering, sanction and embargo violations, bribery, corruption, fraud, financing terrorism, insider trading, market manipulation, transparency requirements, or conflict of interest

>> **Legal:** Segregating client funds, conflict of interest, billing practices, data privacy, or fiduciary duty

Monitor changes in regulations

Are you spending lots of money on compliance, like the 40 percent of businesses spending more than $10 million a year? Would you like to reduce that?

TIP

You can use AI to read and interpret compliance documents, interpret metadata, and pinpoint roles and relationships to cut through all the legalese and techno-speak to identify only the rules that apply to your business.

Maintain data privacy

Data privacy cuts across all organizations that touch money, but some industries have even more rules to deal with, such as those that store health information or personally identifiable information. Anyone who touches legal proceedings faces the task of redacting privileged or restricted information. AI can monitor access to information and perform bulk redaction when necessary.

Maintain data security

Is your data security team like the majority of teams who look at only 5 percent of the alert flags they get because of alert saturation? AI can help make your facility more secure by processing security notifications and categorizing them to help your team focus on the situations most in need of intervention.

Detect fraud and money laundering

The ability of AI to synthesize big data across numerous internal and external sources at a scale that is beyond the capability of humans provides a powerful capability to anticipate risks facing corporations today, such as bribery, theft, fraud, contractual malfeasance, and political corruption.

AI can quickly recognize subtle patterns of fraud previously observed across billions of accounts to detect overlooked forms of suspicious behavior. Traditional approaches to detecting fraud and money laundering involve monitoring transactions and flagging problem transactions for review based on a set of rules, such as transfers to blacklisted people, organizations, and countries, or transactions over a specific amount. The rules can be more sophisticated, but this approach generates up to 98 percent false positives, cases where flagged transactions are actually legitimate, according to Reuters.

In addition, the bad guys are always finding new ways to sneak money out of an account, and a rules-based approach won't detect these innovative methods of committing fraud or laundering money.

TIP

You can use AI-based detection and unsupervised machine learning to learn the characteristics of common behavior (most transactions look like this) and anomalous behavior (this transaction looks different) without labeling them as good or bad. This approach will detect unusual activity that may not fit a known pattern but should be investigated.

You can also use AI to screen names more intelligently. A traditional name search matches one string against another, but if the name is written differently, the system doesn't mark it as a match. It could be something as simple as order (last-name-first instead of first-name-first), or as complicated as colloquial variants, such as using Chuccho or Chuy instead of Jesus, or Pancho or Paco instead of Francisco. When you add the possibilities of abbreviations, titles, and misspellings, you can see a simple text search is unlikely to return a false negative. AI can use fuzzy search and natural-language processing to include not only obscure name variations but also demographic data and other information to overcome these obstacles to name screening.

In addition, AI can go beyond analyzing transaction data to scrape information from websites and social networks and to correlate data from emails with news stories, social mentions and stock prices to spot potentially troubling patterns.

One real-life AI-driven AML pilot saw dramatic results for transaction flagging and name screening. For transactions, the system increased true positives by 5 percent and reduced false positives by 40 percent. For name screening, the system reduced false positives on names of corporations by 50 percent and names of individuals by 60 percent.

Optimize workflow

TIP

You can use AI to automate the workflow of compliance departments, allowing end-users to quickly compile information from multiple data sources and present the results in a consistently formatted document, whether it is a standard report or an ad hoc request regarding a specific issue.

Chapter **24**

Knowledge Assistants and Chatbots: Monetizing the Needle in the Haystack

Sixty years after Peter Drucker coined the term *knowledge worker,* it hardly has meaning anymore. Practically anyone who works in an office steps into the knowledge worker role at some point during the day.

It is the best of times; it is the worst of times. Unlike earlier times when data was scarce and difficult to acquire, you currently live in a data-rich environment. According to some experts, 90 percent of the data in the world was generated in the last two years. Consequently, at any given time, it is increasingly difficult to find the information you need. According to a McKinsey report, employees spend 19 percent of their workweek searching and gathering information. That's one day a week just trying to find what they need to do their job.

Organizations in every market are turning to AI-powered knowledge assistants to remove operational inefficiency by allowing customers to find answers without waiting in a support queue, streamlining back-office processes, reducing risk and compliance costs, and much more.

Missing the Trees for the Forest

Why is it so hard to find things? Because they are scattered all over the place, sometimes locked up in those infamous data silos, sometimes duplicated on multiple platforms — one version on a hard drive (yours or someone else's), another version on a cloud platform, a duplicate or a different version on a different cloud platform, and yet another version in someone's email inbox.

For example, consider the life-cycle of the documents associated with a typical project. The data starts locally on your hard drive, and you share it with internal team members, clients, or partners via email. Some of the relevant information might be in the body of the email, in attachments, or stored somewhere else with a link pointing to it. Eventually, the team migrates some of the documents to a collaboration platform, and now you can add another repository and messaging to the mix. The final work is scattered across multiple platforms, secured in a dozen silos. Not only is it difficult to find information when needed, but it's also difficult to holistically evaluate where things stand because the information is dispersed.

This situation becomes a problem when you need to summarize or act on information that spans multiple repositories or email threads, or when a boss or a client calls to learn the current status of a project. It becomes more problematic when someone leaves the organization and the person who takes on the project needs access to information in the departed coworker's email folders. In some situations, regulations require that information related to a project be archived, such as in the case of a legal hold notification.

Recognizing the problem

This problem isn't limited to internal processes. Customers face similar issues when shopping or trying to resolve a technical difficulty. Many organizations still rely on static web pages and frequently asked questions (FAQs) to help customers and employees complete tasks. And FAQs keep growing. For example, the FAQ on the Canadian open government portal has 59 questions in 12 categories and is 21 pages long when printed out.

Often, the user must leave the process, search for information, and navigate to a different page or call customer support. Failure to find what they're looking for can result in an abandoned transaction, such as booking a hotel or flight or submitting an application.

Consider a customer who has selected a flight and is ready to complete the purchase. Any issue can derail the process, such as trying to find the cost of checking in a bag or determining whether they can add it to the booking at a later date. A customer routed to the FAQ section uses an average of four to five clicks to locate the relevant information.

Enter the intelligent knowledge assistant (IKA), a special kind of virtual assistant optimized to locate data across data types, repository boundaries, and application platforms.

Defining terms

The electronic assistant space is crowded with conflicting terminology and functions — personal assistant, virtual assistant, and intelligent assistant, among others.

Apple calls Siri an intelligent assistant, although that might be debatable because Siri scores lower than Alexa, Cortana, and Google Assistant in providing correct answers to questions, according to a Reuters test. Microsoft calls Cortana a digital assistant. Google calls Google Assistant a virtual assistant. Amazon calls Alexa a cloud-based voice service. No wonder it can get confusing. Whatever they call themselves, they serve a similar function, to provide general information regarding a wide range of topics, from dictionary definitions to weather to business hours for a store, and everything else out there on the Internet.

Then there's the chatbot space. Siri and the other well-known assistants can be thought of as *open domain chatbots.* The helpful little avatar on a webpage that you typically think of as a chatbot is a *closed domain chatbot,* devoted to a specific knowledge base, such as technical support or sales support for a product set or company. Although some think of closed domain chatbots as having limited use, the reality is that they are much more powerful for customer service. Limiting their expertise to a specific domain turns a chatbot into an expert that knows much about a specific topic, as opposed to the open domain chatbots, which know a little about many topics, but can't go very deep into anything.

Although chatbots are improving, a 2018 Computer Generated Solutions report showed that roughly half of customers would rather talk to a human than a chatbot, mostly when they thought the issue was too complex or unusual for the chatbot to resolve.

REMEMBER

Like a chatbot, an IKA is also focused on a defined body of knowledge or corporate knowledge base, but with a more powerful and nuanced search engine behind it. For example, some IKAs generate relevancy scores for metadata fields such as MIME type, content fields like keywords, and work-product fields such as privacy. Like any search, they list specific document results, but also suggest additional search categories.

Hearing the Tree Fall

IKAs are used in diverse contexts, including academic research, fact checking, data security management, customer service, sales support, enterprise search, employee on-boarding, and legal practice.

In the legal profession, it was long assumed that when it comes to legal review, a manual search using a full-text document retrieval system was the most thorough and accurate method of selecting documents for relevancy.

A 1985 study should have derailed this assumption. In the study, a team of two lawyers and two paralegals used full-text computer search to manually review 40,000 documents comprising 350,000 pages and declared they had found at least 75 percent of the relevant documents. However, they had found only 20 percent of the relevant documents. Additional studies have confirmed the fallibility of the manual human review.

Compare that study to an actual 2018 case in which a nonprofit had to respond to broad government subpoenas that affected more than one million documents stored in 125GB of mailbox data. A team of only six lawyers used an IKA to narrow the data. They configured metadata filters to rapidly filter the dataset according to document creation date, sent date, and other time-based filters to eliminate data that was outside the scope of the subpoena. They further culled records based on domain information by filtering out specific custodians and communications that would trigger privilege. Samples that returned rich results were fast tracked into a review workflow aided by predictive coding, an eDiscovery process that uses the principles of supervised learning. The algorithm created a data model that suggested similar documents for review. The team achieved compliance with document obligations pursuant to the government subpoena.

REMEMBER

An IKA goes beyond the simple text and keyword search used by most search engines. When deployed in an enterprise environment, it executes a federated search using concepts instead of keywords. This approach transcends departmental silo boundaries to find key documents, identify relevant authors and internal subject matter experts, and provide a global view of projects.

WHAT AN IKA CAN DO

During document production for legal case, some people's names will be known to the system and will be identified as a judge, attorney, prosecutor, and so on. When unknown names arise, the system can go beyond the knowledge base to a general search to fill in gaps in the knowledge base. Here are a few more examples of what an IKA can do:

- Using an IKA connected to customer care tickets, a customer service agent can easily find out who worked on a specific version of the product.

- An IKA can arrange documents in a timeline to assist in tracking down a specific window and suggest additional queries to pursue, ranked by prevalence to indicate their degree of relevance.

- Multinational organizations can detect and filter documents by desired languages to narrow down the results.

Most IKAs allow you to customize the interface; control user access and security levels; and incorporate expert annotations, ontologies, and taxonomies to influence retrieval and relevance rankings.

Making Trees from Acorns

Knowledge assistants date back more than a decade. Early work focused on creating search interfaces that could access multiple data sources while shielding the user from the complexity of interacting with each data source.

The process of creating a knowledge base is fairly straightforward, if a bit labor-intensive:

1. Convert topics of interest into questions.
2. Expand the questions into tokens, keywords, and query words (who, what when, where, why, and how).
3. Build the knowledge base using machine learning and natural-language processing to identify entities, persons, and relationships.
4. Build the proximity rules to relate tokens, keywords, and query words.
5. Add variants of the tokens, keywords and query words.
6. Insert the official answers into the knowledge base as attributes.

7. Customize and brand the user interface.

8. Configure the knowledge assistant with a text-mining engine.

9. Use the knowledge base (process questions using natural-language processing to match answers in the knowledge base).

AI uses continuous machine learning and conceptual analysis to return more accurate search results. The IKA securely crawls and indexes information from any source, including document management systems, intranets, email archives, contact management databases, and websites. From the indices, based on content and extended metadata, it creates concept models tailored to the information contained within the enterprise. These concept models significantly improve the quality of enterprise search results by identifying related information across different sources and ranking search results by relevance. As documents change and new information is added, the IKA incrementally crawls and updates the models, ensuring that search results are accurate and current.

AI uses entity and concept extraction to identify and automatically redact sensitive information in individual documents or across entire datasets.

Examining the Use Cases

The use cases for an intelligent knowledge assistant are restricted only by the imagination of the developers.

Customer support

In a recent survey, 65 percent of users preferred interacting with a chatbot over waiting in a service queue to get help from a human. And 69 percent of companies using chatbots cited savings on operations as a primary benefit.

You can use chatbots like the one shown in Figure 24-1 to handle large volumes of customer questions and requests, conversing with hundreds of users simultaneously 24 hours a day, which frees up human agents to be more productive handling calls that require the human touch. In addition, you can improve products and services by mining all those text conversations for insight into what customers really want.

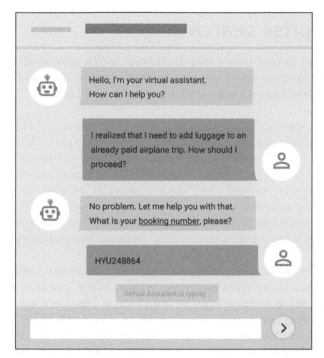

FIGURE 24-1:
A customer support issue handled by a chatbot/virtual assistant.

Legal practice

As a document-rich environment, legal practice is especially suited for IKAs. Predictive coding takes advantage of the strength of continuous machine learning to accurately categorize and tag documents to optimize labor-intensive processes such as eDiscovery, producing the most accurate and defensible predictive coding available.

TIP

You can use a privacy-aware IKA to automatically detect and redact sensitive or privileged information, such as personally identifiable information (PII), payment card industry (PCI), and protected health information (PHI) across document sets instantly and eliminate the need for costly pre-imaging.

You can use a Hypergraph-enabled IKA to illustrate the connections between parties, email conversations, and chat conversations through visualizations, allowing you to understand the connections at a glance and saving valuable time during discovery.

You can add analytics support to an IKA to monitor and share review progress with interactive dashboards, track project data down to the individual coding decisions, or look across entire case portfolios to see aggregated trends.

Enterprise search

It's so hard to find things with traditional search engines that entire websites have sprung up to share complex Boolean phrases, such as this one from the Boolean Search Strings Repository for recruiting on LinkedIn:

```
(cv OR "curriculum vitae" OR resume OR "resum") (filetype:doc
OR filetype:pdf OR filetype:txt) (inurl:profile OR inurl:
cv OR inurl:resume OR initile:profile OR intitle:cv OR
initile:resume) ("project manager" OR "it project manager"
OR "program* manager" OR "data migration manager" OR "data
migration project manager") (leinster OR munster OR ulster
OR connaught OR dublin) -template -sample -example -tutorial
-builder -"writing tips" -apply -advert -consultancy
```

TIP

You can use an IKA to simplify the process of searching by using check boxes to filter the search by repository, date, author, editor, document type, and other elements, and perform a keyword search or, if you don't know the exact word used, a conceptual search. For example, if you don't know which country is mentioned, you can specify a region, such as Asia or Europe, and the search will return results matching every country in the region without your having to create complex Boolean phrases.

Compliance management

Almost daily, the news reports on another breach, another company fined, another settlement.

TIP

You can use an IKA to direct its powerful and versatile search engine to a repository of current regulations, best practice guidelines, breaking news of the current state of the industry and emerging threats, and historical records of litigation, precedents, and outcomes to evaluate relevance to your industry and keep you informed and protected.

Academic research

Every day 5,000 new research papers are published, almost two million a year, adding to the millions of existing papers. Half of them are read by fewer than five people — the author and the editors of the journal that publishes the paper, according to *Smithsonian Magazine*. In addition, information is available in conference reports, articles, heated online discussions, and internal memos at technology companies.

Academic research is also handicapped by the issue that most of these papers are locked up behind a paywall, although there is a growing trend to publish on open access platforms.

TIP

You can use an IKA to scan papers, extract key concepts, cluster the concepts for context, look for synonyms to create conceptual links, and generalize the content across all other scientific papers to accelerate research and development.

Fact checking

TIP

You can use an IKA to scan social media for trending stories, use AI to establish context and sentiment to determine whether the trend is newsworthy and to assess the legitimacy of the source or sources. A journalist can use this information to make a judgment regarding whether to pursue the story.

Chapter **25**

AI-Enhanced Security: Staying Ahead by Watching Your Back

I n every other chapter in this book, the challenge focuses on optimizing processes, streamlining workflows, maximizing revenue, opening new markets, and the like. That's business stuff. A puzzle to be solved, but on the whole, you are working in a nice, friendly, collegial environment with everyone focused on moving toward the same goal.

In this chapter, the challenge is a life-or-death struggle against an actual human adversary, a real living, breathing person whose only goal is to extract as much cash out of you as possible, maybe by siphoning off actual cash, but more likely by hauling off sensitive data that can be monetized elsewhere. And your goal is to stop that bad guy and protect your organization against grievous harm with crippling financial consequences.

It isn't a conference call, it's an arms race. That rather changes things, doesn't it?

The good news is that AI is coming to the rescue with innovative algorithms that make it harder for the bad guys and take much of the load off the good guys. Algorithms that use facial recognition and voice-recognition techniques to recognize malware. Algorithms that find anomalous behavior and block it. Algorithms that isolate the damage and fix it.

Closing the Barn Door

You can assess network and data security in terms of metrics per breach, such as the number of hours unavailable, the number of accounts compromised, the amount of funds stolen, or the size of the fine levied against the organization that failed to adequately secure their data. And those numbers are disturbing enough. But when you look at the bigger picture, the scope of the problem is sobering.

The story in the statistics

The Cisco Visual Networking Index estimates that the number of distributed denial of service attacks will double from 7.9 million in 2018 to 15.4 million in 2023.

Conservative estimates of annual worldwide cybercriminal revenue stack up to $1.5 trillion. According to a Bromium study, if cybercrime was a country, its GDP would equal that of Russia and its economy would rank the thirteenth highest GDP in the world.

Data is the new currency, and everyone from the executives in the boardrooms of corporate offices to the malefactors in the back rooms of the hacker-industrial complex is focused on building a platform to monetize data.

To that end, black-hat coders have commoditized crime, selling easy-to-use, do-it-yourself malware kits, offering cloud-based malware-as-a-service, and scaling their workforce through the use of contingent workers. In recent years, data security engineers have noticed a traditional workday nine-to-five pattern to attacks, even to the point of malicious activity slowing during the lunch hour.

REMEMBER

In the same way that you show up at the office every morning ready to optimize processes to maximize revenue, the bad guys out there show up at the office ready to optimize their workflow to maximize the amount of value they can extract from your network. Somewhere there is a person who stopped by Starbucks to get a skinny iced caramel macchiato with extra sugar-free caramel drizzle before sitting down at their workstation to attack your company. And they are good at what they do. Very good.

Understanding the risk

The first ransomware virus was created in 1989, but it wasn't until 2011 that a wide-scale outbreak hit, facilitated by the development of anonymous payment services and cybercurrency. In 2015, the attackers extended their attention beyond consumers to target county governments and small- and medium-sized businesses. Now, anyone is fair game, from the everyday mobile phone user to city governments such as Baltimore and Atlanta. A 2019 report showed that the average ransom payment was $36,300, the average downtime from an attack was 9.6 days, 8 percent of decrypted data was lost on average, and the total cost of ransomware to businesses and nonprofits was $11.5 billion.

Not only are the cybercriminals expanding the scope of their targets, they are expanding the volume of threats. In 2019, the number of threats had grown to 979 million. At the time of this writing, on average 5,944,111 records are lost or stolen every day, costing U.S. organizations an average of $23.7 million each, and the percentage of companies experiencing a breach has risen more than 27 percent annually. In addition to the cost, new regulations, such as the General Data Protection Regulation and the California Consumer Privacy Act are holding organizations and their executives accountable, adding significantly to the financial impact of an attack.

Without adequate security, malware can stay hidden within your network for days, hoovering up data and causing all kinds of mischief. This is known as *dwell time*. A 2019 Ponemon report found that the average dwell time of a malicious attack was 314 days, including mean time to identify (MTTI, 75 percent) and mean time to contain (MTTC, 25 percent). The cost of a breach increases as the dwell time increases.

Dwell time gives that cybercriminal who found a hole in your defenses time to move laterally within your network, seeking sensitive data and extracting it at their leisure. Consequently, top executives across all industries, both public and private, are focusing their attention on data security risk.

These are possible consequences of a breach:

>> Theft of actual assets

>> Trade secrets exposed

>> Compromise due to espionage

>> Data held hostage

>> Identity theft

>> Compromised or destroyed data

>> Business disruption

>> Regulatory risk

>> Loss of revenue

>> Loss of reputation

Marriott, Equifax, Zendesk, and Capital One are just a few of the many companies that have been sued by their stockholders in a securities class-action lawsuit, with damages calculated by the drop in stock value.

Identifying the source

It may come as a surprise that the person attacking you could be your own employee. Insiders have used their access to stalk people online, sell the personal data of thousands of customers to scammers, and work with foreign governments to track down dissidents.

A 451 Research report named email as the greatest source of security issues (46 percent) and identified these as the top three security pain points:

>> User behavior (28 percent)

>> Phishing (24 percent)

>> Security team staffing (17 percent)

The Ponemon study found that 24 percent of confirmed breaches were caused by human error, 25 percent by system glitches, and 51 percent by malicious or criminal attack, including insiders and external actors.

The state of current solutions

Security solutions available today are generally limited to descriptive and diagnostic analytic capabilities that require manual human intervention. They are increasingly ineffective in responding to the growth in big data, particularly unstructured and hybrid datasets, and are vulnerable to the growing sophistication of the threat vectors used in recent data breaches.

Security teams face numerous challenges, including these:

>> Delayed remediation efforts as a result of the sheer volume of alerts and false positives

- >> Tedious and time-consuming investigation processes that involve using a variety of systems and tools to detect, investigate, and escalate threats

- >> Overwhelmed and over-utilized security operations center analysts

- >> Ever-increasing data volumes as IT infrastructure becomes more diverse

- >> Unresolved security threats

In fact, a 2018 SANS survey found that 32 percent of the respondents were unsure of how many incidents they had not responded to. In the face of a false positive rate of 50 percent, many security teams have taken to tuning the security settings to reduce the number of alerts. The problem with this practice is the potential to increase the number of false negatives, identifying a breach as harmless traffic. It takes only one breach to cause a world of hurt.

Security teams need to effectively prioritize and streamline workloads to focus on what's most important first. But how can organizations quickly identify and investigate threats when they are already struggling as a result of the widespread shortage of security skills? Approximately three million cybersecurity specialist positions worldwide went unfilled for three years running (2017–2019) — this despite 33 percent growth in the number of training programs for cybersecurity skills and 40 percent growth in the number of cybersecurity graduates. With statistics like these, why do three million positions remain unfilled? It's because of a 94 percent growth in the number of job postings requiring cybersecurity skills.

This shortage manifests in oversubscribed workers taking on tasks for which they might not be suited, which in turn leads to more errors, employee burnout, and increased risk of a breach.

Locking the Barn Door

Security analysts spend valuable time sorting through security data using traditional tools. A PwC study revealed that analysts spend more than 50 percent of their time on manual processes. The good news is that this scenario has all the elements of a problem that artificial intelligence is good at solving. It is a data-rich environment. Network logs record the activity of all devices and users. Massive databases document known attack vectors and signatures. Well-defined rules guide the proper response to a threat. All this points to a high chance of success in optimizing the workflow to identify, analyze, investigate, and prioritize security alerts, enabling analysts to focus on coordinating responses.

AI can quickly and efficiently detect cross-channel threats including non-human patterns, spikes of activity outside normal business hours, and other red flags for a more robust and fast-acting response to data security risks that reduces dwell time and thus minimizes the impact of the breach.

Graph analytics uses AI to map the network topology, identify each firewall and its associated rules, and then analyze the logical connections to expose vulnerabilities between endpoints. It catalogs possible routes for an invasion, listing the rules for each firewall in the route. This method helps in thwarting multi-step attacks by identifying possible steppingstones to the target.

TIP

With the ability to sort, classify, and cluster both structured and unstructured data, an AI-enhanced security solution evolves with your organization, continuously improving and using predictive insights to stay ahead of hackers and other data security threats. AI can also be paired with analytics to create powerful slice and dice visualizations and leverage natural-language generation (NLG) to describe notable issues in visualizations to reveal unique threats and anomalous behavior while quickly prioritizing threat events.

An AI-enhanced security solution can also be supplemented with automation and orchestration solutions to execute responsive actions via triggers and workflows. This integration can boost productivity by providing analysts with context about the alerts, recommending next steps, and automating actions to improve the speed of investigations and remediation.

A 2019 Accenture study looked at the cost of cybercrime to enterprises with 5,000 employees to see how they can mitigate those costs and realize savings. They estimated that from 2019 to 2023, $5.2 trillion of total assets will be placed at risk of cybercrime globally.

Automation, AI, and advanced analytics can be used to investigate cybercrime and enhance recovery efforts, while addressing the shortage of technical staff, offering an estimated net cost savings of $2.09 million annually.

Security and user behavior analytics can improve forensic capabilities to achieve an estimated cost savings of $1.72 million annually by efficiently gaining insights on the origin of an attack, how the breach happened, what resources were compromised, and what data was lost, along with a timeline for the incident. Having a mature security program can reduce the time it takes to identify and eradicate a threat. The Ponemon report found that an incident response team with a plan can reduce the cost of a breach by $680,000.

TIP

Using AI to detect and reduce risk can automate data validation and ensure compliance to avoid regulation-related penalties. For example, GDPR authorizes agencies to impose fines of up to €20 million or four percent of a company's total global annual turnover of the prior financial year, whichever is greater, and other governments are considering similar legislation.

Knowing Which Key to Use

As the IT infrastructure extends beyond the corporate firewall to become an IT superstructure via third-party services, SaaS integrations, managed and unmanaged cloud, and mobile, many IT departments are moving to an AI-powered operations model, known as AIOps, to manage the data-intensive environment. AI-enhanced security plays a part in AIOps by stepping in to deflect the teeming hordes storming the castle gate by monitoring traffic, identifying threats, and automating responses.

This list covers some of the algorithms and techniques used in security.

» AI uses supervised learning, graph analytics, reasoning processes, and automated data-mining systems to optimize manual, error-prone breach investigations, predict outcomes, and detect and identify campaigns, originating threat actors, and related alerts.

» AI leverages supervised learning and, especially, artificial neural networks to build a massive library of markers of hostile code, and then scans incoming data for matches.

» AI uses an analytical columnar engine to ingest, blend, aggregate, and analyze massive volumes of data across different sources (structured, unstructured, web, social, traditional databases, spreadsheets) and perform analysis from the general to the row level.

» AI uses machine learning and security analytics, including user- and entity behavior analytics, to detect external and internal risks earlier and more accurately than a traditional rules-based approach.

» AI uses advanced text mining to process social media feeds and enterprise content repositories to uncover hidden interactions between persons, places, mobile phone numbers, and other entities to build advanced segmentation, which is helpful for internal investigations and risk management.

» AI uses NLP to detect email phishing attempts and applies sophisticated log analyses and identification of access patterns to better detect unusual activity.

As powerful as AI can be, like any science, it comes with challenges introduced by the intersection of math and the complexities of the real world. Security professionals would do well to be mindful of these limitations to avoid the pitfall of having an unwarranted degree of confidence in the efficacy of AI solutions. Here are some of the more common challenges in using algorithms to thwart the adversary:

- » **High dimensionality:** Using many different characteristics, also known as features, coupled with sparse amounts of data for each of these features, increases the difficulty of finding clear definition within the data. Superior machine learning has the benefit of depending on a lean collection of features each with sufficient data to glean clear buckets or classes that emerge from the data. These classes may include what is or is not a threat, or in more refined systems, what level a threat may exist as evidenced by a pattern of data.

- » **Class imbalance:** Class imbalance occurs when data for one class far exceeds the amount of data in another class. For example, with fraud detection, far more examples of transactions typically are not fraudulent compared to those that are fraudulent. Here, the fraud and non-fraud transactions may have so many things in common (given the vast amounts of variability in the non-fraud transactions) that it becomes difficult, if not impossible, to differentiate patterns of fraud from patterns of innocent activity.

- » **One-class issues:** This issue is similar to class imbalance. Here, there is one class and then everything else. Think of a spam filter for email. Some messages are indicative of spam, and then there is all other email received. The problem lies in how to define everything else.

- » **Machine-learning model bias:** In a perfect world, a model operates objectively and thoroughly. When it receives data to be classified as one thing or another (in other words, a threat or not), it does so without bias and in a transparent manner. However, in this imperfect world, the model can be misled. Bias can be unknowingly buried in the data itself; it can be unwittingly introduced by those building and refining the model, and in other ways. In the context of investigations, a model may improperly impact our ability to find the truth, which is our goal in any investigation.

Despite these challenges, data science comes equipped with solutions to accommodate the nuances in the data.

Examining the Use Cases

The cybersecurity arms race is a constant real-time battle of threats and detection.

The bad guy tries to sneak in, find the goods, and sneak them out before you notice. The technical terms for these activities are infiltration, lateral movement, and data exfiltration.

The good guy (that's you) works at keeping the bad guys out, kicking them out when they get in, and fixing what they broke. The technical terms for these activities are detection and remediation.

>> **Detection:** To detect an attack, you must be able to differentiate between legitimate and hostile traffic, either through a set of rules (such as searching an access control list or blocking traffic based on a source or destination address, a port, or a protocol), through identifying suspicious behavior, or through matching a known threat marker.

>> **Remediation:** After you detect an attack in progress, you must thwart the attack by stopping it in its tracks in as many ways as you can. This can include closing off ports and other points of entry, disabling compromised accounts, alerting security personnel and reversing any damage imposed by the attacker. More wily measures include letting the bad guys carry out their nefarious activity while tracking them along the way. The security team then tries to follow the breadcrumbs back to the perpetrators in an effort to identify them.

The battle is a never-ending cycle of thrust and parry. The bad guy thrusts his sword at your network by uploading malware to a server, and you parry it by detecting and blocking that malware. The bad guy tweaks his attack, changing things up, and tries again. This is known as a polymorphic attack, and the bad guys can buy malware development kits that offer polymorphism as a feature. Will your system detect the threat in this new variation?

TIP

The secret to deflecting polymorphic attacks is to train your model on sticky markers, aspects of the malware architecture that will take the bad buys lots of effort to change.

AI uses big data and various algorithms to take the two steps (detect and remediate) to the next level.

Detecting threats by matching a known threat marker

Nearly one billion viruses and malware exist out in the wild. Security tools use various resources to identify malware, the most common in legacy solutions being a library of threat signatures. A signature is an identifier for a virus created by taking a section of code that is unique to the virus and running it through a formula to create a fixed, unique string. That string becomes the ID for the threat record in the threat database. However, this solution is vulnerable to polymorphic attacks.

Because the signature is based on a hash of a specific section of code that implements one or more functions, when the code is modified to accomplish the functions a different way, it produces a different signature. It poses the same threat but gets through the filters because it doesn't match any signatures.

Enter file heuristics, an AI technique used in computer vision, voice recognition, and other pattern matching problems. How does a social media platform recognize toxic content that should be censored? "Computer vision" uses heuristics and artificial neural networks to tell whether someone in a photo is holding a guitar or an assault weapon. It doesn't really know what a gun looks like; it just knows that certain combinations of pixels are more likely to be in a photo of a gun than a photo of a guitar.

AI-powered threat recognition uses the same principles to process binary files at the byte level to determine the probability that the code is malicious.

Detecting breaches by identifying suspicious behavior

While detecting a threat at the infiltration phase is vastly preferred to detecting it during the lateral movement or exfiltration phase, and while file heuristics is more effective than detecting anomalous behavior, if an attack gets past your initial defenses, you can still use AI to detect malicious activity.

AI can process thousands of endpoints to analyze behavior, using machine learning to identify compromised accounts, uncover back-channel communications, expose deviations from the norm over time, and pinpoint processes that are propagating throughout your network.

By identifying anomalous behavior, threat hunting can discover the presence of a cyber-thug in your system earlier in the attack life cycle, initiate automated responses to reduce or contain the threat, and send a full report to your security team so they can quickly initiate an informed response, significantly reducing dwell time and the associated damage.

For most attack types, the security team uses an AI-enhanced security tool to collect data by scanning all endpoints, processes, services, drivers, and users. The wider they cast the net, the better, because the more observations in the sample, the more accurately they can characterize legitimate activity and behavior to develop a baseline for normal conditions. With a baseline built from millions of observations, there's a greater likelihood that they will detect the difference between a normal state and an anomalous state. This approach relies on the law of large numbers, which says that the average of the results obtained from a large number of trials should be close to the true value and will tend to become closer as more trials are performed.

Thus, having access to all endpoints and servers is important for accurate detection of malware, because it provides the AI-enhanced security tool with the big-data source information that machine learning thrives on.

After the data is processed, the AI-enhanced security tool creates a frequency distribution histogram based on the number of occurrences of a process or service to isolate anomalies. Then the AI tool transforms the analyzed data into actionable dashboards that help security analysts identify threats and kick-start responses in minutes.

Masquerade attacks

A common method cybercriminals use to get access to sensitive information or resources is to pretend to be an existing user with privileged rights. With higher access, the attacker can run malware by giving it a name similar to a known legitimate process, leading security tools and system administrators to think the process is benign. Then the code uses process injection or process hollowing to insert or map to malicious code.

Process injection inserts code into an existing live process that points to a malicious DLL inside another process, and then invokes execution by creating a remote thread to access resources allocated to the process, such as memory, system or network resources, and possibly elevated privileges. Process hollowing creates a process in a suspended state and then maps the memory to point to malicious code. In both cases, the malicious code is masked under a legitimate process and is more likely to evade defenses and detection analysis.

An AI-enhanced security tool can search for anomalies in processes, services, drivers, module loads, and behaviors to streamline the workflow of identifying existing threats early before they can achieve a high dwell time.

Process, service, or driver anomalies

One method of detecting malware is to search for suspicious processes, services, or drivers. This proactive method is designed to find a breach that hasn't done anything to draw attention to itself yet. The security team runs daily telemetry scans capturing data. For a process, that could be the process filename, folder, originating company, version, and copyright. For servers and drivers, that could be the service name, service file path, service DLL path, service file hash, and service folder.

The AI-enhanced security tool ingests the data to create a single view of all endpoints and presents the team with the information it needs to identify threats.

Module load anomalies

Often, a process with evil intent generates processor loads or traffic loads that differ from a legitimate process. It may hog resources or spawn subprocesses or transmit traffic at higher volumes or to unknown destinations.

The AI-enhanced security tool monitors the activity of all running modules, particularly their use of resources, and compares it to the activity of known legitimate module profiles to isolate anomalies that might indicate malicious activity.

Behavior anomalies

Using the baseline of regular activities established through machine learning for each user and device, the AI tool identifies any activity that deviates from what is considered normal and flags it as an anomaly for security analysts to investigate.

Remediating attacks

If a cybercriminal attacks endpoint devices on multiple continents, an AI-enhanced security tool can scan and analyze hundreds of systems globally in a matter of days to remediate the risks coming from compromised computers.

In one real-life attack, a cybercriminal threatened the executive team with a doxing attack via emails sent over several days demanding payment in Bitcoin not to release video and photos of them doing inappropriate things.

The AI-enhanced security tool quickly identified and remediated the infected endpoints before other machines were infected. This prompted the company to evaluate their current security policy and procedures and to initiate a standard practice of performing monthly threat-hunting jobs and quarterly tabletop exercises.

4

The Part of Tens

Discover ten ways AI will affect the next decade.

Explore ten reasons why AI is not a panacea to solve all problems.

Chapter **26**

Ten Ways AI Will Influence the Next Decade

This book is devoted to exploring the ways that AI can help you achieve your goals right now. But innovation never sleeps. New breakthroughs in AI and supporting technologies show up in the headlines every day — if you're reading the right publications, that is. Here at the end, I'll dust off my trusty crystal ball and indulge in a little prognostication.

But first, let's get the burning question out of the way. Flying cars? No. Or, at least not ones that look like those in *Back to the Future*. Autonomous cars? They're already here. Now, on to real stuff.

Consider this timeline:

» In the late eighteenth century, the steam engine powered the first industrial revolution.

» One hundred and twenty years later, at the turn of the twentieth century, commercially available electricity sparked the second industrial revolution.

>> Sixty years after that, the first silicon-based computer triggered the third industrial revolution.

>> Thirty years later in 1991, the World Wide Web became publicly available, laying the foundation for big data — along with computing and storage — primary drivers of the fourth industrial revolution.

Hmm, 120 years between the first and second, 60 years between the second and third, 30 years between the third and fourth. Given that timeline, are you wondering what powered the fifth revolution you evidently overlooked in 2006?

Do you think that back in 1989, Tim Berners-Lee, who kicked off the World Wide Web by posting a description of the project in the alt.hypertext newsgroup, had an inkling that with the click of a mouse he had laid the foundation for the longest AI renaissance, a renaissance that has no end in sight?

And so it is for us as we try to imagine what AI will look like decades in the future. The future is a big place. I'll narrow it down to a decade and talk about AI in the Twenties.

Proliferation of AI in the Enterprise

Information will rule the future, and AI will continue to be leveraged to process that information to solve complex challenges. Today's limits in AI will continue to be surpassed, and applications will double across a broad range of industries.

In retail, you'll see AI maximize cross-selling by providing hyper-personalizing content through intelligent recommendations, while manufacturers will increase margins through predictive maintenance, which maximizes the usable life of equipment and reduces costly downtime. In real estate, AI will be utilized to analyze massive amounts of data on past home sales, school districts, transportation, and traffic patterns to accurately project future value of homes and cost per square foot. In HR and recruiting, AI will accelerate the talent sourcing process by screening resumes 15 times faster than a human to identify the best candidates. In healthcare, AI will assist in medical, legal, and regulatory review for pharmaceutical companies to verify the development and marketing of new medication that complies with all legal requirements.

As these industries rely on more data from users, AI will continue to advance, learn, and innovate the enterprise.

AI Will Reach Across Functions

Cross-functional teams, sometimes referred to as centers of excellence (CoEs), will empower organizations to create effective AI projects. These teams will represent the entire organization and will include individuals with business knowledge, IT experience, and specialized AI skills such as data engineers, data scientists, subject matter experts, and project managers.

Often they will include members embedded in lines of business — like ops, sales, marketing, and R&D — to ensure the work is aligned to deliver on departmental mandates such as reducing costs, growing revenue, or unlocking new business models. At the same time, the best organizations will have members in a centralized IT or IT-like function to scale learning from different departments across the entire organization, and will ensure compute power and access to data is provisioned. This type of dual hub-and-spoke setup — where the lines of business (LOBs) are the spokes and IT is the hub to help scale — is widely seen as a best practice for AI COEs.

In either case, these teams will identify use cases and manage a digital platform that supports collaboration on key business initiatives. They must also partner with the right vendor who has the tools and expertise needed to help the organization kick-start a successful AI journey. Combining internal and external resources will be imperative to building and executing powerful AI projects that see the light of day and provide real business value instead of getting locked in some corner of the office.

AI R&D Will Span the Globe

Currently the bulk of the new work in AI happens in the traditional loci of technological innovation. But you can't fence in AI. Even now it's escaping the compound and running off to emerging markets like Brazil, Russia, India, and China; however, as the knowledge required and tools to deploy become more and more open and available, AI will and should continue to expand farther, from Kenya to Kansas, Turkey to Trinidad, and beyond. This trend will increase as people all over the world enlist AI in their efforts to address their unique challenges.

The Data Privacy Iceberg Will Emerge

While regulations such as Europe's General Data Protection Regulation (GDPR) and the California Consumer Privacy Act (CCPA) have already been established, new regulatory developments regarding data privacy continue to emerge. Although these regulations have some differences, the fundamental intent of data privacy laws is to give consumers the right to know what types of personally identifiable information (PII) are collected, how the information is collected, and how to exercise the option to remove or take legal action in the event that consumers incur damages from bias or data security breaches.

Until now, most organizations have focused their efforts on structured information, but they must also be able to understand what PII is located in textual data and documents. Archived documents, in particular, are an especially pressing concern for most enterprises. AI-powered solutions will be instrumental in locating sensitive data and managing it through automated workflows. Organizations will also need to establish internal data governance practices to determine who is accountable for data security and enterprise-wide policy, which may include creating teams that blend technical and regulatory expertise, as well as augmenting those teams with AI-powered solutions to help facilitate the same.

More Transparency in AI Applications

In both the private and public sectors, more organizations will recognize the need to develop strategies to mitigate bias in AI and to explain outcomes. With issues such as amplified prejudices in predictive crime mapping, organizations will build in checks in both AI technology itself and their people processes by ensuring that their data samples are sufficiently robust to minimize subjectivity and yield trustworthy insights. Data collection will evolve beyond selective datasets that mirror historical bias to more accurately reflect reality.

In addition, teams responsible for identifying business cases and creating and deploying machine-learning models will represent a rich blend of backgrounds, views, and characteristics. Organizations will also test machines for biases, train AI models to identify bias, and appoint an HR or ethics specialist to collaborate with data scientists, thereby ensuring cultural values are being reflected in AI projects.

At the time of this writing, AI software solutions and features have also been emerging that evaluate AI risk in terms of explainability, bias, fairness, and robustness, to help remediate the same issues the technology enabled to begin with.

Augmented Analytics Will Make It Easier

With a massive amount of information becoming more available to organizations, augmented analytics will become the favored choice for processing data and running business intelligence operations. Through advancements in embedding AI and ML techniques, augmented analytics will help continue to pave new ways to lower the barrier for broader data and analytics use with even less training required, such as asking questions from data with natural-language queries (NLQ), graph and chart recommendations based on the data selected or present, or smart preparation of data based on associative logic, rules, or models. These smart-data discovery features will continue to develop, understand, and optimize analytics experiences.

With it, you'll continue to see major adjustments in the business intelligence market, with an upward trend of enterprise buyers purchasing more of these augmented tools and applications and incorporating them into their data practices. As a result, the roles of computer programmers and software developers will shift back to support building core features for their business. And the roles of data scientists and data engineers in the enterprise will shift from business analyst work they are often pulled away to do because a companies' lack of overall analytics literacy, back to focus on the more complex data projects and models they were hired to tackle from the start.

Rise of Intelligent Text Mining

Organizations will increasingly use sophisticated AI solutions to contextually classify and derive meaning from all types of content, including structured, semi-structured, and unstructured content. Gartner has estimated as much as 80 percent of enterprise content is unstructured, which leaves a vast pool of information for companies to leverage. Data within these emails, customer service transcripts, and other textual documents can provide real business value, as well as insights on which key business decisions can be made. Through intelligent text mining, AI solutions can quickly read and understand huge stores of content for accurate synopses and sentiment analysis, thereby allowing organizations to rapidly access the insights that demand the greatest level of attention.

Chatbots for Everyone

The average consumer may converse with a chatbot more than they speak with coworkers, family members, or even their spouse, as the demand for an instant response at any time continues to bubble up. With their advanced contextual capabilities that can personalize any experience through deep learning, chatbots will prevail as the next preferred digital interface.

As chatbots dominate human interactions more than ever, consumer-facing businesses that want to stay competitive will incorporate these humanlike AI personas into their service. Additionally, chatbot implementation will expand into the workplace in new ways to help with recruiting, training (via knowledge assistants), and overall efficiency (via virtual assistants), becoming more intertwined with all facets of life.

Ethics Will Emerge for the AI Generation

Children born since 2010 make up the AI generation, those who have never known a world without the daily influence of AI. Yet, because many children will use AI-powered toys, programs, and educational software long before they develop critical thinking skills, it is up to adults to enforce ethical uses of AI. This will mean helping children establish logic to question the credibility of information and its sources, along with holding companies accountable for their products and practices intended for young audiences. Companies must establish transparent policies about how information is collected and used in toys, educational software, games, and apps. Specifically, software used in the classroom must be devoid of bias that could deny children educational opportunities. Parents and educators must also familiarize themselves with the products and programs their children are using, supervise their use, and watch closely for any signs of bias or invasions of privacy.

Rise of Smart Cities through AI

Smart cities are coming of age. The next phase in this evolution will be a significant roll-out of smart city AI implementation. Large organizations have long utilized AI and analytics to turn unstructured data into more actionable insights. Now, artificial intelligence is opening the door for applications and networks outside of the workplace to harness big data more intelligently and engage with citizens in new ways and, as a result, make cities more efficient and sustainable.

For example, AI can transform a city's infrastructure and power utilization and can also make strides in public safety and healthcare, and can even make public parking more efficient. Cities will utilize smart technology to find innovative solutions to some of their most pressing urban challenges. AI will usher in even greater opportunities to make the smart city dream more of a reality.

Ultimately, advancements in analytics and artificial intelligence has enabled humans to do so many things that weren't possible just a few years ago, and we are just scratching the surface. With the turn of the decade, AI adoption and implementation will continue to soar to new heights, painting a future that is digital first and full of possibilities.

Chapter **27**

Ten Reasons Why AI Is Not a Panacea

They say it's a poor workman who blames his tools. After all, can humans really blame AI for doing what we built it to do? You should view this not as a list of faults but as a list of limitations.

They also say that a good workman uses the right tool for the job. There are some jobs that AI is not suited for. That's why we still need humans.

Until the robot apocalypse, of course.

The future is already here — it's just not very evenly distributed.
— WILLIAM GIBSON

AI Is Not Human

The world is experiencing an AI renaissance because the technological stars have aligned to give us the gift of practical AI. By the technological stars, of course I mean big data, low-cost storage for that data, advanced computing power, and increasingly effective algorithms.

As we continue to expand the domain of practical AI to address more problems through increases in efficiency and accuracy, some might get the impression that the AI renaissance will usher in a new golden age, a cyber-utopia where we will bask in the shade of a linen canopy while our machine-based servants fan us with palm leaves and peel grapes for us.

Okay, I might have gone a bit too far, but only in the service of making a point. While I am second to none in advocating the value of AI to drive efficiency and accuracy, I don't embrace the view that AI can solve every problem.

AI is just a machine, perhaps the most powerful machine built to date, but still only a machine. Humans build machines to magnify a human capability, to travel faster, lift heavy things, see and hear things that are far away, or calculate solutions faster.

REMEMBER

But machines can't magnify the capabilities we value the most, the attributes that make us uniquely human. I'm talking about curiosity, creativity, empathy, and ethics.

You may recall the story about King Solomon resolving the conflict between two women, each claiming a single baby as her own son. Solomon in his wisdom proposed an extreme form of shared custody whereby they cut the baby in half with a sword, one half for each mother. This ploy revealed the true mother, who offered to relinquish custody to spare the baby's life.

An AI model might come to the same conclusion, but as a serious suggestion, not as a litmus test. Why? Because algorithms don't possess those defining human traits.

Perhaps one day an AI model might be able to detect the difference between an awkward pause and the comfortable silence of two old friends enjoying each other's company, but I suspect that day is at least tens, if not hundreds, of years away.

REMEMBER

With a shockingly small amount of information, humans use subtle skills such as common sense and instinct to make big decisions, and often very good decisions. If we turn to AI to resolve the intractable problems of our age, regardless of its advanced capabilities, it won't come up with a creative solution. It will amplify the bias inherent in the data or in the model or both, because it has no capability to question or evaluate the quality, relevance, and freshness of the data used to train it.

I offer a few examples of why a human must be involved at the beginning, in the middle, and at the end of any decision made by a machine.

Pattern Recognition Is Not the Same As Understanding

Given the right data, machine learning can quickly establish correlations to perform a specific task very well. It learns to connect the dots, but it doesn't *understand* why the dots are connected.

Consider predictive text, which uses an algorithm called *k nearest neighbor (KNN)*. The algorithm looks at the last few words you wrote and compares them to groups of words from the training data. Based on the words that followed similar groups of words in the past, and taking into consideration your personal communication proclivities, it fills in the word that seems most likely to follow.

But here is where we see that pattern recognition is not understanding. The Smart Reply feature in Gmail sometimes suggests "I love you" as an appropriate response to a work email.

That's a raging case of being not clear on the concept. Yes, it's a trivial example, but it is indicative of a larger issue.

WARNING

Because AI can be quick and accurate, humans can be seduced into the illusion that it understands the world, when in reality it is only good at the game of "one of these things is not like the others." Or maybe it *is* like the others, depending on the application.

It took years of work to develop AI to the point where it could recognize a dog in a photo, something a child can do before its second birthday, but it still has a hard time telling the difference between a chihuahua and a blueberry muffin.

The State of California requires at least six hours of in-car driving lessons with a licensed driving instructor to get your license. Compare that to the Waymo algorithm's 10 billion miles of simulation training and 10 million miles of real-world driving, and it's still not licensed to drive in California.

REMEMBER

Pattern matching does not equal understanding.

At the 2018 U.S. congressional hearings, Facebook CEO Mark Zuckerberg said his company was using AI tools to help moderate hate speech, terrorist propaganda, and other toxic content, but the reality is that while machine learning can recognize patterns and perform sentiment analysis, as of this writing it still cannot understand tone, context, sarcasm, irony, or a host of other markers of toxic content.

Certainly, AI is a great tool for streamlining and automating tedious, repetitive tasks, but it will not usher in the next golden era of civic understanding. Bringing AI to bear on mind-numbing bureaucracy might make government more efficient, but it won't automatically make it more inclusive or fair. Because AI doesn't really understand anything. It's just good at finding correlations really fast.

And that's enough for me.

AI Cannot Anticipate Black Swan Events

Before 1606, if you asked a resident of the western hemisphere the color of a swan, you would get one answer: white. The answer would be based on millennia of sightings of millions of white swans. Nobody would have even considered the possibility that a swan could be any other color.

Then, in 1606, the Dutch and the Spanish independently stumbled upon Australia, and a known fact was obliterated.

In his 2007 book, *The Black Swan*, Nassim Nicholas Taleb defines a black swan event using three attributes:

>> It is an outlier, outside the realm of regular expectations, because nothing in the past points to its possibility.

>> It carries an extreme impact.

>> Humans create post facto explanations for how the event was inevitable and predictable.

Other examples of black swan events include Mt. Vesuvius destroying Pompeii and the 1929 stock market crash.

By now, I'll bet you know where this is going. Think about the four kinds of analytics (see Chapter 1 for more details):

» Descriptive

» Diagnostic

» **Predictive**

» Prescriptive

If machine learning can produce predictive analytics, why can't it predict a black swan event?

You know the answer. Because ML is trained on historical data. It can't predict options that aren't represented in the training data. A black swan has no precedent, so ML will not predict it.

In a rather grim example, after the 2015 Paris terrorist attack that killed 130 people and wounded more than 400 others, Facebook built a system to identify terrorist propaganda and flag it for removal. The mission expanded to automatically remove other prohibited content before users see it, such as nudity (96 percent effective) and hate speech (65 percent effective).

But these are all known issues. The system wasn't prepared to intercept live-streaming of the 2019 shootings in Christchurch, New Zealand, where a gunman attacked two mosques, killing 51 people. It took Facebook days to scrub the video from its site, removing 1.5 million copies in the first 24 hours. Twitter and YouTube had similar problems keeping it off their platforms with their own AI-powered moderation tools.

Given the scale of the toxic-content problem, AI is the only tool that can even approach policing social media, but it can't catch everything.

Judea Pearl, who developed Bayesian networks, is taking AI research beyond fitting a probabilistic curve onto the data and toward identifying causal relationships, which might get AI one step closer to speculating a what-if scenario. But we aren't there yet.

AI Might Be Democratized, but Data Is Not

From the dawn of serious AI development in the mid-twentieth century up to the end of the millennium, AI was largely an ivory-tower exercise presided over by the high priests and priestesses of data science. Now, in the early decades of the twenty-first century, the tools for benefiting from practical AI are widely available.

However, of the three pillars of AI — processing power/scalable storage, algorithms (now mostly available "open source"), and big data — big data is the least available to "the people."

Most enterprises have a wealth of internal data, although in some cases it might be trapped in silos like Rapunzel in the tower. In addition to stored data, your organization probably has lots of data flowing through it like a river of potential information in the form of orders, invoices, emails, documents, spreadsheets, and so on. You can use multiple ways to capture that stuff. And you can also buy data or rent it in the form of customer demographic studies and such.

However, for the public sector, it's a different story. In addition to the challenge of the previous paragraph, public sector organizations often lack the resources to take advantage of the data:

>> Private data is usually proprietary, protected by the corporations that use it as a competitive differentiator.

>> Public data is often siloed, buried in bureaucracy, protected by privacy and authorization barriers, or air-gapped in offline archives.

And for the people, individual citizens or groups who desire to engage in grassroots efforts to use AI for the good of mankind, data can be even harder to acquire.

AI Is Susceptible to Inherent Bias in the Data

We are currently not suffering from a shortage of bias in AI. Or in the human world, for that matter — but for now AI is under the microscope.

#RacialBias

In 2013, a Harvard professor published a paper showing that a person's name influenced the ads that Google served. Traditionally black names were served ads about searching for arrest records. Traditionally white names were not served similar ads.

#GenderBias

In 2016, a team of researchers from Carnegie Mellon University noticed a disparity in the ads served to users after a search for executive-level jobs. They created a tool to track how user attributes influence the personalized Google ads served. The tool tracked the ad-delivery results of multiple fake accounts with identical browser histories except for one detail. Some accounts listed the sex as male and others as female. Google showed ads for high-paying executive jobs to the male group at a rate of almost six times that of the female group — 1,852 versus 318.

But that was a long time ago. The industry has probably fixed that by now, right? Well, you might want to take a look at the section on proxy bias later in this chapter.

#EthnicBias

In 2009, HP released the SmartMedia computer with a webcam featuring face tracing through facial recognition. The inability of the system to track faces with darker pigmentation was highlighted in a humorous video of two electronics store employees, one white and one black, when both try it out. It works as advertised on the white employee but fails to recognize the presence of a face when the black employee moves into the field of view of the camera.

HP released a statement saying, "The technology we use is built on standard algorithms that measure the difference in intensity of contrast between the eyes and the upper cheek and nose. We believe that the camera might have difficulty 'seeing' contrast in conditions where there is insufficient foreground lighting."

Odd that the algorithm had no trouble recognizing the faces of white employees under "insufficient foreground lighting" conditions. Could it be that ethnic bias might be present in the population it was developed and trained on? The result was that the face-tracking feature was released as functional when it really was functional only on a subset of the population and literally couldn't recognize the rest of the people. So how does bias creep into AI despite the good intentions of the developers? The primary source of data bias is collection bias. I cover another significant source of bias, framing bias, in the next section.

Collection bias

REMEMBER

Collection bias occurs during data collection when the training data reflects existing prejudices.

Amazon ran into a data collection issue when it created an AI-based hiring and recruitment system. This system was supposed to remove bias from the hiring process by analyzing historical hiring and employee success data and highlighting the applicants who best met the characteristics of their most productive hires. However, because the machine-learning algorithms were trained on a limited dataset that reflected a historical bias (ten years of applications and previous hires), it ended up perpetuating the very biases Amazon was seeking to counteract.

Many advertising algorithms optimize ad service based on the historical preferences of the customer. If a greater number of individuals in a protected group engage with housing ads for rental as opposed to purchase, the model identifies that pattern and perpetuates it, effectively locking members of that class into specific ads.

Proxy bias

Even if the algorithm and the training data are designed to avoid collection bias, the results can still contain bias because of a correlation between a protected class and another attribute.

For example, a loan underwriting algorithm might use the ZIP code of the application as a factor in its decision. Even if the race of the applicant is not present in the data, the U.S. ZIP code is strongly correlated to race, so it will serve as a proxy for race, effectively generating race-based decisions.

In 2019, Goldman Sachs partnered with Apple Pay to issue Apple Card. Within months of the launch, complaints of gender bias cropped up. Ruby on Rails creator David Heinemeier Hansson tweeted that, although he and his spouse share assets and she has a higher credit score, Apple Card offered him a credit limit 20 times greater than the limit it offered her. Apple co-founder Steve Wozniak tweeted that he and his wife had the same experience, with Apple Card offering him a credit limit 10 times the offer to his wife.

Goldman Sachs responded that the algorithm doesn't include gender in credit decisions, but when researching credit history on pre-existing credit accounts, the algorithm takes into consideration whether the applicant is the primary card holder or a supplemental holder.

On the surface, this distinction appears to be a legitimate factor on which to base a credit limit. The algorithm is blind to gender. A primary cardholder will qualify for a higher credit limit, and a supplemental card holder will qualify for a lower limit regardless of gender.

However, if men are listed as primary and women are listed as supplemental on the majority of pre-existing credit accounts, this distinction effectively serves as a proxy for gender.

This example reveals the inherent difficulty in rooting out bias in AI. Credit decisions go beyond shared assets to consider the financial history of the person applying for credit. Although historically the primary-supplemental distinction might map to gender, is it really inherent bias or simply a legitimate basis for evaluating creditworthiness? On the other hand, if Hansson's wife has a higher credit score than he does, why would she be offered a credit limit that is only 5 percent of the size of his?

In many cases, the solutions are not as cut-and-dried as they may appear on the surface.

AI Is Susceptible to Poor Problem Framing

An algorithm maximizes success as defined by the designers. If the designers focus specifically on business objectives and don't intentionally evaluate the model from the perspective of bias, then bias inevitably creeps in. Say a loan approval algorithm is designed to maximize profit. It will likely determine that subprime loans or payday loans provide higher returns in shorter time spans than conventional loans and recommend predatory lending behavior.

Facebook offers several campaign objectives in the categories of awareness (reach), consideration (engagement, lead generation, and so on), and conversion (sales, store traffic). Notice that these are all business goals. These goals do not concern themselves with minimizing bias.

But that's baked into the system, right? Facebook ads wouldn't target housing or job ads based on race or gender.

In the spring of 2019, the U.S. Department of Housing and Urban Development (HUD) sued Facebook for allowing advertisers to target ads by race, gender, and religion, all classes protected from discrimination by U.S. law. The kicker is this practice has been in place for years with investigations and lawsuits going back to 2016.

On the brighter side, just a week before the HUD suit was filed, Facebook settled a $5 million lawsuit for the same practices and said it would change its advertising platform by the end of the year. Facebook agreed to study the potential for unintended bias in algorithmic modeling and meet with the plaintiffs at six-month intervals for three years to review their practices. Facebook also agreed to create a separate portal for job, housing, and credit advertisements that wouldn't allow advertisers to target ads based on protected classes or ZIP codes, and to subject the ads to automated and human review.

AI Is Blind to Data Ambiguity

AI operates in a VUCA world, a world rife with volatility, uncertainty, complexity, and ambiguity, and although all are problematic, ambiguity poses the biggest challenge. In the context of training AI to accurately categorize inputs and recognize correlations with historical data, ambiguity refers to the potential for misreads due to the lack of clarity in real-world data.

Remember the situation earlier in this chapter in which a computer vision algorithm identified a chihuahua as a blueberry muffin? That misclassification illustrates a weakness in machine-learning systems. The system relies on the training data to develop its understanding of the world. When it encounters a new image, it works as it was trained to do. It dutifully matches the new image to something it already knows about, not taking into account that there may be ambiguity in the data, that if you take a photo of a chihuahua from a certain angle, it can look surprisingly similar to a blueberry muffin.

TIP

If you haven't done so before, search the Internet for "chihuahua or muffin," and, unlike the computer vision system, you will see the ambiguity immediately.

AI is often used to assess risk, which is essentially quantifying the certainty, or uncertainty, of the distribution of possible outcomes. However, the accuracy of the result is influenced by ambiguity, which indicates the level of uncertainty of the distribution in the training data. As the degree of ambiguity in the training data increases, the accuracy of the result plummets. If the system has no mechanism to gauge the degree of ambiguity in the data, it is impossible to place confidence in the result. Confidence levels can be cut in half due to even small increases in ambiguity.

As I mention earlier in this chapter, this issue shows up in the inability of AI to recognize cause-and-effect relationships.

For example, one neural network project was designed to reduce deaths due to pneumonia by identifying high-risk patients who should be admitted to the hospital immediately and low-risk patients who could be sent home with antibiotics. The model was accurate, but it had a significant flaw. It identified patients with asthma as low risk, meaning they were less likely than the general population to die from pneumonia, a conclusion that was the opposite of reality.

How did this happen? The model correlated fewer deaths to less susceptibility. However, the real correlation was between having asthma and getting treatment immediately. Individuals with asthma were highly aware of any irregularities in their ability to breathe and thus sought medical attention as soon as symptoms surfaced — which was why the training data showed a lower risk of dying.

AI Will Not, or Cannot, Explain Its Own Results

When people use AI to make important, even life-changing decisions, they stand a good chance of eventually ending up in court.

AI sends you to jail

In 1998, Northpointe Inc., now Equivant, launched Correctional Offender Management Profiling for Alternative Sanctions (COMPAS). The system, which is deployed in dozens of jurisdictions across the U.S., uses a proprietary algorithm that evaluates attributes from a 137-item questionnaire to estimate the likelihood that the defendant will commit another crime, boiling all that information down to a single number from 1 to 10. COMPAS has come under attack for generating what some consider to be racist outcomes.

In 2016, Loomis, a defendant in a criminal case in Wisconsin, demanded to see how the system calculated his score, claiming that the black box nature of the process violated the requirement that a sentence be individualized. Northpointe responded that its algorithms are proprietary and thus constitute a trade secret. In 2017, Loomis filed a motion for post-conviction relief in the trial court, claiming that the use of a proprietary instrument violated his constitutional right to due process by preventing him from challenging the accuracy and scientific validity of the risk assessment. The motion was denied, the Wisconsin Supreme Court affirmed the lower court ruling on appeal, and the U.S. Supreme Court declined to hear the case.

AI cuts your medical benefits

Also in 2016, 700 miles south in Arkansas, beneficiaries of a state Medicaid waiver program suddenly found their benefits cut. The culprit? A newly implemented algorithm from InterRAI that replaced the subjective assessment of human administrators. The algorithm consists of 20 pages of code and processes 60 attributes to sort program recipients into categories that determine the number of hours of home care they are eligible for. However, it was so complex that only an expert could explain why any given case was assigned a specific category.

When a lawsuit was filed and the expert witness was challenged on the stand to manually walk through the process to sort a plaintiff into a category, the court took a short recess. The expert returned to admit that in this case, the algorithm had used the wrong calculation. Counsel observed that filing a federal suit and spending hundreds of hours and thousands of dollars wasn't a scalable process for transparency.

In these cases and many others, it is possible to backtrack the decision process by examining the code. However, with the development of deep learning and neural networks, that level of transparency has become even more opaque. Even the data scientists who develop the models have problems explaining any individual decision.

AI and the black box

Neural networks have been around for decades. They mimic the structure of the human brain with its mind-numbing layers of interconnected neurons. They are used to address problems such as image captioning, voice recognition, and language translation.

A neural network has an input layer, an output layer, and multiple hidden layers in between. Imagine each layer as a window screen, with a neuron at each intersection of the fabric. Only the screen isn't just an arrangement of horizontal and vertical connections. It is a mesh with possible connections between all neurons on the layer.

Got it? That's one layer. Now imagine dozens or hundreds or thousands of layers between the input and output, with myriad connections between layers, each layer refining the resolution of detail in the information from the previous layer. Add to that a feedback process known as *back propagation* that detects errors at the output layer and routes that information back through the network to refine the accuracy of future output.

For image recognition, the input layer has one neuron per pixel. The network filters the connections by proximity, which means that pixels are analyzed in relation to adjacent pixels to establish discrete regions of significance, for example, to identify a collection of pixels that correlate to the shape of a head or a hand. At each layer, neurons associated with a significant pattern analyze smaller parts of the shape, such as the eyes, nose, mouth, ears, and so on. The output layer delivers a vector of probabilities that predicts the likelihood that the detected pattern belongs to a known category.

It's currently impossible to know with precision the steps by which the algorithm generates the result.

Some algorithms are more transparent than others. Here are seven commonly used machine-learning models in decreasing order of explainability, from transparent to opaque:

>> Rules

>> Naive Bayes

>> Logistic regression

>> Decision trees

>> Random forests

>> Boosted trees

>> Neural networks

AI diagnoses your latent schizophrenia

In 2015, Mount Sinai Hospital in New York used deep learning to train a neural network algorithm using hundreds of attributes from 700,000 patient records. The system, called Deep Patient, predicts a wide range of diseases better than any of the hospital's existing systems. In fact, it appears to anticipate the onset of psychiatric disorders, something physicians have difficulty doing. The doctors and data scientists who created Deep Patient have no idea how it does what it does. It is a diagnostic black box.

So what happens when doctors act on Deep Patient's diagnosis and things don't go well? Will the family sue Deep Patient for malpractice?

Remember the system that rated asthmatics as low risk for pneumonia? The tool was never deployed. Not because of the asthma-pneumonia snafu, but because, like Deep Patient, it too was a block box neural network, and the creators had no way of knowing how many other weird conclusions and unknown unknowns were lurking in the model.

The question remains. For high-stakes situations such as legal, medical, and military decisions, how long will it take, or what conditions must exist, for humans to be comfortable with a non-human black box decider?

AI can be fooled

There's chihuahua versus blueberry muffin, and then there's turtle versus rifle. The former is nothing more than an insufficiently rigorous pattern matching algorithm. The latter is an adversarial image.

Human eyes can easily be tricked by optical illusions. Is the dancer spinning to the left or the right? Is the dress blue and black or white and gold? Are the lines parallel or angled? It turns out that AI eyes can also be fooled. Of course, not by ordinary folks such as ourselves. It takes skills.

For example, when was the last time you created an optical illusion that fooled a human? Probably around the last time I created an adversarial image that fooled an AI tool. If you find the topic interesting, search for "adversarial image," and you'll soon find yourself hours deep down a rabbit hole of cat versus guacamole, piglet versus airliner, or puppy versus ostrich. For some reason, critters are popular in the adversarial image world.

Although these examples can be amusing, adversarial attacks can be targeted for serious applications. Data scientists at Carnegie Mellon University printed specially designed patterns on cheap drugstore glasses and wore them while being scanned by current state-of-the-art facial recognition software. They were able to create unique patterns to target specific identities in a round of "choose the celebrity you want to be for the airline boarding facial scan software," turning one average-looking male researcher into a famous female supermodel and cover girl. Once again, it's an amusing example, but with serious security implications. One Cornell University experiment rendered an adult invisible to the people-detection capabilities of a security camera by giving the intruder a specially designed image printed on a 12-inch cardboard square to point toward the camera.

In experiments with serious implications for the autonomous vehicle market, researchers were able to accomplish these tricks:

» Position two pieces of white tape and two pieces of black tape onto a stop sign, leaving the sign perfectly legible for human drivers but causing a self-driving car to interpret it as a 45-mph speed limit sign.

» Place three small stickers on the pavement to trick a self-driving car into crossing the lane marker into the oncoming traffic lane.

REMEMBER

Until data scientists find a way to make smart machines smarter, humans will always have to be in the loop to counter the work of other humans trying to throw a monkey wrench in the works.

On the other hand, bringing it back down to typical enterprise applications, I will hazard a guess that you aren't working on autonomous vehicles or facial recognition algorithms. When it comes to adversarial attacks on the enterprise, the most vulnerable stage of the data science project methodology is data preparation. If there were a malicious person seeking to sabotage your project, the simplest way would be to insert intentionally dirty data into the training dataset, increasing data ambiguity and reducing the validity of the model and the quality of the results.

You can address this possibility the same way you address any other data security issue, by employing good physical and digital security.

AI Is Not Immune to the Law of Unintended Consequences

Complicated systems produce unexpected outcomes.
— GENERALIZED UNCERTAINTY PRINCIPLE, SYSTEMANTICS, JOHN GALL

I bet another thing Tim Berners-Lee didn't see coming back in 1989 when he clicked the button that launched the World Wide Web is that he would spawn a brand new mental disorder. Only 27 years after that mouse click, the American Psychiatric Association added Internet Gaming Disorder to the Diagnostic and Statistical Manual for Mental Disorders (DSM).

Dating way back, history is rife with examples of technology and unintended consequences. It's hard to narrow them down to just a few, but I'll try.

In 1450, Johannes Gutenberg, who was a devout Catholic, invented the printing press. The first thing to come off the press was the Gutenberg Bible, the wide availability of which helped fuel the Reformation and reduced the power of the Catholic Church.

In 1855, the British army equipped its troops with the P53 Enfield rifle, a significant improvement over the muskets currently in use, to assure Britain's hold over its vast empire. However, a rumor circulated that the cartridges were greased with pig and cow fat, which caused a problem in India where part of the population considers cows sacred and another part of the population considers pigs unclean.

In 1857, the Bengal army refused to use the rifle. The ensuing mutiny sparked a rebellion that marked what is commonly seen as the first step in a 90-year struggle that ended with Indian independence in 1947.

The pioneers of the smartphone probably didn't realize they would be responsible for endangering the lives of millions of people. Owning a smartphone significantly increases the risk of having an automobile accident, at least for those who can't resist using them while driving and anyone who happens to be proximate when they do.

The risk of a car crash or near miss increases with cell phone use:

>> 1.4 times higher when reaching for a cell phone

>> 2.8 times higher while dialing a cell phone

Move to a truck, and the odds get worse:

>> 6.7 times higher when reaching for a cell phone

>> 5.9 times higher when dialing a cell phone

And when it comes to texting, that's bad news for everybody no matter what they drive; the odds of having a wreck are 23.2 times higher.

In 1987, computers caused the stock market catastrophe known as Black Monday. Program trading uses computers to automatically balance portfolios to reduce risk efficiently at a lower cost than manual trading. It has become standard practice for institutional investors. In 2018, program trading accounted for 50 to 60 percent of all market trades placed during a typical trading day, rising above 90 percent during periods of extreme volatility. On October 19, 1987, in response to a market downswing, program trading systems automatically sold off large volumes of stock, exacerbating the downward trend. The Dow Jones Industrial Average lost more than 20 percent in a single day and within two weeks most of the major exchanges worldwide had also dropped 20 percent. So much for all those efficiency gains.

REMEMBER

Given the power of AI and the potential opacity of black box algorithms, it is imperative to have humans in the loop to anticipate unintended outcomes and steer clear of them. These include making sure the human element is given full consideration, bias is avoided, and privacy and security are kept top of mind.

Index

hosting AI
  affordability, 79
  cloud hosting, 77–78
  data gravity, 79–80
  hybrid approach, 78
  on premises, 77–78
  regulatory requirements, 80
  scalability, 79
  security, 80
human resources
  natural-language processing, 188
  virtual assistants, 39–40
hybrid approach, hosting AI, 78
Hypergraph-enabled IKA, 271

I

IBM Deep Blue computer, 15
ICD-10 (International Classification of Diseases-10), 54
ICO (Information Commissioner's Office), 250
ICR (intelligent character recognition), 241
IKA (intelligent knowledge assistant)
  academic research, 272–273
  compliance management, 272
  customer support, 270–271
  defined, 267
  enterprise search, 272
  fact checking, 273
  legal services, 271
  overview, 267–269
industrial revolutions, 289–290
Industry 4.0, 100, 106
Information Commissioner's Office (ICO), 250
Information theory, 15
in-house AI solutions, 75–76
Inside Out (film), 192
Instagram, 17, 218
insurance industry, 37–38, 247
Insys Therapeutics, 92
intelligent character recognition (ICR), 241
intelligent knowledge assistant. *See* IKA
intelligent recommendation system
  collaborative filtering, 223–224
  content-based filtering, 224
  credit card offers, 227
  cross-validation, 224–225

  customer retention, 219–220
  data mining, 219, 222
  data visualization, 225–226
  finance sector, 226–227
  market-basket analysis, 220
  media and entertainment industry, 194
  overview, 217
  popularity-based recommendations, 220
  practical AI, 31–32
  propensity modeling, 220–222
  retail industry, 228–229
  social media, 218–219
  text mining, 222
  upselling, 219
Intelligent Retail Lab (IRL), 156
Intermountain Healthcare, 85
internal data, 52
internal partnerships, 74–75
International Classification of Diseases-10 (ICD-10), 54
Internet Gaming Disorder, 311
Internet of Things data. *See* IoT data
InterRAI algorithm, 308
inventory management
  manufacturing industry, 106
  professional services, 188
IoT (Internet of Things) data
  asset performance optimization, 210, 214–215
  biotech/pharma, 96
  manufacturing industry, 101–105
  oil and gas industry, 114–115, 186
  retail industry, 154, 156
  smart cities, 130
  telecom industry, 167, 170
  transportation and travel industry, 163
  utilities sector, 136, 139, 186
IRL (Intelligent Retail Lab), 156
Iron Triangle of Medicine, 84–85
is a relationship, 19
item-based collaborative filtering, 223–224

J

Jacquard, Joseph Marie, 121
Jobs, Steve, 218
Johnson & Johnson, 92

About the Author

Zachary Jarvinen is a product & marketing executive, AI technologist, and member of the Forbes Technology Council, known for translating technical concepts into benefits the broader community can grasp and use. Zachary's current focus is to demystify confusing and intimidating jargon found in the AI and tech space and to present AI in a palatable and approachable way so organizations can benefit and grow their company. Zachary has become known for taking seemingly foreign technological concepts and presenting them in ways that are easy to understand and implement.

Over the course of his career, Zachary has served as the Head of Technology Strategy and Product Marketing for Artificial Intelligence and Analytics at OpenText, has helped expand global markets for Fortune 500 Epson, has grown an analytics startup to #87 on the Inc. 5000, and was part of the famed digital team for the 2008 Obama Presidential Campaign. He speaks fluent Spanish and Portuguese and holds an MBA/MSc from UCLA and the London School of Economics.

In addition to his professional career, Zachary also serves as AI track lead at several industry conferences in Europe, Asia, and North America, where he delivers breakout and keynote sessions. He is regularly quoted in the press and is a contributor to *Forbes, TechRadar, TechTarget,* and other enterprise media outlets on the most pressing and important AI topics of today. Zachary can be reached at www.zachononomics.com and followed at www.twitter.com/zachonomics.

Dedication

This book is dedicated to all the medical professionals fighting COVID-19 on the front lines right now — my wife among them — and all the data scientists who are going to have to tune their models to account for the 2020 pandemic — for many years to come.

Author's Acknowledgments

I have discovered that it takes a village to create a book. I would like to thank Brad Whittington for helping with the writing. His steady hand and deft wordsmanship as we went through iterations on this journey meant so much. I thank my wife, Laura, for her love and support during all the long days and nights required to finish.

I'd also like to thank the analyst and journalist community for inspiring this project: Mike Gualtieri, Kjell Carlsson, Dave Schubmehl, Nick Patience, Alan Pelz Sharpe, Peter Krensky, Carlie Idoine, and Erick Brethenoux, among others. We are fighting the same good fight of educating on this topic — and are now happy to be able to provide the answer to all the journalists who've said over the years, "If only there was a guidebook available on Enterprise AI." I'm looking forward to handing you a copy when next we meet!

Furthermore, I thank all my professional and practitioner colleagues in the industry, including Paul Starrett, Marc St. Pierre, Sheila Woo, Ivan Kirigin, and the many others who read parts of this book to help refine the approach or provide input to help make sure it hit the mark. Their volunteer support and encouragement meant so much and I owe them all copies and in-kind contributions for their own works to come.

Finally, I would like to thank Katie Mohr for her early collaboration, guidance, and encouragement through the process, and Marty Minner for his detailed guidance and inputs in the middle, and the rest of the editorial and production staff at Wiley for all their work to get this book into its final state and out the door.

Publisher's Acknowledgments

Associate Publisher: Katie Mohr

Project Editor: Martin V. Minner

Copy Editor: Gwenette Gaddis

Technical Editor: Steve Wasick

Production Editor: Siddique Shaik

Cover Image: © Just_Super/Getty Images

PERSONAL ENRICHMENT

Staying Sharp dummies
9781119187790
USA $26.00
CAN $31.99
UK £19.99

Facebook dummies
Carolyn Abram
9781119179030
USA $21.99
CAN $25.99
UK £16.99

Guitar dummies
Mark Phillips
Jon Chappell
9781119293354
USA $24.99
CAN $29.99
UK £17.99

Investing dummies
Eric Tyson, MBA
9781119293347
USA $22.99
CAN $27.99
UK £16.99

Beekeeping dummies
Howland Blackiston
9781119310068
USA $22.99
CAN $27.99
UK £16.99

Digital Photography dummies
Julie Adair King
9781119235606
USA $24.99
CAN $29.99
UK £17.99

Meditation dummies
Stephan Bodian
9781119251163
USA $24.99
CAN $29.99
UK £17.99

Pregnancy ALL-IN-ONE dummies
9781119235491
USA $26.99
CAN $31.99
UK £19.99

Samsung Galaxy S7 dummies
Bill Hughes
9781119279952
USA $24.99
CAN $29.99
UK £17.99

iPhone dummies
Edward C. Baig
Bob "Dr. Mac" LeVitus
9781119283133
USA $24.99
CAN $29.99
UK £17.99

Crocheting dummies
Karen Manthey
Susan Brittain
9781119287117
USA $24.99
CAN $29.99
UK £16.99

Nutrition dummies
Carol Ann Rinzler
9781119130246
USA $22.99
CAN $27.99
UK £16.99

PROFESSIONAL DEVELOPMENT

Windows 10 dummies
Andy Rathbone
9781119311041
USA $24.99
CAN $29.99
UK £17.99

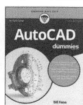
AutoCAD dummies
Bill Fane
9781119255796
USA $39.99
CAN $47.99
UK £27.99

Excel 2016 dummies
Greg Harvey, PhD
9781119293439
USA $26.99
CAN $31.99
UK £19.99

QuickBooks 2017 dummies
Stephen L. Nelson, MBA, CPA, MS in Taxation
9781119281467
USA $26.99
CAN $31.99
UK £19.99

macOS Sierra dummies
Bob "Dr. Mac" LeVitus
9781119280651
USA $29.99
CAN $35.99
UK £21.99

LinkedIn dummies
Joel Elad, MBA
9781119251132
USA $24.99
CAN $29.99
UK £17.99

Windows 10 ALL-IN-ONE dummies
Woody Leonhard
9781119310563
USA $34.00
CAN $41.99
UK £24.99

SharePoint 2016 dummies
Rosemarie Withee
Ken Withee
9781119181705
USA $29.99
CAN $35.99
UK £21.99

Fundamental Analysis dummies
Matt Krantz
9781119263593
USA $26.99
CAN $31.99
UK £19.99

Networking dummies
Doug Lowe
9781119257769
USA $29.99
CAN $35.99
UK £21.99

Office 2016 dummies
Wallace Wang
9781119293477
USA $26.99
CAN $31.99
UK £19.99

Office 365 dummies
Rosemarie Withee
Ken Withee
Jennifer Reed
9781119265313
USA $24.99
CAN $29.99
UK £17.99

Salesforce.com dummies
Liz Kao
Jon Paz
9781119239314
USA $29.99
CAN $35.99
UK £21.99

Coding dummies
Nikhil Abraham
9781119293323
USA $29.99
CAN $35.99
UK £21.99

dummies.com

dummies
A Wiley Brand

Printed and bound by CPI Group (UK) Ltd, Croydon, CR0 4YY

27/10/2024

14580182-0001